JOURNEY TO
BRITANNIA

*

FROM
THE HEART
OF ROME
TO
HADRIAN'S
WALL,
AD 130

*

JOURNEY TO

BRITANNIA

*

FROM
THE HEART
OF ROME
TO
HADRIAN'S
WALL,
AD 130

*

Bronwen Riley

First published in 2015 by Head of Zeus Ltd

1 3 5 7 9 10 8 6 4 2

A CIP catalogue record for this book is available
from the British Library.

ISBN (HB) 9781781851340
(E) 9781781852675

Printed and bound in Germany by
GGP Media GmbH, Pössneck
Designed and typeset by
Ken Wilson | point918

———

HEAD OF ZEUS LTD
Clerkenwell House · 45–47 Clerkenwell Green
London EC1R 0HT
www.headofzeus.com

PATRI QUI PRIMUS MIHI MONSTRAVIT
VESTIGIA ROMANORUM MATRIQUE
QUAE VIAM PATEFECIT

Contents

———

List of Maps

—

N

Vallum Aelii
Pons Aelius
Eboracum
Deva
Britannia
Isca
Rutupiae
Londinium
Gesoriacum
Augusta Treverorum
Gallia Belgica
Lutetia
Gallia Lugdunensis
Lugdunum
Aquitania
Burdigala
Alpes Graiae
Gallia Narbonensis
Narbo Martius
Massilia
Forum Iulii
Antipolis
Alpes Cottidae
Barcino
Hispania Citerior (Tarraconensis)
Lusitania
Baetica
Gades
Mauretania Tingitana
Mauretania Caesariensis
Saldae
Lambaesis
Numidia
Germania Inferior
Germania Superior
Pannonia Superior
Raetia
Noricum
Alpes Maritimae
Italia
Burnum
Aequum
Salona
Dalmatia
Camerinum
Centum Cellae
Portus
Roma
Ostia
Sardinia et Corsica
Sicilia
Oea
Leptis Magna
Sabratha
Africa Proconsularis

0   300 miles
0   500 km

The Roman Empire AD 130

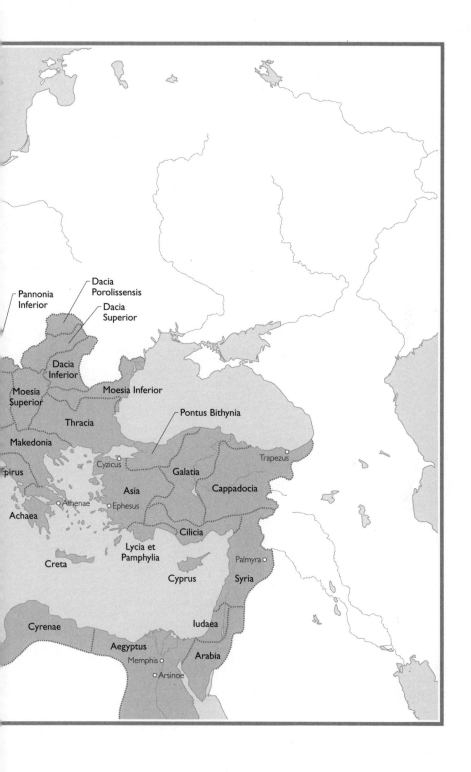

Pannonia
Inferior

Dacia
Porolissensis

Dacia
Superior

Dacia
Inferior

Moesia
Superior

Moesia Inferior

Thracia

Pontus Bithynia

Makedonia

Trapezus

pirus

Cyzicus

Galatia

Asia

Cappadocia

Athenae

Ephesus

Achaea

Cilicia

Lycia et
Pamphylia

Creta

Cyprus

Palmyra

Syria

Cyrenae

Iudaea

Aegyptus

Arabia

Memphis

Arsinoe

Evoking the Past

*

Bowness-on-Solway in Cumbria was the north-westernmost limit of Hadrian's Wall. In AD 130 it was also—apart from a handful of outposts north of the Wall—the most north-westerly point of the entire Roman Empire. From here, according to my online route planner, it is a distance of 1486.9 miles (2392.9km) to the Capitoline Hill (Piazza del Campidoglio) in Rome. The itinerary tells me that were I to travel by car, the journey would take 22 hours and 8 minutes.

The suggested route is not, of course, the only way of getting there, simply the most direct, along the fastest roads. Such a concept would have been familiar to the Romans, who used itineraries based on similar principles: routes drawn as a series of straight lines, giving distances between suggested stopping points, with symbols denoting towns, ports, temples and various types of accommodation available along the way.

Motorways now bypass the towns and cities through which the Romans once travelled and the stopping places where they would have sought refreshment for themselves and their horses. Scanning the modern route through England, I look for the Roman towns, forts and settlements that I might pass on my journey and find them straight away. Soon after leaving Bowness-on-Solway (Maia), I would pass by Carlisle (Luguvalium), a Roman military base and later Romano-British town. A little further south in Lancashire, having sped by Lancaster, I would cross the River Ribble, just a few miles west of Ribchester. Both these places were Roman forts, indicated by the -*caster* and -*chester* in their modern names: from the Latin *castrum*, via Old English *cæster*, by which the Anglo-Saxons denoted a place of Roman origin. What the Romans called Lancaster is unknown, but Ribchester went by the splendid name 'Bremetenacum Veteranorum'. This comes from the Celtic for a roaring river, *Bremetona* (an apt name, as the Ribble has devoured a third of the fort), and the Latin for 'of the veterans', indicating that soldiers—at one time Sarmatian cavalry originally from the Ukraine and southern Russia—had settled here on retirement.

Just off the M6 Toll Road in Staffordshire is Wall (Letocetum), which provided a well-appointed government rest house or *mansio* for official travellers on Watling Street, a key military road between the south coast and North Wales. Once on the M1, I would pass by St Albans (Verulamium), a town that came to prominence soon after the conquest thanks to its strategic position north of London on Watling Street and its pro-Roman inhabitants. The rather less amenable Queen of the Iceni, Boudicca, torched the place in AD 61. She did the same to London (Londinium), massacring its citizens and burning the future provincial capital so effectively that it left forever a glaring red scar of burnt clay in the earth, which archaeologists refer to as the 'Boudiccan destruction layer'.

The twenty-first-century route now bypasses London on the M25 and joins the M20 at Dartford, following a much more circuitous way to the coast and the Channel Tunnel south of Dover than the old Roman road. By contrast, Watling Street runs south of London in a no-nonsense line, directly connecting the capital with the ports of Dover (Dubris) and Richborough (Rutupiae) via Canterbury (Durovernum Cantiacorum).

The way in which Rome's tentacles reached even the most out-of-the-way places, in what for the Romans was our really faraway island, never ceases to amaze me, as does the origin of the men and women who ended up here from all corners of the empire. Just down the coast from Bowness-on-Solway, at the fort of Maryport (Alauna) on the Cumbrian coast, Caius Caballius Priscus, born in Verona, was a tribune here between AD 128 and AD 131.

Marcus Censorius Cornelianus, from Nîmes in the south of France, served here in AD 132 before being sent to Judaea. Lucius Cammius Maximus, prefect of the camp between AD 133 and AD 135, came from Austria, returning to the region to serve on the Danube. And at some point in the second or third century, Gaius Cornelius Peregrinus, a town councillor from Algeria, prayed for a safe return to his sunny home after his stint as an officer on the northwest frontier.

Over at Corbridge (Coria), just south of Hadrian's Wall, Diodora described herself—in Greek—as a high priestess on the altar she dedicated to the exotic oriental cult of Herakles of Tyre. She probably came from Asia Minor. Further east along the Wall at South Shields (Arbeia), Barates, a Syrian merchant, erected a handsome tombstone in honour of his British wife, a freedwoman called Regina.

Many who came to Britannia as high-ranking officers and officials were cultured and affluent men who enjoyed remarkable careers: men such as the slick and extremely rich Spaniard L. Minicius Natalis, who arrived in Britain in about AD 130 fresh from winning a four-horse chariot race at the Olympic Games. Would he have been appalled by life on this gloomy old island or been thrilled by the hunting, the famously sensitive noses of the hounds, and the archaic skill of the British charioteers who, as late as AD 83, had ridden their war chariots into battle against the Romans at Mons Graupius? It was in thinking about these diverse characters from such varied backgrounds that I began to wonder not just why they came here and what they might have made of this place but *how* they got here. What means of transport would they have taken? How long would it have taken them to get to Britain? How would they have got about the place when they arrived?

In attempting to evoke a journey to Britain in the Roman period, to capture the flavour of life for any of these people, the first hurdle is to confront the fact that Roman Britain spans a period of more than 450 years—beginning with Julius Caesar's expeditions in 55 and 54 BC. This is the same amount of time that separates the era of Elizabeth I's reign from the the present day. Unsurprisingly during these centuries, both the Roman world and Britain changed profoundly: the Roman Republic fell and 'chief citizens' became emperors. The empire expanded greatly and then was carved up several times over. Christianity triumphed over paganism, and power shifted ever further east, away from Italy until, in AD 330, the Emperor Constantine the Great dedicated Constantinople in his name as the New Rome.

For these reasons a journey in the first or early second centuries would have been profoundly different to one in the third and fourth centuries, featuring personalities from widely different backgrounds, both in terms of their country of origin and their social class. Their journeys would have taken them along different routes, and those travelling in the later period would have had to face more uncertainties, including a greater threat of pirates on the seas and armed conflict on land. Britain was also administered in completely different ways; the province was split in two in the early third century, and into four in the fourth century, and her political and economic organization changed markedly.

In order to evoke a journey as it might have been experienced by any one person, it was therefore necessary to choose a period. There are a number of reasons why I decided on AD 130. It is a time when a most complex and compelling emperor, Hadrian, ruled an empire whose boundaries he was keen to consolidate and delineate, most famously with Hadrian's Wall. He himself spent several years of his reign travelling through the empire and visited Britain in AD 122. It was at this time that he gave the orders to build the Wall, and he very possibly stimulated the construction of many other monumental buildings in the province, the remains of which may still be seen today. By AD 130 the main towns and cities of Britain were established, conforming more or less to a Roman model, albeit with some idiosyncratic flourishes. Both the Wall and other monumental civic building projects were well under way. We also know—and this is rare for most of the Roman period in Britain—the names of several high-ranking officials who served in the province in the early 130s and who may have overlapped: the governor Sextus Julius Severus (in Britain AD 130–133); the aforementioned Minicius Natalis, who took up his post as legionary legate in command of the Legion VI Victrix based at York (Eboracum) at about the same time; and Maenius Agrippa, who is thought to have been appointed 'prefect of the British fleet' (*praefectus classis Britanniae*) in the early 130s.

In this period, Rome was still the radiant centre of imperial power, the city where both the emperor and the ruling class needed to have a base and the place from which many high-ranking officials would have set out at the start of their postings to the provinces. It is the city that provided a model for the provincial towns and cities of the empire. To understand what was happening in a place like Britain in the second century, one must first glimpse the shape of things in Rome. And although people coming to live and work in Britain in the AD 130s would have arrived by diverse routes, many of them from places outside Italy, Rome was still the measure of all things, which is why this journey begins in the heart of the imperial capital.

Bearing in mind the fact that for this period and place there is simply not enough evidence to piece together an exact journey made by one particular person, I have attempted to reconstruct a journey as it might have unfolded at this time using what literary and archaeological evidence we have. For reasons of fluency and readability I have tried to limit the many potential 'might haves', 'probablys' and 'possiblys', but I hope that speculation, doubt or dissent is adequately treated in the footnotes and endnotes, which will enable interested readers to follow up the relevant sources and arguments.

I have had to be very selective about the places I mention to avoid this becoming a gazetteer and have tried to choose sites where there is a significant Hadrianic story, and which contain good examples of a particular type of building of the period, or where a theme can best be exemplified. It has been difficult to leave out some towns beyond the briefest mention, but places such as York and

Cirencester (Corinium), together with many significant villas, for example, have at present more to tell us about the later history than Hadrian's era. St Albans, a key town on major routes north and east of London, figures greatly in the early and late Roman periods, but the record is quieter in the second century.

That said, one of the excitements of Roman history in Britain is that archaeological discoveries are constantly being made, which sometimes add a piece to the puzzle and occasionally show that two pieces have previously been fitted together in entirely the wrong way. Recent discoveries at Maryport mean that many books on Roman military history will have to be rewritten. At Colchester (Camulodunum)—the first provincial capital of Britain, which figures so greatly in the early conquest period—Britain's only known Roman *circus* or racetrack has recently been discovered. One of the many pleasures and excitements of writing this book has been hearing of new discoveries, and then thinking about how they could help inform the narrative.

One of the major problems with writing about any period of Roman British history is the paucity of evidence and fragmentary nature of our sources. Most of what we know about Roman Britain is based on archaeological evidence. The main written sources for Hadrian's reign are from later: the flaky but titillating *Historia Augusta* (fourth century) and the account in the third-century *Roman History* of Cassius Dio, which only survives in a much later, abridged form. In both, only the odd sentence refers directly to Britain. For the second century, however, we do at least have several works of literature written by authors who were contemporary with Hadrian, or one generation removed. Tacitus, who was possibly still alive in the early part of Hadrian's reign, offers our best written source for Britain in the first century, in the *Annals* and *Histories*, and in his biography of his father-in-law *Agricola*, who was governor of Britain for an unusually lengthy period between AD 77 and AD 83. The *Letters* of Pliny the Younger (*c.* AD 61–113) supply us with an enormous amount of information about the character, interests and career of an upper-class Roman who served as governor of a

Roman province under Hadrian's predecessor Trajan—albeit on the other side of the empire, in Bithynia. Arrian, too, who is contemporary with Hadrian, also gives us a few snippets about his time as governor of Cappadocia in the early 130s, although he is rather more informative about hounds and hunting—the great passions of the emperor and of many army officers throughout the empire, including those in Britain. And Suetonius Tranquillus, author of the entertaining *Lives of the Caesars* became Hadrian's chief secretary (*ab epistulis*), although he was later sacked.

Writing about Roman Britain, as has been said many times, is like trying to fit together a complicated jigsaw puzzle when most of the pieces are missing. For one thing, the story is very one-sided— practically all from the Roman point of view. The British before the conquest did not have the literary habit: whatever laws, histories, songs and poems they might have had were passed on by means of an oral rather than a written tradition. Even after the Romans arrived, they do not seem to have taken to writing, or at least not for the purposes of erecting monumental inscriptions. Of those inscriptions that survive from Britain, only the tiniest fraction commemorate native Britons; for the most part it is the incoming soldiers, merchants and their families whose names are inscribed on tombstones, altars and buildings on the island. In the third century, even the military inscriptions dry up.

Miraculously preserved, though, in the boggy conditions of Northumberland and Cumbria, and discovered primarily at Vindolanda, just south of Hadrian's Wall, are letters written on pieces of wood. They give wonderful everyday details of life on the frontier, albeit often in tantalizing fragments. The letters span the period from the AD 90s to the 120s and complement other letters with similar details of daily life in the army found in dumps of papyri thousands of miles away in Egypt. Excitingly, work continues on the Vindolanda tablets and others recently found in London. We also have hundreds of lead and pewter curse tablets, such as those, mainly from the third century, that were thrown into the thermal waters of Aquae Sulis (Bath), together with a substantial number of second- and third-century curses deposited at a shrine at Uley, Gloucestershire. Here, at last, even if through the most fragmentary filter, we can hear the voices of ordinary people, sometimes with distinctively Celtic names. Their odd spellings and grammar and use of colloquial words give a thrilling, but fleeting, insight into the idiosyncratic and accented way in which they might have used the imported Latin language.

These disgruntled individuals at Bath were visiting the only place in Britain to have made it into any sort of international guide. Unlike Egypt and Greece, this remote province was not one of the empire's touristic hotspots. Like Julius Severus and Minicius Natalis, most travellers to Britain came here strictly for business rather than pleasure. It took courage to travel such a distance. According to the second-century jurist Ulpian, the hazards of travel included being killed by bandits, having the inn you are staying in collapse on top of you, and being run over by a cart. To these perils, any traveller to Britain might have added the dangers of crossing *Oceanus*, that immeasurable expanse of sea full of monsters and unfathomable tides at the ends of the earth.

Having made such a perilous journey, what awaited the second-century traveller on arrival on Britannia's shores? Expectations, as far as we can tell, seem to have been low. The natives were considered to be uncultured and generally unpromising, though their plain clothes were of most excellent quality wool and their hunting hounds were deemed to be effective, if unprepossessing in looks. The climate, too, left much to be desired. Here was a place where the rain fell, the sun was seldom seen, and a thick mist was said to rise from the marshes 'so that the atmosphere in the country is always gloomy'.

Welcome to Britannia, AD 130.

BRONWEN RILEY

CHAPTER I

Rome, Heart of Empire

Ἄγεται δὲ ἐκ πάσης γῆς καὶ θαλάττης ὅσα ὧραι φύουσιν
καὶ χῶραι ἕκασται φέρουσιν καὶ ποταμοὶ καὶ λίμναι καὶ τέχναι
Ἑλλήνων καὶ βαρβάρων· ὥστε εἴ τις ταῦτα πάντα ἐπιδεῖν
βούλοιτο, δεῖ αὐτὸν ἢ πᾶσαν ἐπελθόντα τὴν οἰκουμένην
οὕτω·θεάσασθαι ἢ ἐν τῇδε τῇ πόλει γενόμενον.

Here is brought from every land and sea all the crops of the seasons
and the produce of each land, river, lake, as well as of the arts
of the Greeks and the barbarians, so that if someone should wish
to view all these things, he must either see them
by travelling over the whole world or be in this city.

AELIUS ARISTIDES, *On Rome*
(Oration XXVI.11)

*

IT IS APRIL, AD 130. Rome is the teeming capital of an empire that stretches from the blustery north-western shores of Britain to the fringes of Mesopotamia, 2,500 miles to the east, and as far south as Africa and the desert of the Sahara. The Roman Empire's boundaries extend from the ocean where the sun god rises to the ocean where he sinks.[1] Publius Aelius Hadrianus, a most complex and compelling man, has been emperor for fourteen years.

All over Rome, as all over her empire, people, animals and produce are on the move. Along roads, rivers and seas—a vast network stretching tens of thousands of miles—men and women of every age and class are travelling through towns, ports, provinces and continents. Many are soldiers, employed in their manifold imperial duties, or merchants and craftsmen, off to sell their goods

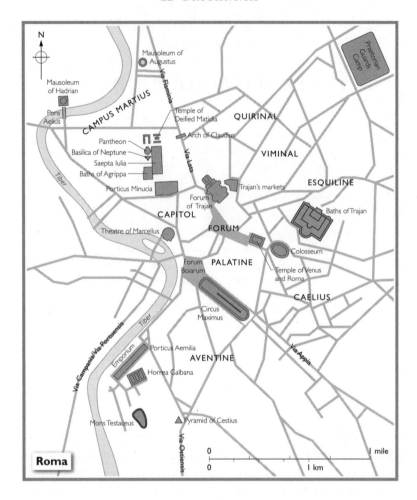

N

Mausoleum of Augustus

Praetorian Guards Camp

Mausoleum of Hadrian

CAMPUS MARTIUS

Via Flaminia

Pons Aelius

Temple of Deified Matidia

QUIRINAL

Arch of Claudius

Pantheon

VIMINAL

Basilica of Neptune

Saepta Iulia

Baths of Agrippa

Via Lata

Tiber

Porticus Minucia

Trajan's markets

ESQUILINE

Forum of Trajan

Baths of Trajan

CAPITOL

FORUM

Theatre of Marcellus

Colosseum

Forum Boiarum

PALATINE

Temple of Venus and Roma

CAELIUS

Circus Maximus

Tiber

Via Appia

Via Campania/Via Portuensis

Emporium

Porticus Aemilia

AVENTINE

Horrea Galbana

Mons Testaceus

Pyramid of Cestius

Via Ostiensis

0   1 mile

0   1 km

Roma

or services abroad. Other people are travelling at leisure, full of expectation for the marvels they are to see in two of the empire's most popular tourist destinations: Egypt and Greece. The Emperor Hadrian is particularly attached to Greece, where he spent much of the past year. This summer he is due to arrive in Egypt, where he will stay for the rest of the year. Hadrian travels the empire constantly. This year alone, he wintered in Antioch, visited Palmyra in early spring, and is currently making his way through Arabia and Judaea.[2]

Less happy to be travelling are the slaves being brought to market, to be bought and sold in shame; and the wild animals, captured as far away as Caledonia and Africa, being shipped in great numbers to meet their miserable fates (together with condemned criminals) in amphitheatres around the empire. Performers of various types and abilities are also on the road—bands of hired gladiators, celebrity charioteers and the imperial troupes of approved *pantomimi* or dancers and mime artists, who are off to play Italy and the provinces.[3] Groups of slave prostitutes are being taken to ply their trade at religious festivals, where carefree tourists, with holiday money in their bags and belts, offer rich pickings for their pimps. Touts, pickpockets, dodgy guides and souvenir-sellers, who congregate around temple boundaries in large numbers on high days and holidays, are also the hopeful beneficiaries of the sightseers' largesse.

Among those travelling to more legitimate purpose is Sextus Julius Severus, who has been appointed the new governor of Britannia. Rated as one of Hadrian's best generals, he will need to travel across the entire continent to take up his post, for he has been serving as governor of Moesia Inferior, a province that has the shore of the Pontus Euxinus (the Black Sea) as its eastern border.[4] One of the most dashing young men to take leave of Rome for Britannia at this time is L. Minicius Natalis the Younger. He has been appointed legionary legate in command of the VI Victrix Legion at Eboracum (York).[*] Now in his early thirties, he was born in Barcino (Barcelona), in the province of Hispania Tarraconensis, where his fabulously rich family has recently erected a large public baths complex.[5] He is a keen sportsman who, only last year, won the four-horse chariot race at the 227th Olympic Games.

Minicius Natalis also holds a number of offices in prestigious religious colleges, including that of *augur*, which holds huge social cachet. He is of senatorial rank (for which there is a property

---

[*] The position of legionary legate, or commander, was reserved for those of senatorial rank (except briefly under the Emperor Commodus, in the later second century, when equestrians became eligible).

qualification of 1 million sestertii) and his family move in the high-est social circles. As a teenager, he served on one of the most socially prestigious boards of magistrates in Rome, the *tresviri monetales*, which oversees the mint, and his early senatorial appointments were marked by the emperor's favour. Natalis's family have an estate less than 20 miles east of Rome, at fashionable Tibur (Tivoli), where Hadrian has nearly finished building his own breathtaking 900-roomed palace, the Villa Tiburtina.[6]

HADRIAN'S IMPERIAL CITY

Most people, especially those embarking on a journey, get up early to make the most of the daylight hours. In Rome at this time of the year, the first hour of the day is about 6.30am. In winter, the first hour, which is reckoned by the time the sun rises, will be nearer 7.30am—although no one can give you the precise time, should you stop to ask. It is true that some people carry pocket sun-dials and have water-clocks as status symbols (and the fancier the better); but it is rare to find one device that runs to the same time as another, and most people find the position of the sun in the sky and the length of the shadows enough to guide them through the hours of the day. Everyone, rich or poor, needs to make the most of day-light hours when artificial light comes only from the flicker of an oil lamp or a smoking torch.

Time may be measured imprecisely, but there is still a sense of urgency and a huge amount of noise. With a million inhabitants, Rome is the largest city in the world. The majority of its populace lives packed together in the 46,000 or so apartment blocks (*insu-lae*) that glower over narrow streets.[7] The *insulae* in the poorer areas look—and are—distinctly unsafe, jerry-built by unscru-pulous landlords who cram in the tenants but fail to maintain the properties, which are constant fire hazards. This is despite the best efforts of successive emperors to at least limit the heights of buildings in Rome—to 21 metres (70 feet), by Emperor Augustus, and more recently to 18 metres (60 feet), by Emperor Trajan, enough for a four-storey apartment block plus attic space.[8]

The streets are already busy. Among the earliest to rise are school-children, accompanied by slaves. If it is the Ides of the month—the 13th or 15th day (depending on whether it is a short or long month; April is short)—they will carry money to pay their impecunious teachers. Other Romans hurry, tickets (*tesserae*) in hand, to the Portico of Minucia, hoping to get there before the queue for the privilege of the corn dole becomes too big.[9]

The elaborate litters of the rich, carried by six or so bearers who are skilled at barging their way through the throng of pedestrians, have not yet surfaced; but the crowds on the street still have to compete for space with laden mules and wagons dangerously overloaded with building materials—wood and brick and marble. Although there is a ban on vehicles in Rome during the day (which makes for rather noisy late afternoons and evenings), wagons carrying material for work on public buildings are exempt.[10] Since Hadrian came to power, in AD 117, he has instigated enormous architectural projects in the city and elsewhere, building monuments to assert his taste, authority and vision of imperial rule as quickly and as magnificently as possible. For the past hundred years or so, emperors keen to leave their mark and assert the validity of their dynasties on the Senate and populace have transformed Rome. The first emperor, Augustus (r. 27 BC to AD 14), claimed to have found the city made of brick and left it made of marble; his (at times) deranged successors have all tried to emulate or outdo him.

Hadrian's immediate predecessor, Trajan, built his grand forum at the very heart of Rome. This magnificent complex of buildings includes baths, markets, a library and the famous column (over 38 metres/126 feet high), whose frieze tells the dramatic story of Trajan's campaign against the Dacians which ended in crushing victory in AD 106. Hadrian has at present no wars to commemorate monumentally. Instead, he has been creating a landscape all over Rome, and across the empire, that affirms him not only as Trajan's heir—and his family as worthy rulers—but as a successor to Augustus, whom he emulates above all. Hadrian uses a portrait of

Augustus as his personal seal and keeps a small bronze bust of him as a boy among the images of household gods in his bedchamber.[11] As Augustus did, so Hadrian is adopting a policy of consolidation in the empire and is attempting to raise standards of morality and discipline in public life. He is, likewise, keenly aware of the power of architecture in projecting a political message, and nowhere does Hadrian demonstrate the promotion of his family more strikingly, not to say surprisingly, than in the construction of a gigantic new temple to his deified mother-in-law, Matidia, who died in AD 119.

As new monuments are erected, the legacy of former emperors is swept away. It took twenty-four elephants to remove Nero's 9-metre (30-foot) bronze statue of Helios the sun god, which had been erected outside the entrance to his notorious Domus Aurea (Golden House), for which Nero had demolished countless people's houses and businesses.[12] Now, up on the Velian Hill at the eastern end of the forum, and just north of the Via Sacra (Sacred Way), the Temple of Venus and Roma is rising in its stead, on a massive platform measuring 145 by 100 metres (475 × 330 feet). Although it was inaugurated nine years ago, in AD 121, it will not be completed for several years.

To accompany the temple, Hadrian has also transformed an ancient festival, the Parilia, into a new one, the Romaia, a cult to commemorate Rome's birthday (*Natalis Urbis Romae*).[13] The event is celebrated on 21 April, just one of the 159 days a year when one can expect to see processions and games in the city marking one cult or other. It is an anniversary celebrated throughout the empire, nowhere more solemnly than by the army, which steadfastly maintains Rome's traditions wherever stationed. Every year, in celebrating this birthday, dutiful soldiers dedicate altars and carry out sacrifices in honour of *Roma Aeterna*, even in the remotest parts of distant Britannia, in outpost forts north of Hadrian's great Wall.[14]

Of all the innovation in building and engineering now taking place, Hadrian's newly rebuilt Pantheon is pre-eminent. Its massive unreinforced concrete dome is twice as big as any other in existence. Lying south-west of the new temple to Matidia, and abutting the elegant Saepta Iulia shopping district, it is approached across an exquisite square paved in travertine and surrounded by raised porticoes with columns of grey Egyptian granite, crowned with white marble capitals. The Pantheon itself is raised on a platform above the square and approached up two flights of steps, with a fountain on either side. The monolithic columns supporting its portico are 40 Roman feet high (almost 12 metres), made of marble quarried in the eastern desert of Upper Egypt. The interior dazzles with coloured marbles and stones: porphyry from Egypt, serpentine from the Greek Peloponnese, *giallo antico* from Numidia (Tunisia). Here are statues of the imperial family and the gods, arranged in such a way that the beam of light pouring through the central oculus is said to highlight each one on their feast day.[15]

Hadrian has also been making his architectural mark outside Rome. On visiting Britannia for a few months in AD 122, he seems to have sparked something of a building boom there as well. Ambitious *fora* and *basilica* are now being constructed throughout that province, mini-Romes going up in this far-flung place—not only in Londinium (London), the province's main city, but also at smaller towns such as Calleva Atrebatum (Silchester) and Viroconium Cornoviorum (Wroxeter). And, stretching across the northern boundaries of Britannia is the great Wall bearing Hadrian's name, which separates the Romans from the barbarians.[16] During the course of his reign, over a hundred cities throughout the empire east and west, north and south, will benefit from his personal attention, most notably his beloved Athens. From sweltering Africa to shivering Britannia, architecture serves everywhere to reinforce the union of state, religion and soldiery.

In the next month or so in Judaea, very possibly with Hadrian present at its foundation ceremony, a new and highly controversial city, Colonia Aelia Capitolina, will be instigated at the site of the legionary fortress built on the destroyed city of Hierosylma (Jerusalem). It will take Hadrian's family name, Aelius, and that of the god he closely associates with, Capitoline Jupiter, for whose great temple on the Capitoline Hill in Rome the Jews have been paying the levy they once contributed to their own temple until it was razed when Jerusalem was sacked in AD 70. There will soon be far-reaching repercussions for the Jews, for the Romans—and for Britannia's newly appointed governor, Sextus Julius Severus.

To service the current building boom, huge quantities of construction materials are being transported in ships, barges and wagons throughout the empire. In Rome, cranes and scaffolding can be seen everywhere. Workshops have sprung up all over the place, some of them specialising in different types of marble, others in specific architectural details: three alone are devoted to producing capitals for public buildings in the city, and skilled craftsmen have been brought in from Greece and Asia Minor to help.[17]

The vast quantities of white and coloured marble that are needed for Rome's imperial and other building work are shipped in from Turkey, Greece, Tunisia and Egypt. They arrive at Rome's great harbour at the mouth of the Tiber, Portus Ostiensis. The marble is transported by barge as required, first on a canal, the Fossa Traiana, which links Portus with the Tiber, and then up-river to the foot of Rome's most southerly hill, the Aventine. Here, vessels arrive at Emporium, the ancient river port of Rome. Boats and barges moor along the whole 500-metre (1,640-foot) length of its wharf,[18] which is accessed by steps and ramps that descend to the river. Behind it stands the massive Portico of Aemilia, which serves as a monumentally splendid depot for the huge number of goods arriving here. The entire plain is crammed full of buildings, especially warehouses storing the food, such as grain and olive oil, that serves the voracious and subsidized appetites of the population of Rome.*

At the southern end of the Emporium, behind the Portico of Aemilia and the state warehouses, carts laden with broken pots can be seen ascending the ramp up the Mons Testaceus (Monte Testaccio). This 'mountain of potsherds' is a gigantic rubbish dump of discarded olive-oil amphorae.[19] Olive oil—a fundamental ingredient of Roman culture—is used not only for cooking but also as fuel

---

* The area later acquired the name 'Marmorata', from the huge quantities of marble (*marmor*) that were once unloaded and stored here.

for lamps, and it takes the place of soap in the baths. Up to 95 per cent of the broken pots being deposited here come from Baetica, in south-western Spain. Smashed up after their contents have been decanted into other vessels, they are then doused in lime to disguise the smell of the rancid oil seeping into the clay, which makes them useless for recycling.[20]

Many Spanish olive-oil merchants have amassed great wealth and considerable power, organizing themselves into formidable trade organizations complete with influential patrons in Rome.[21] For some time now, the Spanish elite, such as Minicius Natalis and his family, have done much more than set up advantageous business deals and trading associations. They have used their vast fortunes to wield political power and influence. Even by the time of the Italian Flavian dynasty (emperors Vespasian, Titus and Domitian), at the end of the first century AD, something like a quarter of the Roman Senate was of Spanish origin. And now two successive emperors, Trajan and Hadrian, have themselves come from Spanish families, the Ulpii and the Aelii.

Although many senators now come from outside Italy, they are nevertheless expected to keep official residences in Rome and are required to gain permission from the emperor should they wish to travel abroad.[22] Trajan decreed that all Roman senators had to invest one-third of their property in Italy, so it is no surprise that rich provincials like Minicius Natalis's family, with their place near Hadrian's palace at Tibur, have acquired considerable estates, especially in the area around Rome.[23]

ROME AND BRITANNIA

Unlike Spanish goods, British products of any description are a rare sight in the empire's capital. Shoppers are daily seduced by dazzling wares for sale from within the empire's borders, and even from beyond them too—exquisite Chinese silk, Arabian spices, jewels from India; Rome is awash with Greek and Gallic wine, and Romans can choose whether Belgian or Spanish ham makes the better accompaniment.[24] But if asked whether they can identify any British products, Roman consumers might be stumped for an answer. Slaves, blankets or rush baskets (*bascaudae*)[25] perhaps? Roman gourmands are said to enjoy oysters from Kent but this may be a poetical joke at their expense rather than proof that British shellfish is readily available in Rome.

Curiosities and collectors' items from the remote island are few. In the first century BC, Propertius the poet described Augustus's friend and ally, the rich aesthete Maecenas, riding around in a painted British chariot outside Rome.[26] If such vehicles are still on the market, they will surely appeal to a dashing character like Minicius Natalis, for his passion is breeding and racing horses, which he does with great success: he is the first (known) Spaniard to have won at the Olympic Games. Following his triumph there last year, he made a votive offering of his victorious chariot and had it mounted near the Hippodrome at Olympus.

When Julius Caesar first landed in Britain, in 55 BC, he marvelled at the British charioteers who were able to run along the chariot pole, stand on the yoke and then jump back into the chariot with lightning speed.[27] He admired, too, their ability to retain control of their horses at full gallop down a steep slope and to rein them in and turn them in an instant. But that was some 170 years ago, and although chariots were used against the Romans by the Caledonians at the Battle of Mons Graupius in AD 83 it is unlikely that the warriors of conquered Britannia were allowed to retain their war chariots for anything other than ceremonial use. Despite their literary fame, neither British horses nor their riders appear on Rome's racetracks. Most of the successful horses to race in the city come from countries where the climate is dry and the going is sandy or rocky—conditions that produce the hard hooves that are essential for racing.[28]

So many foreigners have settled in Rome—often creating their own distinctive neighbourhoods—that it can sometimes seem as though whole populations have emigrated here *en masse*. The British, however, seem to be less successful than other provincials at cultivating contacts and patrons in the capital. As with their exports, few of these immigrants come from Britannia.[29] Thus, while men such as Minicius Natalis or Julius Severus will have encountered in their careers plenty of Britons serving as auxiliary troops in the army, scattered across the empire, the British remain a much rarer sight on the capital's streets than the large numbers of rich Spaniards, learned Greeks, or Gallic and Syrian merchants who have settled in the city or who trade with it. Rarer still—practically non-existent—are Britons who have made it to the top rungs of Roman society as senators.[30]

Years ago, before Britannia's conquest by Emperor Claudius in AD 43, certain British kings sent embassies to Augustus and paid court to him in Rome, even setting up votive offerings on the Capitoline Hill.[31] Augustus received two British kings: Tincommius, who ruled territory south of the River Thames; and Dubnovellaunus, whose kingdom lay north of the river, with a major centre at Verulamium (St Albans) and stronghold at Camulodunum (Colchester).* In the end, Augustus wisely decided to leave Britannia alone, although connections were maintained. As was the custom with other peoples from the fringes of empire, during those embassies and submissions to Rome the British probably left their sons as hostages in the great city, where they would have acquired a smattering of Roman tastes, manners and language and received training in the Roman army. Southern British rulers benefited from all manner of imported goods: food, drink and olive oil, as well as luxurious items of clothing, decoration and furniture. They also gained some knowledge of Latin, if only enough to write their names and status (*rex*) on the coins they began to mint.

It was the flight of Verica, a client king from southern Britain, to the court of Claudius in AD 41 that provided the emperor with a pretext for invasion. Claudius himself, accompanied by elephants, spent all of sixteen days in Britannia during the conquest two years later, arriving conveniently in time to capture Camulodunum and

---

* Tincommius was also known as Tincomarus (*fl. c.*25 BC to AD 5). The kingdom of Dubnovellaunus (*fl. c.*30 BC) was centred on Hertfordshire and the Chilterns.

thereafter receive the submission of many kings.[32] On his return to Rome he celebrated his magnificent triumph, to which he invited the governors of all the provinces. Among the proudest tokens of his victory was a naval crown: he set it on the gable of the Palatium (Palace) next to the civic crown, to show that he had not only crossed the terrifying *Oceanus* but also conquered it.[33] He and his son were awarded the title 'Britannicus', a title by which his son became known.[34]

The conquest of Britannia was also celebrated in more concrete terms. Within a year or so of Claudius's triumph, few citizens of the Roman Empire could have been unaware of his victory. In Aphrodisias, in the province of Asia (Turkey), Britannia's fall was commemorated in a marble relief depicting Claudius—in a pose of heroic aggression—brutally tugging back the hair of a distraught, personified Britannia, who lies on the ground, her face staring pitifully at the viewer. Her short slave's tunic has come adrift, rising up her bare legs and exposing one of her breasts; in vain she tries to adjust it with her one free arm.[35] Commemorative coins were also struck throughout the empire, some no doubt still in circulation in Hadrian's time. In Rome, a series of *aurei* and *denarii* was issued with Claudius's portrait on one side. A victory arch surmounted by a rider with trophies and the words '*de Britannis*' running across the architrave of the arch appeared on the reverse.[36] In Caesarea, in Cappadocia, a silver *didrachm* was struck with Claudius riding a triumphal chariot on the reverse and that phrase '*de Britannis*', below it.[*]

Two arches were constructed to commemorate Claudius's victory, one in Gesoriacum (Boulogne), from where he had set sail to Britannia, and the other in Rome. Unusually, the Arch of Claudius in Rome was integrated into the structure of the Aqua Virgo aqueduct, which Claudius had restored magnificently.[37] The arch was erected at the point where the aqueduct crossed the Via Lata

---

[*] One gold *aureus* = 25 silver *denarii*; 1 *denarius* = 4 brass *sestertii*; 1 *sestertius* = 2 brass *dupondii*; 1 *dupondius* = 2 bronze *asses*. In the eastern part of the Empire, the *drachma* was used: 1 silver *didrachm* = 2 silver *drachma*.

(Broad Way).* The dedication of the Roman arch, some nine years after the conquest of Britain, took place in the same year, AD 51, as the spectacular capture of the British leader Caratacus, son of King Cunobelinus, who was brought in chains to Rome. During the time of Claudius's invasion, Caratacus had become the dominant British leader, providing a focus of resistance to the Romans. His tactics of guerrilla warfare had proved so effective that he had managed seriously to harass the Romans for nine years. In the end, however, he had been forced to make a desperate last stand in the territory of the fierce Ordovices in North Wales.

Here, he was decisively defeated by the Roman governor, Publius Ostorius Scapula, and his wife, daughter and brothers were captured. Caratacus himself managed to slip through the net one more time. He fled further north, seeking refuge with Cartimandua, Queen of the Brigantes—who promptly threw him in chains and handed him over to the Romans. His story seized the Roman imagination. The historian Tacitus related the whole gripping episode, describing how the fame of Caratacus 'sailed over the islands and travelled through the neighbouring provinces to Italy... Everyone wanted to see the man who had defied us. The name of Caratacus was even known at Rome.'[38]

When the captive Caratacus and his family arrived in Rome, Claudius, who never needed an excuse to put on a show, invited the populace to see this notorious prisoner. Soldiers of the Praetorian Guard stood at arms outside their camp, while booty from Britain was put on display—horse trappings and torcs, typically barbarian Celtic items of treasure, guaranteed to send a shiver down the spines of the populace of Rome.[39] Next, Caratacus's brothers, wife and daughter were brought forward. They were extremely frightened and showed it. But when Caratacus stood before the emperor's *tribunal* (platform), he did so proudly and delivered the following speech, according to Tacitus:

---

* Later known as the Piazza de Sciarra.

If my moderation in prosperity had been equal to my birth and fortune, you would not have thought it beneath your dignity to receive a descendant of illustrious ancestors, ruling over many peoples. My present fate is as repugnant to me as it is magnificent to you. I had horses, men, arms and wealth. How astonishing is it, that I was unwilling to lose them? For if you wish to rule over everyone, does it follow that everyone is to accept servitude? If I had immediately been given up and handed over, neither my ill fortune nor your glory would have found fame and my death would have been followed by oblivion: but if you were to save me unharmed, I will be an eternal example of your clemency.

It is not known what Caratacus's *exact* words were, nor whether he spoke Latin or through an interpreter.* But whatever Caratacus really said, upon hearing his words Claudius pardoned him, together with his wife and brothers.[40]

Tacitus implied that Caratacus was exhibited outside the Praetorian Camp, in the north-eastern part of the city; but Claudius's new victory arch surely played a part in the proceedings. It would have provided a theatrical architectural backdrop, its friezes of Romans fighting barbarians and a procession of the Praetorian Guard mirroring the living tableaux below of conquered natives, barbaric treasures and stalwart Roman soldiers.

It is not known what then happened to Caratacus, but another no-doubt apocryphal story describes him wandering about the city after being pardoned. Beholding Rome's size and splendour, he is said to have exclaimed: 'How can you, who have such possessions and so many of them covet our poor tents?'[41] It is unknown how long Caratacus stayed in the capital and where he died; but in Hadrian's time it is conceivable that there are still people in Rome who,

---

* The words that Tacitus gave him are stirring pieces of rhetoric, reflecting this conservative upper-class writer's concerns about the demoralizing effects of imperialism and the decline of noble and dignified behaviour: that quality of *virtus* which he feared was now so lacking in Roman citizens.

even if they were too young to remember Caratacus's appearance in chains 75 years before, came across him in subsequent years.

With so few Britons apparently in Rome, and Britannia so far away, travellers to the province, such as its new governor, must rely for information on the eyewitness accounts and written reports of returning officials, merchants and soldiers. Julius Severus has no previous personal connection with the north-western provinces. All his foreign postings to date have been east of Rome—although he will have encountered Britons serving in Dacia while governor of Dacia Superior in AD 119–125. Dacia, like Britannia, has proved a troublesome place, dangerous because of its position on the edge of empire, with barbarian forces to its north and east.[42]

Now in his early forties, Severus comes from the colony of Aequum (near Sinj), in Dalmatia. His family are evidently of senatorial rank and well connected in Rome.[43] In common with other boys of his background, he was very likely sent to the capital to finish his education and ensure an early introduction into Roman society, so that he could meet eminent patrons to put forward his name for the right sort of job.* Despite his obscure origins, the strategy evidently worked. Severus was elected, aged about seventeen or eighteen, to one of four boards of minor magistrates of the city. He was a *quattuorviri viarum curandarum*, one of four magistrates who, together with the more senior aediles, were responsible for the maintenance and cleanliness of Rome's streets.† While this job may not have been quite as socially prestigious as the mint on which Minicius Natalis served, it was nonetheless a route to high office.[44]

Severus has enjoyed imperial favour from early in his career. He

---

* Sons of senators could begin to wear the broad stripe (*latus clavus*) on their togas, which signified senatorial status, shortly after formally entering manhood at the age of sixteen or seventeen. They were allowed to attend meetings in the Senate but could not officially take their seats there until the age of about twenty-four. They were expected first to gain experience in civil administration in Rome and complete service in the army abroad.

† The others were concerned with the coinage, the Centumviral Court (Court of Chancery), and capital cases.

served under the governor of Macedonia as quaestor, the first office available to young men on taking up their place in the Senate at the age of twenty-four. As a 'Candidate of Caesar', Severus was again backed by the emperor for the prestigious post of Tribune of the Plebs, a position that required him to be based in Rome. At around the age of thirty, he returned as praetor to command the Legion XIV Gemina, stationed at Carnuntum on the banks of the River Danube in Pannonia Superior (Lower Austria, between Vienna and Bratislava), a legion he had served as a callow military tribune. Few men return to command their old legions—perhaps because unforgiving career soldiers, signed up for twenty-five years, are all too ready to reminisce about any slip-ups they made as junior officers.*

The XIV Gemina 'Twin' Legion took part in the invasion of Britannia, where its men helped to destroy the Druids and their sacred groves on the isle of Anglesey in AD 61. Their victory over Boudicca, Queen of the Iceni, in the same year—following her butchery of the inhabitants of Camulodunum, Londonium and Verulamium—earned the legion its title of 'Martia Victrix' (Victorious by Grace of Mars), and later Nero singled it out as his best legion.[45] By now, unless there are some ninety-year-old veterans of the legion still around, there will be no one left alive who witnessed those blood-curdling scenes in Britannia, and Severus will need to familiarize himself with the province through official records and first-hand accounts from those men who have served there more recently.

One man with such insight is Marcus Maenius Agrippa. Originally from Camerinum (Camerino, in the Italian Marches), Agrippa has been commanding a British auxiliary unit, the Cohort II Flavia Brittonum, in Severus's current province of Moesia Inferior; he also has first-hand experience of Britannia itself. Agrippa served as tribune of the Cohort I Hispanorum at Alauna (Maryport), a

---

* Although most military tribunes were aged only nineteen or twenty, in their first military posting they were technically second in command of a legion. It may seem remarkable that someone so young and inexperienced should be put in such a position, but the idea was that a young man of promise should gain experience at the very top by shadowing the person whose role he would one day take up. See Birley (1981), xx.

fort on Britannia's north-west coast, just south of Hadrian's Wall, and earlier took part in a military campaign on the island, almost certainly in the north. He is personally acquainted with Hadrian, and three years ago even acted as host to the emperor, probably at Camerinum.[46] Severus may well have had a hand in the promotion of Maenius Agrippa to prefect of the British fleet.

Despite the insights that can be gleaned from old hands like Maenius Agrippa, general background information about Britannia's native population seems to be patchy, poetic and neither particularly well informed nor up-to-date. Romans have a disconcerting habit of recycling old information and perpetuating stereotypes in their geographies and histories. The attitude seems to be that if a topic has been covered by writers in the past, then the research has been done and all that remains is to collate it.[47]

For the educated Roman who reads his Horace and Virgil, Britannia represents the remotest shore, the untamed and unknown; there is a frisson of danger about it. Although the tentacles of Roman administration—via the army—have now reached into just about every corner of the province, and the island has been scrupulously measured and recorded, at least in terms of potential revenue, the inhabitants of the island are not necessarily more deeply understood.[48] Occasionally, the British are represented in literature as proud and noble as a means by which writers can criticise contemporary Roman life, with its taste for unmanly vices, excessive consumption and spoiling luxury. But the Britons are always presented as almost impossibly remote and somewhat uncouth, their bodies tattooed with patterns and pictures of all kinds of animals.[49] This viewpoint is more than a literary topos and is reflected in reality. Serving officers on Hadrian's Wall refer to the British disparagingly as '*Brittunculi*' (or 'Britlings') in the second century.[50] Clearly they have not progressed very much in their view of the native inhabitants since the days of the orator Cicero, who joked during Julius Caesar's expedition to Britannia in 54 BC, 'I don't suppose you're expecting any of them to be accomplished in literature or music.'[51]

WHAT TO PACK FOR BRITANNIA

With such thoughts in mind, cultured travellers bound for Britannia might well be keen to take some decent reading material with them, not to mention those small treats and necessary luxuries that they would be assured of in other, more civilized, parts of the empire. The *Letters* of Pliny the Younger (*c.* AD 61–113) were available in the bookshops of cosmopolitan Lugdunum (Lyon), in Gaul, during his lifetime; but who knows what will be on offer—if anything—in Britannia?[52] As this is not the kind of place to which friends can pop over easily, and it takes at least a month for letters, let alone packages, to arrive in Britannia from Italy, it may be advisable to stock up before you go. Affluent travellers from Rome can choose to make a last-minute trip to the luxurious shops in the huge porticoed piazza of Saepta Iulia, east of the Pantheon, adorned with paintings and sculptures. Selecting what and how much to take can be tricky. It is not done to be too overladen or flashy, of course. Having the kind of luggage which looks as though it has been around a bit and can be jostled without harm is better than being seen with the excessive bags of the *novus homo* (nouveau riche).[53]

A basic traveller's requisites can still, though, be considerable. During the First Jewish War (AD 66–73), the senior officers' baggage train formed a separate part of the Roman army's marching order and included members of their private households—slaves, freedmen, family members—as well as a change of horses, pack animals, portable bathing equipment and mobile kitchens.[54] For a serving army officer or government official, it is certainly important to have the right clothes. Officers are expected to have a proper mess kit, which includes dining capes and scarves, being required to wear appropriate attire at dinner, even in that most remote outpost of Britannia.[55]

Men of the world, such as Minicius Natalis and Julius Severus, can be relied upon to be properly equipped; but as the new governor of Britannia, Severus is subject to certain specific rules and allowances. Years before, in order to cut down on extravagances and make savings on the public purse, the Emperor Augustus introduced a fixed 'mule-and-tent' allowance for provincial governors. This replaced a system by which they contracted baggage handlers and then charged them to the Public Treasury.*[56] While away on tour, especially for a posting that will be for three years or more, the prudent should also think about what they will leave behind. They need to put items into storage for safe keeping, including furniture, clothing and medicines.[57]

As well as rules about what to pack, there are certain regulations about when to go. Emperor Claudius had decreed that governors who were appointed by lot (that is, to senatorial provinces) should leave Rome before 1 April, though this deadline was extended to mid-April; governors had apparently been in the habit of hanging about in Rome too long.[58] Perhaps, in their tardiness, some had missed the official start of their posting on 1 July.[59] An April departure from Rome should give everyone plenty of time to reach even far-off provinces comfortably, as well as the opportunity to make diversions to see friends, or visit estates, on the way. Unless there is an emergency, imperial governors going to distant provinces will set out at the same sort of time in spring, when the sea is officially open again after the winter.[60]

Governors travelling to an *imperial* province such as Britannia, however, are subject to different rules to those of *senatorial* provinces, as the former take their instructions from the emperor. A new imperial governor such as Severus is appointed formally by

---

* The specifics of what a governor setting out for his province was allowed to take in Hadrian's time is unclear, but a century later, during the reign of Severus Alexander, it is recorded that governors could expect to be provided with 20 pounds of silver, 6 she-mules, 1 pair of mules, a pair of horses, 2 ceremonial garments for use in public, 2 sets of clothes for private use, 1 set of clothes for bathing, 100 gold *aurei*, a cook, a muleteer and—if the governor did not have a wife—a concubine. On returning from his governorship, all the mules and horses, the muleteer and cook had to be returned to the central office, but the rest could be kept—according to the sometimes untrustworthy source—if he had conducted himself well. If he had performed badly, the ex-governor would have to pay back fourfold, in addition to being condemned for embezzlement or extortion.

letter, in a *codicillus* issued directly by the emperor,[61] and the new incumbent will correspond directly with his emperor while abroad, ruling the province on his behalf. In Julius Severus's case, he may conceivably have taken leave of Hadrian in person while the emperor was wintering in Antioch.[*]

All returning governors and procurators are obliged to leave their provinces as soon as their successors arrive and to travel to Rome without delay, to arrive back within three months of departure.[62] Leaving a province in early July will enable them to get back in time to oversee the grape harvest at their estates in September, when the majority of the Senate is absent from Rome.[63] Quaestors and other officials follow the same sort of timetable, leaving their posts in the provinces at the end of the 'proconsular' year (that is, at the end of June/start of July).[64] Governors of senatorial provinces— who wear civilian clothes and are not permitted to carry swords at their belts—assume the insignia of their office as soon as they leave the *pomerium*, the boundary of Rome, and continue to wear them until they return. Imperial governors, on the other hand, who are operating as the emperor's deputies, may only adopt the military uniform and badges of office on entering their appointed provinces.[65] It would be potentially provocative and destabilising—for the emperor as much as anyone else—to give them such privileges before they are safely confined within their provinces, where they are expected to stay until finishing their terms of office.

Setting out (*profecto*) on a journey and returning (*reditus*) from it are momentous events, charged with personal, religious and— if you are an important person—political significance. Emperors understandably expect from Senate and people overt demonstrations of respect and loyalty on their own departures, complete with prayers, sacrifices and libations for a safe journey.[66] Even if you are

---

[*] Julius Severus could well have travelled to Rome prior to taking up his governorship in Britannia, somewhat in the manner of a modern diplomat returning to his country's capital before a new posting. He might well have had business or political matters to attend to in Rome, too. But it is also possible that he travelled to Britannia direct from Moesia along the Rhine, or via Dalmatia if he had family estates there.

young and relatively unimportant, the start of a journey is marked in several ways, especially when it is as significant as a voyage to Britannia across the unpredictable *Oceanus*. In the weeks leading up to departure there is formal leave-taking, of patrons, older relations and important family friends, and in turn there will be visits from dependants and clients.

Everyone, of whatever rank and travelling for whatever purpose, has to be extremely flexible about the date, time and method of transport for the entire length of the journey. All travellers are dependent on the elements and the tides, not to mention in some cases the whim of the emperor, and must be prepared for delays and changes along the way. No one travels alone. High-ranking officials and their families will be escorted by a retinue of friends, family advisers, freedmen and household staff; and those close friends, family and clients who stay behind will make the effort to accompany them at least to the city's boundaries to bid farewell.[67]

CHAPTER II

Setting Sail from Ostia

τειχῶν γε μὴν οὐκ ἠμελήσατε, ταῦτα δὲ τῇ ἀρχῇ περιεβάλετε,
οὐ τῇ πόλει· καὶ ἐστήσατε ὡς πορρωτάτω λαμπρά τε καὶ
ὑμῶν ἄξια, ὁρατ<έ>α τοῖς εἴσω τοῦ κύκλου, ἡ δὲ πορεία ἐπ' αὐτά,
εἴ τις βούλοιτο ἰδεῖν, μηνῶν τε καὶ ἐνιαυτῶν ἀρξαμένῳ
βαδίζειν ἀπὸ τῆς πόλεως.

You have not neglected walls but you built them
around your empire, not your city. And you erected them
as far away as possible, splendid and worthy of you,
ever visible to those who live within their bounds
but for anyone from Rome who wishes to see them
the journey would take months and years...

AELIUS ARISTIDES, *On Rome*
(Oration XXVI.80)[1]

*

JUST AS all roads are said to lead to Rome, so there are many roads
out of the city, which ultimately lead to all corners of the empire.
Although Britannia is hardly the most convenient place to get to
from the capital of empire, there are several options open to those
wishing to visit the remote island.

Anyone travelling there will probably sail a significant part of the
way, weather permitting, for travel by sea is much the quickest and
cheapest form of transport for both people and goods. The River
Tiber is only navigable with small boats, and Rome's nearest port
for sea-going vessels is some 17 miles (27km) from the city. Until
the reign of Claudius, Ostia, at the mouth of the Tiber, was the port
of Rome. Under that emperor, a phenomenal feat of engineering

resulted in the creation of a new port (Portus) less than two miles to the north of Ostia. In Hadrian's day, the old and new ports are regarded as a single entity, and referred to as Portus Ostiensis or interchangeably as Portus and Ostia.

High-ranking officials such as Julius Severus and Minicius Natalis will have staff to make their travel arrangements for them; but the average prospective sea traveller can glean valuable information about ships likely to be sailing in their direction at the agencies or offices (*stationes*) of representatives from foreign ports in Rome. They may be able to tell you of a ship soon expected or already sailed into Portus Ostiensis and even secure you a place on board. Such *stationes*, once found around the Forum of Caesar, have since moved to other parts of the city. Some can be found on the Via Sacra, where the air is fragrant from the Horrea Piperataria—the warehouses built by Emperor Domitian to store pepper and spices from Egypt and Arabia.[2]

Although it is possible to sail down-river to Ostia from the centre of Rome—as Claudius did when setting out to conquer Britannia—it is an easy journey by road. Ostia lies 14 miles (23km) from Rome, and both Ostia and Portus are perfectly manageable in a day. Pliny the Younger, who had a superbly designed (in his view) seaside villa at Laurentum, near Ostia, described how it was possible to do a day's work in Rome and get to the villa for the night without feeling unduly rushed. Pliny described the trip as a pleasant ride, though once off the main thoroughfare parts of the road could be sandy and heavy-going in a carriage.[3] While some among Minicius Natalis's party, such as his wife and children, may travel by covered carriage or by boat down the Tiber, riding to the port could well be an attractive option for Natalis and other members of his retinue, especially when faced with the prospect of being cooped up on a ship at sea for the next few days—or even weeks.

There are two routes out of the city, depending on whether you are making straight for Ostia or for Portus. For those heading to Ostia, the Via Ostiensis runs along the left (southern) bank of the Tiber, while the Via Portuensis flanks the right (northern) bank.

There were no direct links to Portus until Trajan's time, when he extended the old Via Campana, which connected the salt marshes of the Campus Saliniensis, north of Portus, with the salt warehouse close to Porta Trigemina in the Forum Boarium.

In Rome, the Via Portuensis (Campana) crosses the Tiber on the bridge named Pons Aemilius into Trans Tiberium (Trastevere) district.* This populous area, with its many warehouses and workshops, is also the principal residential quarter for foreign merchants. Many freedmen and Jews of eastern Mediterranean origin have settled here, and anyone who takes the Via Portuensis out of the city will be struck by their highly decorated and distinctive tombs, which lie a little further along the road.

Between the banks of the Tiber and the road's first milestone is the Naumachia Augusti. A huge flooded basin, 536 metres long by 357 metres wide (1,758 × 1,171 feet), with an island in its middle, it was built by Augustus in 2 BC for the re-enactment of naval battles. Close by are the barracks where a detachment of the Ravenna fleet (*classis Ravennas*) is stationed, handily close to the Naumachia, where they no doubt help to stage the mock fights. They may even serve as harbour police and have official escort duties when the emperor travels along the river.

After about two miles, the road temporarily splits, with the new Via Portuensis taking a higher route to the west, while the old Via Campana follows the meanderings of the river, before reuniting again (at Ponte Galeria).[4] The newer stretch of road thus avoids the crowds of people along the Via Campana who, on high days and holidays, make their way to two ancient sanctuaries between the fifth and the sixth milestones.

One sanctuary belongs to the Dea Dia, a cult which is said to have been founded by Romulus. In addition to the ancient sacred grove—now within a monumental enclosure—there is a whole complex of buildings attached, including baths and an adjoining *circus*, or racetrack. Augustus revived the cult and made it chic. It is

---

* The remains of the bridge in later centuries will become known as the Ponte Rotto (Broken Bridge).

officiated over by the *fratres arvales* (Arval brethren), a select group of senators to whom Hadrian, automatically enrolled as a member on becoming emperor, is much attached. He consented to become their *magister* in AD 126, a job which entails officiating at arcane rites at the sanctuary, sacrificing on public occasions in Rome and holding convivial dinners for his fellow priests.

Rather less socially exclusive are the celebrants at the temple of Fors Fortuna a little further along the road at the sixth milestone. During the three-day festival of this goddess of (good or ill) fortune, held in late June, both road and river are choked with people. Parties of young men hire boats festooned with garlands, and they waste no time in breaking open the wine mid-river. A couple of days later they will attempt to make it back to Rome, hailing the stars, blind drunk.[5] Even on non-festival days the small boats on the Tiber make a colourful sight; many are painted, covered in bright pictures and patterns.[6]

On the opposite bank of the Tiber, visitors taking the Via Ostiensis can leave Rome from the heart of the Emporium, with the mound of potsherds on their right, or come down directly from the Aventine and pass through the Porta Ostiensis, one of the gates in the city's massive Servian Wall. (Named after Rome's sixth king, Servius Tullius, the wall is in fact a later construction from the early fourth century BC—but now the city has long expanded beyond it.[7]) Travellers coming from either direction pass the spectacular pyramid tomb of Caius Cestius, built in about 18–12 BC, and within a short distance they enter a suburban landscape of tombs, among which may lie the burial place of the Christians' St Paul. Many of the funerary monuments lining the roadsides are large and elaborate, even if not as spectacular as Cestius's pyramid.

Roadside tombs are not always the most salubrious places. They are notorious hangouts for the cheapest sorts of prostitutes, the bottle-blonde tarts (*flavae lupae*) otherwise known as *bustariae*—'grave girls'.[8] Tombs also have the reputation of being used as public conveniences. In Petronius's *Satyricon*, written in the previous century, the lavishly ludicrous Trimalchio declares that he is going to appoint a freedman to watch over the tomb he is about to commission so that people won't 'run up and shit on it'.[9] His solution might be typically extravagant but, as Romans know, the problem is certainly not confined to fiction. An inscription on the Roman tomb of Julia Fericula and Evaristus begs: 'Passerby, do not urinate on this tomb, the bones of the man housed here beg you. If you are an agreeable man, drink and give to me a mixed drink [of water and wine].'[10] Most messages along similar lines are rather less delicately put—blunt warnings along the lines of 'Whoever shits here, beware of bad luck!'[11] It is not only tombs that suffer this fate. Similar injunctions and pleas can be found outside the doors of private houses as well as on public monuments.[12] Just as people put out signs warning *cave canem* ('Beware of the dog!'), so there are signs threatening *cacator cave malum* ('Watch out for bad things, shitter!').

Once past the necropolis, the Via Ostiensis takes on a more pleasant aspect and runs close to the river again.[13] At the third milestone, where it reaches Vicus Alexandri, a small river port with docks, the route reveals olive groves, gardens, villas and farms.[14] Between the seventh and the eighth milestones, the road passes near to many fine villas in the possession of senatorial families.[15] Travellers to Britannia may spare a thought for M. Stlaccius Coranus as they pass his family's richly decorated funerary monument along the way. He was a local landowner and served as equestrian tribune in Britannia in the Legion II Augusta during the Claudian conquest, a legion now based at Caerleon, in South Wales.[16]

About 11 miles along the Via Ostiensis there is a fork in the road; this is where the younger Pliny would have branched off along sandy roads to his seaside villa.[17] Shortly afterwards, the road climbs, dips, then rises again to its highest point, passing over a ridge of hills. On this high land (Monti di San Paolo), there is a last view back towards Rome, as well as the first sight of the sea. Here, too, is the source of Ostia's water supply, brought to the port by aqueduct. From here, the road gently descends into the wooded and marshy coastal plain, where the climate is mild and the landscape pleasingly varied, with woods and meadows. Flocks of sheep and herds of horses and cattle graze in the fields; soon they will depart for their summer pasture in the hills.[18]

The coastal plain can be prone to flooding. (After the great fire of Rome in AD 64, Emperor Nero proposed sending burnt rubble from the city to fill up the marshes.[19]) For this reason, as it nears Ostia, the road is raised up on a low causeway.

OSTIA—BOOM TOWN

Founded on the southern side of the mouth of the Tiber in 386 BC, Ostia is a river port with only limited facilities for larger ships. This means that they have to anchor off the mouth of the river and transfer their cargoes onto smaller vessels. As a consequence, many larger boats, such as the gigantic grain ships that come annually from Egypt, formerly had to use Puteoli (Pozzuoli) in the Bay of Naples, 124 miles to south. This was a less than satisfactory arrangement, especially for something as crucial as the city's grain supply.

As demand in Rome grew for 'all the products of all the places in every season',[20] it was critical to improve the logistics for transporting these goods into the city. It was also important for Rome, as the centre of an empire that ruled over so many maritime lands, to have control of a large sea port in proximity to the city. In Hadrian's era, Ostia remains an attractive place to visit, even for those ultimately heading for the glossy new gateway of Portus. In fact, Ostia is buzzing, profiting hugely from the state investment in Portus. Far from being sidelined, Ostia has also grown in size and prestige.

Many foreign ship-owners have retained their offices here, and since the end of the first century AD, senators and members of Rome's equestrian class have been investing heavily in Ostia's development. Hadrian himself has been closely involved in the town's affairs and has served as *duovir*, or chief magistrate, on more than one occasion. Early in his reign a large area of shops and warehouses between Ostia's forum and river was rebuilt,[21] and the town now boasts new, state-of-the-art apartment blocks, warehouses, shops and luxury baths.

Coming from Rome, the visitor enters via Ostia's east gate, the Porta Romana. At this point, the Via Ostiensis becomes the Decumanus Maximus, the main street running through the town, 9 metres (30 feet) wide and flanked by continuous porticoes of gleaming marble. Right by the Porta Romana stands a new baths complex (Terme dei Cisiarii—'Baths of the Wagon Drivers') and a little further along, before the theatre and set back behind a portico, another enormous baths development (Terme di Nettuno—'Baths of Neptune') is under state-funded construction.

Hadrian's largest project here is his complete remodelling of the forum, which is now dominated by the Capitolium, a temple dedicated to the Capitoline triad of deities—Jupiter, Juno and Minerva—and flanked by porticoes of grey granite. The temple to these gods, who safeguard the health and security of Rome, stands opposite an earlier temple dedicated to Rome and Augustus, erected during Tiberius's reign. Urban development is particularly intense in the part of the town facing the sea, where a complex of pleasant, purpose-built apartments with central courtyard gardens (*case a giardino*) has recently gone up.

Ostia is a giant distribution centre for Portus. From here, cargo that has arrived at Portus can be dispatched, traded or stored, including wine and hides from Gaul, olive oil from Baetica (in southern Spain) and numerous goods from North Africa, such as lamps and cooking wares, fish sauce and olive oil.[22] The huge amount of marble being shipped in to supply building projects here and in Rome from Greece and Turkey, North Africa and Egypt, needs especially large spaces for unloading and storage. It is housed at a special Marble Depot (Statio Marmorum) lying between Portus and Ostia on an island known as the Insula Portuensis (Isola Sacra), which was created when the Fossa Traiana canal was dug to link Portus with the Tiber.

Few of the goods distributed from Ostia come directly from Britannia. As demand for British products in Rome is not high, the majority of British exports to the Mediterranean and imports from the region are probably sent via Gaul and the River Rhine, along trade routes that pass through the prosperous cities of southern and central Gaul and the great military bases and their associated towns in Germany. This route is also less dependent on the weather. By contrast, a journey sailing directly to or from Britannia hazards the stormy Atlantic coast and necessitates entering or exiting the Mediterranean through the straits of Gibraltar. This direct route was the one Emperor Claudius chose at the time of the conquest; but because of bad weather, he was forced instead to land at Massilia (Marseille) and continue his journey to Gesoriacum (Boulogne) along the roads and rivers of Gaul.[23]

In the second century, high-ranking officials, with a small convoy of boats at their personal disposal, may also favour this more direct route to and from Britannia—unless they have business in Gaul or along the Rhine. Travelling via the Straits might be a particularly attractive option for Minicius Natalis as it means he can visit family estates in Hispania before his three-year stint in Britannia.

According to Pliny the Elder, writing in the early first century AD, it was possible to sail from Gades (Cadiz) to Ostia in six days, while journeys from Hispania Citerior ('Nearer Spain', being the coast of Spain nearest Italy) could be done in three days and Narbo Martius (Narbonne) in two.[24] These are quick times; in unfavourable conditions, the journeys can take much longer.

Anyone travelling to Britain independently can elect to make contact with ships sailing to Gaul, which will be able to take them on the first leg of their journey.[25] Gallic ship-owners in Ostia have offices in a large rectangular colonnade with a small temple at its centre (Piazzale delle Corporazioni), which can be found behind the stage of the theatre. The office spaces are all tiny—but then most business is conducted outside and, as shipping is strictly seasonal, takes place mostly during the warmest, most clement months of the year. Outside each office is a decorative mosaic, identifying its occupants' business.[26] One depicts a ship next to a lighthouse bearing the inscription '*Navi [cularii] Narbonenses*' ('Shipowners of

Narbonne') above it. Here too is the office of the *stat(io) Sabraten-sium*, the North African city of Sabratha, represented by an ele-phant, as well as the agencies of Alexandrians and Carthaginians. Other offices in the square are occupied by associated trades, such as tow-rope and cord makers, tanners and the barge owners who transport goods from the large ships up to Rome.[27]

The Gallic ship-owners of Ostia are geared, as are their col-leagues from Africa, Egypt and elsewhere, towards cargo rather than passengers and many have made fortunes out of the import–export trade. Some run very large-scale operations. M. Sedatius Severianus from Lemonum (Poitiers), for example, who comes from a family of ship-owners on the Loire, is one such magnate with extensive interests at Ostia. He is destined for the consulship, the only known senator from that part of Gaul to achieve this.[28] International businessmen of his standing do not themselves hang about in the poky little offices at Ostia, but rather employ freedmen as their agents.

FINDING A SHIP

No one, however, not even an emperor or a general with an entire fleet at his disposal, can expect to arrive at the harbour, board a ship and set off at a fixed time. Indeed, only a minority of VIPs can even have an expectation of travelling on any particular vessel. The emperor himself might have to be kept waiting or change his plans if weather conditions are unfavourable, as Claudius had to do when he sailed for Britannia. Journeys by sea are very *ad hoc* expe-riences and everyone, of whatever status, needs to be flexible about the arrangements.

Most people travelling independently or in small groups simply go to the harbour and take the next available ship sailing in roughly the direction they wish to take.[29] As vessels hug the coast where possible, and stop frequently in ports and harbours along the way, travellers have many opportunities to disembark and find other ships that may go nearer to their ultimate destination. Each stage of such a journey involves a separate negotiation with the captain of the next ship.

While awaiting embarkation on the first leg, travellers can at least take lodgings in Ostia. The wait might be a matter of hours, days or even weeks if the weather suddenly changes. But at Ostia, at least the would-be travellers have an excellent choice of places to bathe, dine, worship, acquire last-minute provisions and rest in comfort before the long sea journey.

As is to be expected in any large sea port, there are bars and taverns to cater to those living or working here or simply passing through. Some of the establishments are a little on the seedy side, the haunts of 'hitmen, hangmen, sailors, thieves, fugitives, eunuch followers of Cybele and makers of paupers' coffins', according to the satirist Juvenal.[30] The landlords of such bars, often freedmen and women, enjoy as dubious a reputation as their clientele, ever ready to exploit the vulnerable traveller or drunken customer, and to part them from their purses.[31] There have been various restrictions placed on *popinae* (bars or cookshops) over the years, such as limiting the type of food they are permitted to offer, although it is not clear exactly why. Tiberius banned them from selling bread and cakes, while Nero forbade them from serving any cooked food except for vegetables and beans. Frugal Vespasian further reduced the menu to beans.* Perhaps the *popinae* kitchens were too much of a fire hazard, being typically situated in the heart of towns, or gave off too many vexatious fumes or too much smoke.[32]

In contrast to the paucity of food on offer, one can expect the bars of Ostia to stock a good selection of wines, from all over the empire and to suit all tastes, backgrounds and pockets. Romans have acquired a taste for Spanish, Greek and French wine, traded at Ostia's *forum vinarium*. The wine, which is stored in large jars on the bar floor or in racks on the wall, is decanted into jugs through a funnel and diluted with water. Regrettably, many a barman's hand

---

* Large pots from the bars of Herculaneum have been found containing very parsimonious ingredients—dried fruit, beans or chickpeas—suggesting that the regulations were adhered to at the time.

strays with the water, leading to customer complaints, sometimes scrawled in graffiti: 'What a lot of tricks you use to deceive, innkeeper. You sell water but you yourself drink unmixed wine.'[33] In the face of such jibes and accusations bar owners fight back, pointing out that you get what you pay for: 'You can get a drink here for only one coin. You can drink better wine for two coins. You can drink Falernian for four coins'.[34] Falernian is the most venerable Italian wine, an expensive tipple associated with high living.

It isn't only food and wine that is on sale here. Scrawled on bar walls throughout the empire, from the sweltering dives of Pompeii to the smoky taverns of Bonna (Bonn), are claims along the lines of 'I screwed the barmaid'.[35] While some of these brags may be drunken jokes or fantasies, the law certainly regards innkeepers and tavernkeepers as guilty of procurement if they are found to have girls offering more than just drinks.[36]

Perhaps it is possible to find among this shady crew an honest bartender to run up some honeyed wine for the journey. It is a soothing drink, which keeps well and is easy to make: just combine ground pepper with skimmed honey in a *cupella* (small cask) and, at the moment you want to drink it, mix as much as you like with the wine. If you use a thin-necked container, dilute the honey mixture first with some wine, so that it pours freely.[37]

Having been to the baths, a bar, a brothel—or perhaps all three— and after having eaten, prayed, rested or shopped, travellers must return to their lodgings at some point to await the summons to sail. Word may come from a sailor with an unkempt beard—it is considered unlucky for sailors to shave on board ship or to cut their hair[38]—or from a slave sent to enquire about when the ship is due to set sail. Once you are summoned, there is no time to waste as the ship needs to take advantage of the now favourable conditions, which means not just the wind but also the omens, for sailors are notoriously superstitious people.

THE GRANDEUR OF PORTUS

Connecting Ostia with its newer neighbour, Portus, is the Via Flavia, a late-first-century road that runs north–south through the Insula Portuensis. On either side of this road are the monumental mausolea and numerous graves of a large cemetery.* At its northern end, the Via Flavia crosses the Fossa Traiana canal by way of the Bridge of Matidia, another construction in honour of Hadrian's mother-in-law (and Trajan's niece).

As the gateway to Rome from the sea, Portus is much more than an enormous transport hub. It is monumentally impressive, proclaiming Rome's domination over the world. Goods arriving here on merchant ships from all over the empire are unloaded as quickly as possible and then either stored in gigantic warehouses, or taken straight on by barge through the Fossa Traiana and into the Tiber to Rome, or shipped on to other destinations. Along the canal, broad towpaths run either side, raised above the surrounding landscape and accessed at intervals by steps. Co-ordinating all this traffic to and from Rome is a constant logistical headache.[38]

Sailing daily into Portus Ostiensis, too, are crowds of people with many diverse reasons for visiting Italy. They include officials, merchants, tourists and military recruits—men such as young Apollonarius, a hopeful, Greek-speaking Egyptian recruit to the Roman navy, who, arriving into Portus on a ship from Alexandria, immediately sends a letter back home to his mother Thaesion to let her know that he has arrived safely.† His correspondence is proof indeed as to the efficiency of Roman communication systems. For, on reaching Rome the same day, a second letter informs his mother that he will be assigned to the main base at Misenum; and, having been suitably impressed by all that he sees on his first day at the heart of empire, he tells her not to worry because he has come

---

* It remained in use until the fourth century AD and left to posterity some of the most significant examples of Roman funerary architecture.
† He sails in the month of May, at some time during the second century, though the exact year is not known.

to 'a lovely place',[40] (καλον τοπον).

This is precisely the favourable impression that visitors are meant to have, from the moment their ships first reach the huge outer basin of the Claudian harbour. At its mouth stands the great lighthouse, modelled on the famous one at Alexandria. It is built on a man-made island, created out of the ship on which Emperor Gaius Caligula brought the giant obelisk from Egypt, which he erected in his new Circus.* From the harbour's mouth, ships travel more than two-thirds of a mile, passing a monumental series of colonnades, which stretch all around the harbour. As they manoeuvre into the unique hexagonal inner basin built by Trajan, they pass what looks like a palace (the Palazzo Imperiale), surrounded by administrative buildings, and a series of imposing warehouses and porticoes on the south side. The inner basin is absolutely calm, with a gigantic statue of the Emperor Trajan rising above it. A temple and surrounding enclosure forms its central focus, flanked by the almost continuous frontages of warehouses and offices.[41] Ships are able to moor in the dead calm of the centre of the basin while awaiting their allocation for a berth—each one marked by numbered columns on the sides of the hexagon.[42] The basin accommodates up to 400 large ships, so that a considerable proportion of the entire grain fleet can be in port at any one time.

For travellers arriving at Portus, this gateway into the heart of empire represents their first glimpse of Rome—and to those leaving it, their last. As ever, the emotional and political resonance was not lost on the port's architects. Portus is, as Juvenal put it, 'more wonderful than anything nature made'.[43]

The majority of the ships that dock in Portus arrive between May and October. During winter, the sea is all but closed to shipping, owing to the dangers of sailing in inclement weather, when moody skies obscure both sun and the stars. The most crucial commodity to be landed is grain, and it is North Africa that is Rome's principal

---

* The Circus was situated in what became the Vatican. The obelisk remained there (to the left side of St Peter's basilica) until 1586, when it was moved to the Piazza San Pietro.

bread basket. Late spring and early summer are not only the open seasons for travel by sea, but also the time of the Mediterranean harvest. Rome imports 20 million *modii* of grain each year from Egypt alone, more than 136,000 tonnes, with twice that amount from elsewhere in North Africa.[44] The spring and summer months are therefore ones of frantic activity and potentially great anxiety: bad weather, a shipwreck, a poor harvest or lack of capacity in harbour—all spell disaster. As each grain ship from Alexandria can only make a limited number of journeys to Rome a year, it is imperative that they are able to land safely in harbour, be unloaded and then set out again as quickly as possible. Everything at Portus is thus geared towards maximum efficiency and a speedy turnaround for both goods and passengers.

Emperors must keep Rome fed. Claudius almost lost his life in AD 51 when, with only fifteen days' supply of grain left in the city, he had to be rescued from an angry mob that drove him to the far end of the forum.[45] In order to prevent supplies falling so perilously low again, Claudius tried to tempt ship-owners to sail with corn during the winter months by guaranteeing them compensation in the event of loss and by providing perks and incentives.[46] His new harbour of Portus meant that ships were not riding at anchor in open sea.

The tall-masted grain ships make a splendid sight, not just because they are the biggest ships in harbour but for the hope they bring for the coming of summer and the season of plenty. The sudden appearance of the Alexandrian mailboats in spring, heralding the imminent arrival of the grain ships, used to send crowds hurrying down to the waterfront at Puteoli in the days before the harbour was built at Portus.[47] No doubt the sight of their arrival offers similar promise at Ostia.

The grain carriers may be the largest ships in port, but others are no less eye-catching. There are triremes of the Roman fleet, whose *rostra* (beaks) at their bows are sheathed with gleaming bronze and perfectly designed to inflict maximum damage on an enemy ship, while at the same time helping to spring the ships apart and prevent entanglement. The great swooping curves of their sternposts are carved in the form of animal heads, such as those of geese or swans. Some boats have giant eyes painted on their prows to avert the evil eye. Others have cows' horns hanging from the rigging and giant phalluses or heads of Medusa painted or carved around the ship to neutralize evil spirits and ward off ill omens. Their great iron and lead anchors are also carved with signs to avert bad luck, together with the name of whichever deity watches over the fortunes of the ship: some have Hera's shining star which, the sailors pray, will provide a guiding light on their journey.[48]

The ships of the fleet have sails but also banks of oars, with which they can manoeuvre in and out of harbour in the event of a dead calm. The sails themselves are also full of colour and symbolism and are made from rectangular pieces of linen, reinforced at the edges with leather. With Hadrian away from Rome, emperor-watchers will look in vain for the imperial titles emblazoned in gold letters across a sail, or one of purple, the colour that has denoted an imperial ship since the time when, in Pliny the Elder's phrase, 'Cleopatra arrived with Mark Antony at Actium on a ship with such a sail, and fled with the same sail'.[49]

Altogether, there are so many ships in port that the sight is quite overwhelming; indeed, such is the traffic endlessly coming into sight or pulling out of the harbour that it is hard to imagine how even the sea has enough room to hold them all.[50] The name of each ship is conveyed pictorially on either side of its prow. Here is a warship known as *Armata* (Armed), while others are optimistically (or perhaps euphemistically) called after Roman virtues such as *Pax* (Peace) and *Concordia* (Concord). There is a *Draco* (Dragon) and a *Taurus* (Bull), while the ship called *Europa* derives her name from the unhappy princess abducted by Jupiter, when disguised as a bull, and carried across the ocean on his back. Ships named after deities associated with the sea or rivers are also popular: *Neptunus*, *Nereis* and *Triton, Castor et Pollux*,[51] who were worshipped by sailors through their association with St Elmo's fire.[52]

The ships may be less lavishly painted than their smaller

counterparts on the River Tiber, but they are still a splendid sight, bearing decoration to match their proud names. The bows are painted with encaustic (paint mixed with wax) in a variety of colours—white, blue, yellow, green and red—and the hulls of some ships are painted too, the waxy mixture laid on while still hot to form a protective layer against the elements. Many hulls are also simply left black with a coat of tar.[53]

In contrast to the gigantic grain freighters and the long sleek ships of the fleet, the average *navis oneraria* (cargo ship) is the packhorse of the seas. It is broader than its purely military counterpart and sometimes nicknamed '*corbita*' (basket), because of the stout, round shape of its hull. The majority of ships sailing from Portus around the Mediterranean use a combination of oars and sails. Larger boats depend mainly on sails and use oars only for going in and out of harbour or rounding a point when battling with the wind. Among the smaller types of boats visible along the coast are the *celox* ('speedy'), a small, swift, single-banked boat often used by the military to carry dispatches and passengers on urgent business, and the long slender *phaselus* which can range in size from a skiff to a large ferry, and which uses both sails and oars.[54]

While the average merchant ship will only have room for a modest number of passengers in addition to her cargo and crew, the super-sized grain ships can accommodate several hundred people: Josephus travelled to Rome on one such vessel with 600 passengers, while the boat that carried St Paul as a prisoner on his journey to Rome had 276 passengers on it, even during the dangerous closed season.[55]

FINAL FAREWELL TO ROME

For all seafarers, travelling on whatever type of ship, the moment of embarkation must finally arrive. While only an emperor or general going off to war can expect a large formal leave-taking from Rome, with speeches, sacrifices, crowds and festive garlands, even the most ordinary traveller will expect some sort of a send-off from friends and family, who might accompany them as far as the edge of the city, or even down to the harbourside. At the water's edge, as the poet Statius describes, the 'heartless captain's shouts divides last embraces, ends faithful kisses and denies a lingering hug around a beloved neck', as the ship, with her narrow gangplank lowered into shallow water, makes ready to cast off her cables.[56]

If they have any sense, passengers detained by lingering hugs and kisses will already have dispatched a servant, slave or companion up the gangplank to secure a place on deck. On most ships there are very few cabins—usually just one for the captain or owner at the stern of the ship, with 'the helmsman's rudder hard by [his] bed'.[57] He may have to make his cabin available to other passengers, according to their rank. Depending on the size of the ship, there may also be other cabins adjoining the captain's.

One can expect passengers of the standing of Minicius Natalis and his family to be able to secure a comfortably appointed cabin. Otherwise, passengers will have to find a space on deck as best they can. Some ships might also accommodate people in the shadowy space below deck, a place to which passengers may retire to sleep, to get some privacy—or do something clandestine.[58] The hold may be damp as well as dark. Ships often carry some sort of pump to keep the hold free of bilge—and if there is no mechanical pump, then a weak or junior member of the crew has to do the job by hand.[59] Automatic bailers are also used to evacuate water flowing onto the deck. Excess seawater runs into a lead tank with a grille over the top, fitted just below the deck, which has two long lead pipes on either side running the width of the boat so that the overflow runs out of one pipe or another into the sea, depending on which way the ship is tilting.[60]

The only facility that the ordinary traveller can expect to be included in the price of their passage is access to fresh drinking water, which is kept in a large tank in the hold. Everything else, such as food and bedding, passengers must provide for themselves, so they need to come well equipped with blankets, leather cushions and mattresses if they are to have hope of passing the journey in anything approaching comfort.[61]

The main shrine of the ship is located on the poop deck, and on a ship of the fleet this is where the ship's standards can be found.[62] Before the start of any journey, crew and passengers sing hymns and prayers, make offerings, light a lamp and pour a libation either over the side of the ship or at the ship's main altar, invoking the ship's tutelary god and any other deities who (they hope) might look favourably upon them during their journey and make it auspicious.[63]

Although ships stop at harbours along the way, everyone has to be prepared for the possibility that for one reason or another, such as rough weather or being becalmed, the ship might be stuck out at sea for longer than planned. It is important, therefore, to bring emergency rations and food that will not perish or go off easily in warm weather. Hard, dry ship's biscuits are the staple for the crew; but dried fruit and nuts, preserved meat and fish, as well as grain to make gruel or porridge, not to mention the honey wine, all make good rations. Few will be allowed access to the ship's galley, which is small, its roof tiled as a fire precaution, with a hole in the middle to let out smoke. The cook prepares food on an iron grille fixed in clay above a floor of flat tiles. The bulkheads are filled with cupboards where cooking utensils and dinner plates and cups are stored, and there is a large water jar to hand. The crew guard their personal property jealously and scratch their names onto their own crockery.[64] Sometimes the crew bring fresh produce on board in the form of live animals, such as goats or chickens, if the journey is likely to be a long one.[65]

As the boat makes ready to leave harbour, it is probably best to keep a low profile while the captain shouts his orders to the sailors. His crew will be running around frantically, hauling up rigging, unfurling the sail, heaving the yardarm around and raising the anchors. Under the gaze of the huge statues of the gods and protecting deities of the port and the ocean which adorn the harbour, only the passengers have the leisure for reflection as the ship gradually leaves the harbour behind, 'the land receding by slow degrees as if it were setting sail rather than you'.[66] Many a traveller must experience a pang as they leave the magnificent embrace of Portus—and the protection and triumph of Roman organization and orderliness that it represents—and sail towards wilder, most distant shores. When, weeks later, travellers to Britannia disembarking at Rutupiae are greeted by a huge triumphal arch, they might cast their minds back to one of their last sights at Portus: an arch crowned by a chariot drawn by four elephants, and driven by the Emperor Domitian.[67]

And so the ships sail out of the inner basin and pass the Tyrrhenian lighthouse between huge breakwaters whose arms, in Juvenal's words, 'stretch out and leave Italy far away'.[68]

THE OPEN SEA

Once at sea, everyone gradually begins to adjust to life onboard. If you do not have a cabin, conditions may be not merely uncomfortable but as unsanitary as those suggested by the satirist Lucian in his *Zeus Tragoedus*. In the topsy-turvy ship he describes, a criminal is honoured with a seat next to the captain, while crowds of good people are packed together in a corner of the ship, 'not daring to stretch out their bare legs because of the filth'.[69] Passengers and crew, not to mention any chickens and goats on board, will produce quite a lot of filth between them in the course of a journey.[70]

Sickness is an inevitable hazard, as everyone lives so closely on board for days and perhaps weeks on end. A well-equipped ship or travelling party carries a medical chest stocked with remedies to cure stomach problems, eye complaints and seasickness. Pliny the Elder, who was admiral of the Praetorian fleet based at Misenum (Miseno), recommended wormwood (absinthium) taken as a drink to help prevent nausea at sea.[71]

Open-plan, on-deck living, where passengers camp out with their own food and bedding, is tolerable on journeys in the Mediterranean during the summer months, with regular stops at harbours along the way to stock up on provisions, to bathe and generally to relax on dry land. This is just what St Paul was able to do, even as a prisoner, on his way from Caesarea to Rome: after just a day at sea, the ship called in at Sidon, and Julius the centurion allowed Paul to go ashore 'to see his friends and refresh himself'.[72] When Gaius Caligula sailed to Egypt along the coast of Asia Minor and Syria, he went ashore each night, causing enormous logistic and supply headaches for local officials along the route.[73] They were obliged to get in large quantities of food and fodder to cope not only with the imperial entourage (including family, friends, retainers, guards, marines and animals) but also with the vast crowds who were turning out by land and sea, following the emperor's train ever since it had left Italy. Provincial governors such as Julius Severus and high-ranking officials such as Minicius Natalis will, however, be expected to travel a little more discreetly than an emperor. When onshore, they will stay with friends and acquaintances where possible, so that they can be assured of accommodation more comfortable and salubrious than the average wayside inn.

Over a period of days—or weeks—at sea, friendships will be struck up and confidences made over shared food and gossip, board games and music.[74] Those seeking peace and quiet and a tasty supper may try their hand at fishing over the side of the ship. But however passengers choose to pass the time, their most abiding and deep-seated fears will remain those of storm, shipwreck and drowning. The theme of shipwreck is, of course, as old as Homer, and the fear of drowning and the consequences of death at sea are vividly expressed by poets such as Ovid. While condemned to his own living death in exile, on the shores of the Black Sea, he wrote:

> I don't fear dying but… save me from drowning and death will be a blessing… if you die of natural causes or even by the sword at least your body rests on solid ground, as you fade away, and you can make requests to others and hope for a tomb—not to be food for the fishes in the ocean.[75]

Everyone dreads the sudden gloom that presages a storm, as the sea swells and one side of the ship plunges into the waves as the other rises into the air. The Greek novelist Achilles Tatius describes how, during a terrible storm at sea, wicker shields are set up on all sides of their ship and his protagonists Leucippe and Clitophon vainly seek shelter together with their fellow passengers, by crawling under them 'as if into a cave... abandoning ourselves to fortune and giving up all hope'.

If the captain gives the order to jettison all cargo, passengers know that they are in serious trouble, and they must heave everything over the side, including personal possessions. Ships are usually equipped with a lifeboat in the form of a smaller boat, or *scapha*, tied to the ship by a cable and manned at all times by a crew member or slave. On Achilles Tatius's fictional voyage, there is a terrible panic on board when the captain at last gives the order to abandon ship. The crew in the lifeboat tries to cut it free from the ship without letting desperate passengers climb into it, threatening them with swords and axes. At this point, 'ties of friendship and decency break down as each man seeks only his own safety and suppresses his more generous impulses... the passengers on the ship curse and pray that the lifeboat will sink'.[76]

The threat of shipwreck is all too real and the Mediterranean is littered with the skeletons of thousands of ships. All passengers and crew can do is observe the correct rituals to the gods, pray for a fair wind and distract themselves as best they can as they leave the Port of Rome behind them.

CHAPTER III

Through Gaul to Ocean

Narbonensis provincia... agrorum cultu,
virorum morumque dignatione, amplitudine opum
nulli provinciarum postferenda breviterque Italia
verius quam provincia.

The province of Narbonensis... by its agriculture,
the high repute of its men and manners and the vastness
of its wealth it is unrivalled by any other province and,
in short, is a part of Italy rather than a province.

PLINY THE ELDER, *Natural History*
(III.5.31)

*

PROVIDED that the gods and the weather stay favourable, the journey from Portus Ostiensis to the southern sea ports of Gallia Narbonensis, on Gaul's Mediterranean coast, should be relatively pleasant and straightforward. The journey from Rome takes, at its quickest, the best part of a week.[1] The boat will sail close to the coastline, calling into ports along the way and allowing passengers to disembark, eat, bathe and perhaps even sleep on dry land for the night, depending on the circumstances.

The first substantial port, just a few miles up the coast from Portus Ostiensis, is Centumcellae (Civitavecchia). Built by Trajan, it is a mini version of Portus, with an inner basin entered from the main harbour, which is protected by sea walls and an island built as a breakwater on the seaward side of its entrance.[2] Centumcellae provides safe harbour for ships bound to and from Portus and serves as an auxiliary port for cargoes arriving from Gaul and Spain: they can be unloaded here and then sent along the Via Aurelia to Rome, some 35 miles (56km) away.[3] The number of ports called at along the Italian coast is determined partly by the weather and partly by the requirements of the captain, including whether or not he needs to collect or deposit cargo *en route*. A senior official with a ship entirely at his disposal might choose to stop at particular places along the way, so that he can meet up with old friends or conduct business.[4]

During the summer season in the Mediterranean, the prevailing winds are northerly, which means that ships sailing north, such as those from Rome to Gaul, do so in the teeth of the wind. It can be strong, especially when the cold, sharp Mistral blows along the coast of Gallia Narbonensis,[5] or when the dry northerly etesian winds make life difficult in the Aegean and eastern Mediterranean. Sailing back to Rome is much swifter, and the journey from Gallia Narbonensis can be done in as little as three days.[6] Ships sailing from Narbo can reach the coast of Africa in five days (a distance of 500 nautical miles), whereas in the other direction a thirty-day sail from Alexandria to Massilia can still be counted as a good journey.[7]

Gallia Narbonensis (roughly, Languedoc and Provence) has been a Roman province since 121 BC. Up to the time of Augustus, it was known simply as 'Provincia'—*the* province*—and was, according to the Elder Pliny, second to none, 'in short, a part of Italy rather than a province'.[8] Its Mediterranean climate, its landscape studded with vineyards and olive groves, and its urban culture make it home from home for Romans. The province attracted a large number of Roman settlers early on, and now many families from here have attained as great a prominence in Italy as they have in their native land.

As ships sail past Antipolis (Antibes), travellers may get a strong whiff of *muriae*, a sauce made from tunny fish, for which the port

---

* It would later give its name to the French region of Provence.

is famous. They should breathe more deeply at Forum Julii (Fré-jus) just along the coast, a former naval base of the Roman fleet, where both the air and the milk are said to be beneficial for people with respiratory complaints.[9] An ancestor of Julius Severus, named Julius Silvanus, was born here. A veteran of the Legion VII Claudia Pia Fidelis, he settled in Aequum, Severus's birthplace, when it became a new *colonia* during the reign of Emperor Claudius.[10]

At Massilia, down the coast from Forum Julii, passengers may find much that is pleasingly old-fashioned and even still quaintly reminiscent of Greece. This former Greek colony, founded in about 600 BC, has also had much longer associations with Britain than has Rome. As early as the fourth century BC, the city had overland trading links, acquiring tin from the island, and the Greek explorer Pytheas partially explored Britain from here.[11] Agricola, governor of Britannia in the AD 70s, was born at Forum Julii and brought up in Massilia; he was, according to his pious son-in-law Tacitus (also, very probably, from Gallia Narbonensis), sheltered from unsuitable company by growing up in a place 'which so well combined a Greek sense of beauty with provincial frugality'.[12]

ARRIVAL IN NARBO

By contrast, Rome's first colony in Gaul was founded a mere 250 years or so ago, in about 118 BC. Narbo Martius (Narbonne), lying west of Massilia, is the seat of the provincial governor and the centre of the imperial cult. It sits at the crossroads of two great roads: the Via Domitia, which links Italy with Spain; and the Via Aquitania, which runs some 245 miles (395km) via Carcasso (Carcassonne) and Tolosa (Toulouse) to Burdigala (Bordeaux), thus connecting the Mediterranean and the Atlantic.

On approaching Narbo, sailors begin to decorate their ship with garlands and olive branches, and on arrival the most senior person on board will offer a libation in thanks. Crew and passengers might also offer a sacrifice and, especially if the journey has been a difficult or anxious one, they might wish to make an *ex voto* offering at a temple in the port, respectfully propitiating the local presiding deity.[13] This practice occurs in all corners of the Roman world. Just as the Greek protagonist of Achilles Tatius's novel offers a sacrifice (to the Phoenicians' great goddess Astarte[14]) for his safe arrival at Sidon, so Gallic and British merchants at the Rhine delta make offerings to the mysterious goddess Nehalennia, attended by her faithful hound, in thanks for a safe crossing of the perilous North Sea.

Everyone will be relieved to have safely completed the first leg of their journey and to spend a night or two on dry land in a civilized place like Narbo. But as the ship has now docked in a new province, there will first be the inevitably irksome customs to get through—as there are at all ports and boundaries between provinces and frontiers. Duty, which is generally between 2.5 and 5 per cent of an item's worth, is charged on the value of the goods (*ad valorem*) being conveyed from one province to the next. It is payable on everything other than items necessary for your journey (*instrumenta itineris*) and those for your own personal use (*ad usum proprium*).

Customs officials are no more popular than any other sorts of tax collectors, and there are endless complaints about them throughout the empire. One edict against them, issued by the prefect of Egypt, declared:

> I am informed that the customs collectors have employed fraudulent and clever tricks against those who are passing through the country and that they are also demanding what is not owing to them and are detaining those who are on urgent business, in order to get them to pay for a speedier release. I therefore order them to desist from such greed.[15]

The pettiness of customs officials and the upset they cause by their rifling through bags are also common sources of exasperation. The biographer Plutarch, who died *c.* AD 120/7, held up customs officials as examples of intrusive busybodies: 'we are annoyed and displeased with customs officials, not when they pick up those articles which we are importing openly but when in the search for concealed goods they pry into baggage and merchandise which are another's property'.[16] Some enterprising individuals resort to tricking the customs men, by pretending that the goods they are importing are for their own use rather than for sale.[17]

Elsewhere in the port there is furious activity, as hundreds of people engage in the unloading of goods and in making ready the ships. Here are heavy barrels of Gallic wine, each being steered by two men up the gangway and over the sides of ships. Huge frames stand on the quayside ready to receive the large spiky-bottomed amphorae, full of Spanish olive oil, which are then closely stacked onto the frame in a pyramid shape. Once on board, the amphorae are kept in the hold, their spikes wedged into the gaps between the amphorae in the layer below.

Slaves carry sacks and smaller amphorae over their shoulders. They are bent almost double as they trudge down the gangplanks. Heavy amphorae need to be carried by two men, who slot poles between the handles. For extra protection during the journey, amphorae can be wrapped carefully in plaited straw or nestled in twigs and branches.

A governor on his way to a new province, such as Julius Severus, or a legionary legate, such as Minicius Natalis, can be assured of hospitality at the provincial governor's residence, even if the latter is not at home. Other well-connected travellers might have family friends, business associates or, through letters of introduction, friends of friends who can put them up for a night or two. Even if the owners of a local estate are away in Rome or at properties elsewhere in the province, it is to be hoped that they will have written to their estate managers on their guest's behalf, to ensure that their housekeeper is expecting visitors and will have food and a bed prepared.[18]

Comfortable and convenient though such arrangements might be, there remain all the constraints that giving and accepting hospitality demand of guest and host alike. Plautus's comment in his second-century BC play *Miles* is still just as relevant in the second century AD: don't overstay your welcome. Three days is okay, but after ten days 'it's an *Iliad* of disagreements. The slaves begin to talk.'[19]

With a far-off province to get to, no one is likely to stay in one place for more than a day or two unless delayed by illness or bad weather. Writing after Caesar's expedition to Britain, in the first century BC, Strabo observed that there were four sea crossings commonly used in getting there from the Continent, namely from the mouths of the rivers Rhine, Seine, Loire and Garonne.

If the sailing conditions are unpromising, then there are long-established overland routes up to the *Oceanus Britannicus*, the English Channel. Trade routes between Britain and the Mediterranean were in operation centuries before the Roman conquest. Diodorus Siculus, writing *c.*60–30 BC, but using third-century sources, relates how it took traders thirty days to travel across Gaul on foot with their packhorses, bringing British tin to the mouth of the Rhône, at Massilia and Narbo.[20] Their route went along the estuary of the Gironde and the valley of the Garonne by way of Burdigala, Tolosa—an ancient trading post between Gallia Narbonensis and the Celtic tribes of Gaul before their conquest[21]—and on to Carcasso and Narbo.[22]

Today's travellers from Narbo to Burdigala may also follow the ancient tin traders' route, now transformed into the Via Aquitania. At Burdigala there will be plenty of merchant ships heading up the Atlantic coast, perhaps even ones sailing straight for Britannia and distant northern British ports.[23]

LUGDUNUM—EPICENTRE OF
THE THREE GAULS

Travellers taking the overland route now have the option to continue north by road or river into Tres Galliae (Three Gauls), an altogether different entity from Gallia Narbonensis. Acquired much more recently, during Julius Caesar's conquests of 58–51 BC, the region was once referred to as 'Gallia Comata'—Long-haired

Gaul—after the outlandish hairstyles of the natives. Tres Galliae consists of three provinces: Aquitania, Lugdunensis and Belgica.* During the first century AD, the region was further restructured when a military zone along the Rhine was established and two additional provinces of Germania Superior and Germania Inferior (Upper and Lower Germany) created.†

The effective capital of Tres Galliae is Lugdunum (Lyon), which sits at the confluence of the rivers Rhône and Saône. It is readily accessible from most parts of Gaul and from the Rhine via the great rivers and network of roads that converge on it. The majority of goods reaching Britannia from the Mediterranean probably do so via Lugdunum, being shipped along the Rhône and the Rhine in consignments destined mainly for the large civilian and army populations in the Rhineland. Any onward shipments bound for Britannia will then arrive in the province via ports on the North Sea.[24]

Although the route to *Oceanus Britannicus* from Lugdunum pre-dates the conquest of Gaul, it was under Augustus that M. Vipsanius Agrippa established a military road system centred on Lugdunum, with roads leading west to the Atlantic coast and north to Colonia Agrippina (Cologne) via Andematunnum (Langres, in Champagne). One road led north-west up to Gesoriacum (Boulogne) via Augusta Suessonium (Soissons) and Samarobriva (Amiens).

A centre of the imperial cult of Rome and Augustus was founded in Lugdunum by Drusus in 12 BC. It was served by priests drawn from the Gallic nobility. At the sacred precinct of Condate above the rivers, the aristocratic high priest still performs sacrifices at the great altar, which is faced in marble and glitters with the gilded names of the Gallic states inscribed on it. Here, once a year, prominent members of town councils from every state in Tres Gallia

---

* Aquitania was bordered by the Bay of Biscay to the west and the Pyrenees to the south; Lugdunensis comprised central and eastern France, and Belgica northern France, Belgium, Luxembourg and a part of western Germany, including Trier.

† Germania Superior (Upper Germany) comprised parts of eastern France and western Germany; Germania Inferior (Lower Germany) included the southern part of the Netherlands, the eastern part of Belgium and part of Germany.

gather at an assembly in the magnificent amphitheatre, next to the altar, to vote for the annually elected *sacerdos*, or priest of the cult, and for other officers of the assembly. To be elected priest is the highest honour in Gaul, and the Gallic aristocracy have embraced both the cult and the assembly enthusiastically, taking advantage of the opportunities they offer for enhanced prestige. At Lugdunum, nobles vie with each other in other ways too—in erecting monuments at their own expense, and in mounting increasingly spectacular and costly gladiatorial shows.[25]

Worshipping the *numen* (divine spirit) of the emperor through the imperial cult is required of everyone in the empire, military or civilian. But it is, in religious terms, unproblematic for people who view the whole world as alive with many spirits and deities, and where each locality has a presiding spirit, which it is wise to propitiate. The only peoples for whom worship of the imperial cult is impossible are the Jews and Christians, whose belief in a single deity excludes the worship of any other, including the emperor. And it is because the Christians refuse to honour the imperial cult that they are persecuted as a dangerously subversive and disloyal group.[*]

As a hugely important commercial and administrative centre, Lugdunum offers all the attractions of a great city. Many emperors have used it as a base while on their travels further north, including Claudius, who was born here.[26]

PLEASURES AND PERILS OF
GALLIC HOSPITALITY

While men of the status of Julius Severus or Minicius Natalis, and their companions, can expect to be entertained in the style to which they are accustomed at Lugdunum, anyone making their way independently to Britannia, or travelling in less elevated company, will have to take pot luck among the many private establishments

---

[*] The account of the horrible persecution of Christians in the amphitheatre at Lugdunum in AD 177 is preserved in Eusebius (*Ecclesiastical History*) 5.1.

available in the city and along the main roads out of town. While small hotels can typically be found in the centre of towns, larger establishments are often on the outskirts, where space is at less of a premium and carriages, horses and mules can better be accommodated, especially as there are restrictions about bringing them into town centres.

Hotels and inns go by all sorts of names. Some are called after a feature of the building, such as *ad Pictas* (At the Painted Houses), or take their names from the surrounding landscape, such as *ad Pontem* (At the Bridge). They might be known after a sign painted on, or hung from, the building, such as *ad rotam* (The Wheel), or named after beasts: *ad aquilam* (The Eagle) or *ad draconem* (The Dragon).[27] The signs are attractive enough, and they ensure that strangers can locate a hotel in a world that lacks formal street names and house numbers. But with so many places on offer, innkeepers and hoteliers have to work hard at marketing their businesses. In Lugdunum, one owner, Septumanus, hopes to attract plenty of customers with the upbeat advertisement he has pinned to the wall of his hotel: 'Mercury here promises wealth; Apollo, health; Septumanus hospitality, with a meal. Whoever comes will feel better afterwards. Guests, take care where you stay.'[28]

'Take care where you stay': Septumanus brilliantly plays on the fears of many travellers. As with bars or *popinae*, the inns and innkeepers have, at best, ambiguous reputations. The medical writer Galen mentions dodgy innkeepers passing off human flesh as pork.[29]

Innkeepers are not always male, and the vivid world conjured up in Apuleius's second-century novel *Metamorphoses* offers a rare glimpse of feisty, witty and seemingly independent women running the show. One of them, Meroë, 'an old but still very beautiful woman', cooks a big free meal for any male guests she likes the look of, as well as inviting them into bed with her; but then—and here is the catch—she turns them into animals if they displease her. One of the worst fates is that of the man she turns into a beaver, 'because the beaver, when alarmed by the hunt, bites off its own testicles and leaves them lying by the river bank to put the hounds off the scent'—a lot she hopes will befall her disappointing lover. While such startling metamorphoses are confined to the story books, there is certainly sex on offer at many establishments.[30]

Even the most basic provincial inn must provide stabling for horses and mules, as well as an enclosed courtyard where carriages can be parked securely, so that they do not need to be unloaded completely. A gatekeeper will be on twenty-four-hour duty to guard the entrance against intruders and to prevent guests leaving without settling their accounts.[31]

Guests expect to be able to secure their rooms—against non-magical intruders at least—by means of a lock and bar. Rooms tend to be sparsely furnished. Uncomfortable beds, with uneven legs or bases, always that little bit too short, are a hazard the empire over.[32] Unless the inn has its own bath house, guests will be directed to the nearest one in town, private or public, reputable or otherwise, depending on their requirements. Some hotels include free admission to nearby baths in the price of the room.[33]

Having finally settled into their lodgings and bathed, travellers' thoughts can naturally turn to food and drink; unless, through drinking brackish water, their stomachs have rebelled and they are forced to sit and watch their companions tuck into dinner. Such a fate befell Horace during his poetic journey to Tarentum in the twilight years of the Roman republic.[34] It is to be hoped that the human flesh that Horace speaks of [35] will be off the menu, and that instead there will be appetising food on offer, such as prawns, African snails, ham and sausages, all of which—Horace tells us—line the stomach for a night of serious drinking.[36]

As everyone knows, the Gauls' capacity for feasting and drinking (a barbarian hallmark) is legendary: they are said to have the habit of drinking their wine unmixed and in such excess that they either fall into a stupor or lapse into a state of madness. As a consequence, they become flabby and unfit, 'quite incapable of running or hardship and when required to exert themselves they get breathless and sweaty and soon became exhausted'.[37]

Before the Roman conquest of Gaul, its inhabitants were said to have had such a thirst for Italian wine that they were prepared to pay over the odds for it: a slave in exchange for a jar of wine.[38] Nowadays, the Gauls produce their own wine and export it to the Romans, though they still import *grands crus* from the eastern provinces. Their own sweet, strong wine of Massilia, produced in limited quantities, can command as high a price as Falernian.[39] Vienna (Vienne) produces 'pitch-flavoured wine', while wine from Baeterrae (Béziers) is extremely popular in Rome,[40] although Pliny the Elder was scathing, claiming that many Gallic wine-dealers adulterate it, adding colour and doctoring it with herbs and harmful drugs.[41]

If you are drinking good wine in elevated company, then elegant receptacles will be provided, such as crystal glasses. For the consumption of beer, punch or *vin ordinaire* in more casual surroundings, there are jokier sorts of cup, perhaps even of the kind inscribed with bar-room banter in colloquial Latin, complete with abbreviations, shifting vowels, dropped 'h's and slipshod grammar: (*H*)*ospita, reple lagone*(*m*) *cervesa* ('Hostess, fill up my flagon with beer') or *Reple me, cop, conditi* ('Fill me up with punch, boss.')[42]

On finally repairing for the night, travellers—it is to be hoped—will not be kept awake as Horace was on his journey to Tarentum (Taranto). First there were the tedious voices of those who had drunk too deeply from the punch and cheap wine, such as the sozzled boatman singing too loudly of his distant lover, and the inevitable fellow who joined in, trying to outdo him. All this in addition to the mosquitoes and the fantasies about the girl who promised to come to his room but failed to show up.[43]

A traveller might or might not end up sharing a bed with a companion, paid for or otherwise. Slaves will sleep on a mattress on the floor, possibly in the same room, and in readiness for whatever services they may be called on to perform during the night—regardless of whether anyone is in bed with their master or mistress. Even if you retire alone, the probability is that at some point during the night you will realize that you are, after all, sharing your bed with not one but many miniature companions: the bedbugs that so many writers mention in their descriptions of a night spent at an inn or lodging.

Before going to sleep it is advisable to check that there is a chamberpot under the bed, to avoid the fate of the unfortunate guests at Pompeii's Inn of the Mulekeepers, who scrawled outside the door of their hotel: 'We have wet the bed, my host, I confess we have done wrong. If you ask "Why?" There was no chamber pot.'[44]

The hope is that the next morning you will wake up with neither a hangover nor bites from bedbugs, nor as a castrated beaver, but feeling alert and ready for the rigours of the journey ahead.

TO GESORIACUM... AND OCEANUS

Outside the towns, Gauls in their vast country may still indulge in quaint barbaric habits. But most imperial travellers, unless they are curious Greeks collecting ethnographic information about the locals, will be more interested in getting safely to their destinations along the fastest routes. As you go further north, however, you cannot fail to notice dramatic changes in the landscape and climate, and, while passing through smaller towns and roadside settlements, you will hear the Celtic language spoken more often than Latin. Different types of buildings appear in the countryside, including roundhouses, and there are unmistakable changes in the dress and appearance of the people, who wear trousers or short tunics, with scarves tucked into their necks and long capes.[45]

For the most part, though, Roman travellers will be able to cocoon themselves from anything too foreign or rustic, riding on well-maintained roads with *stationes* (service stations) at regular enough intervals, and staying where possible among people of similar background in private residences or perhaps in *mansiones*— the official guesthouses for government officials, provided at key stopping places along the major roads.

Conveyed by various means (boat, barge, carriage, ox cart or on horseback), and following their various routes—by land or by river through Gaul, or by ship along the Atlantic coast—our travellers to Britannia eventually arrive at Gesoriacum (Boulogne), the Continental base of the *classis Britannica*, or British fleet. Those who left Portus Ostiensis could well have been in transit for three weeks or more by now, and those arriving here via family estates or from distant postings will also have been travelling for some time.

Any members of Severus's new staff who have come from elsewhere in the empire will be able to meet up with him at Gesoriacum if they have not already joined him along the way.* With such a large number of soldiers stationed in Britannia, Julius Severus will have more posts to offer than do the governors of most other provinces. Although senior military positions are in the emperor's gift, Julius Severus has undoubtedly had a say in the appointment of Minicius Natalis as the new legionary legate and Maenius Agrippa as commander of the British fleet, both of whom he has worked with in the past: Natalis may have been serving as a tribune in the Legion XIV Gemina in Pannonia Superior at the time when Severus was commanding that legion, while Agrippa was the prefect of the *ala Gallorum et Pannoniorum catafractaria*, a heavy armoured cavalry unit in Moesia Inferior.[46] If there is trouble in Britannia, and war or the reorganization of the province is looming, Severus will be keen to have these men by his side as soon as possible.[47]

On a clear day, Julius Severus will have a fine view of the coastline of Britannia from the British fleet's base, which is built on a hill overlooking the harbour. Enclosing an area of about 31 acres, it houses around 3,500 men.[48] On high ground, roughly a mile to the north-west of the base, a lighthouse built by Gaius Caligula helps ships navigate the Channel.[49] An answering light across the water in Britannia shines from lighthouses on the cliffs of Dubris (Dover).† Alongside Gesoriacum's harbour are extensive *navalia* (shipyards),

---

* Those coming from the Rhineland, for example, could have travelled from Cologne (Colonia) via Tongres (Atuatuca Tungrorum), Bavay (Bagacum), Tournai (Turnacum) and Cassel (Castellum Menapiorum).

† Remarkably, one of those lighthouses, among the most astonishing Roman remains in Britain, may still be visited at Dover Castle.

where boats can be brought out of water during the long winter months when the sea is 'closed' and when maintenance and repairs can be carried out: prows painted, sails repaired and hulls recoated with pitch and wax to make them more watertight. Nothing goes to waste, and should a vessel be damaged beyond repair, every scrap of it will be recycled, right down to the bolts, nails and even the wax.[50]

The British fleet is one of the two most important provincial fleets of the empire, the other being the *classis Germanica*, which patrols the Rhine and has its main base at Altenburg, near *Colonia Claudia Ara Agrippinensium* (Cologne). Only the Italian fleets based at Misenum and Ravenna are ranked higher. The *classis Britannica* patrols the Channel and the seas around Britannia, ensuring that supplies are maintained for the province's army and that any goods exported from there on behalf of the emperor, or to supply the army on the Rhine—such as tin, lead, wheat and hides—reach the Continent in safety. Organized along the lines of the auxiliary sections of the army, the fleet is recruited largely from non-citizen provincials who sign up for twenty-six years (one year longer than in the army) and are awarded the prize of citizenship on discharge.

The commander of the British fleet needs to be a senior officer of equestrian rank with sound administrative experience, someone who can deal with logistics and keep complicated supply networks running smoothly. Maenius Agrippa is just such a man.[*] He and his deputy, the *subpraefectus*, will be supported by staff such as clerks and accountants, quartermasters, messengers and doctors based in Gesoriacum and Dubris, in addition to several likely outposts around the British coast.

Although the *classis Britannica* still counts men from the Mediterranean area, such as Syrians and Thracians, among its ranks,[51] these days there are many more from the north-western provinces. The Romans were swift to enlist men from tribes such as the Batavii, Chauci, Frisii, Morini, Menapii and Veneti after the conquest

---

[*] He clearly excelled at his new role and flourished in Britain, afterwards being made procurator of the province.

of their territories. Living along the coastline of Gallia Belgica and Batavia (northern France, Belgium and the Netherlands), these people have crucial experience of sailing in the strong tidal waters of the Atlantic and North Sea, and of the different types of vessels and skills needed to navigate these waters. By AD 69 the commanding officer of the *classis Germanica* was a Batavian officer, Julius Burdo,[52] with large numbers of his fellow Batavians serving as oarsmen. The Batavians had a crack cavalry force, which could swim the Rhine in perfect formation in full armour while holding on to their mounts.[53] Sailing men from Britannia were also swiftly recruited into the German fleet.[54]

In the harbour are vessels better suited to the tidal waters of the north-western provinces, with high bows and sterns to protect against heavy seas and storms, than the Mediterranean ships. While the latter are constructed using interlocking timbers, the northern vessels are made of stout planks laid edge to edge which are secured to massive, closely spaced framing timbers by large iron nails. The northern ships' flat bottoms help them ride in shallow waters and on ebb tides, and better enable them to be drawn up on a beach, where they sit upright on the shore. Their sails, like the river boats of northern Gaul, are made of raw hides or thin leather,[55] and their anchor chains differ too, being made of iron rather than rope.[56] Larger ships have additional masts and sails, including a triangular 'lateen' sail, which allows them to sail more directly into the wind.[57] All in all, these vessels make ideal transports for soldiers, horses and supplies. They were swiftly adopted during Caesar's second expedition to Britannia and used in Germanicus's naval expedition from Rhine to Ems in AD 15.[58]

At Gesoriacum ships will now be put at Julius Severus's disposal and that of his retinue of friends, family advisers, freedmen, household staff, bodyguards, horses (and hounds) and all their various baggage, to transport them over the *Oceanus Britannicus* (English Channel).[59] But before Julius Severus sets sail, he must first write to the outgoing British governor to confirm the day on which he expects to arrive. He is required to do this not only as a matter of courtesy, but also to prevent any fears among the provincials of a hiatus in government, which might lead to unrest or prevent business being carried out.[60]

Julius Severus might have the option of sailing ceremoniously to Britannia in a conventional trireme: there is one based at Gesoriacum called *Radians*, 'Gleaming'.[61] But he can also take a smaller, nippier type of naval galley which has been specially adapted for use in the north-western provinces.[62] Although the boats have oars, sails are used whenever possible, and it is only ever when under duress—during a battle or when required to go at top speed to carry an urgent message—that all the oars are manned.

On board these vessels, the crews are jealous of their status as military men, describing themselves as soldiers rather than sailors.[63] They have undergone rigorous training, having been taught to row on dry land on special practice benches before being let loose on a ship; now, when the *pausarius*, or chief oarsman, calls out the stroke they all row together, perfectly in unison.[64] There are no pitiful galley slaves in the Roman fleets.

As they take leave of the Continent, Julius Severus and his retinue pass under the most prominent monument in the port: the victory arch granted to Claudius, commemorating the place from which he launched his successful invasion of Britannia in AD 43. The distance they will travel, from Gesoriacum to Rutupiae, is approximately 40 nautical miles. Provided all goes well, the journey will take between six and eight hours, benefiting from the prevailing south-westerly winds. If the ships cast off about the time of the third watch, around midnight (as Caesar's did in 55 BC), they should reach Britain at about the fourth hour of the day, around 9am.[65]

The route across the Channel to Rutupiae may be short in comparison with the many miles travelled to get to Gesoriacum, but the symbolic distance is immense. For to step foot on a ship bound for Britannia is to venture into *Oceanus*, that immeasurable expanse of sea full of monsters and perilous tides, beyond which lies a land of unfathomable people.

CHAPTER IV

Arrival in Britannia

*Ex his omnibus longe sunt humanissimi qui Cantium
incolunt, quae regio est maritima omnis, neque multum
a Gallica differunt consuetudine.*

Of all the Britons, by far the most civilized
are the inhabitants of Kent, a wholly maritime region,
who in their way of life do not differ
greatly from the Gauls.

JULIUS CAESAR,
Gallic War (V.14)

*

UNLIKE Julius Caesar's arrival in Britannia, the first sights and sounds to greet travellers now, as they near the long anticipated province, are not war cries from ranks of ferocious painted people but the screeches of seabirds circling above the line of white cliffs. In earliest times this land was referred to as 'the island of the Albiones'; but contrary to what the newcomer may think, looking at those gleaming cliffs, 'Albion' does not derive from the Latin for white (*albus*) but from the British stem *albio-*, meaning 'the land' or 'the country'.[1] Now, of course, it is 'Britannia', originally from the Greek Πρεττανια (Prettania).

As Julius Severus approaches the island's shores he is at last allowed to assume the insignia of his office, something he is expressly forbidden to do until he enters his new province.[2] As the new governor of an imperial province, Severus must wear military uniform and carry a sword—with which he is permitted to execute

Caledonia

Vallum Aelii

○ Pons Aelius
○ Coria
Luguvalium ○
Alauna ○

○ Glannoventa
○ Cataractonium

Oceanus
Germanicus

Manavia

Isurium Brigantium ○
○ Eboracum
○ Bremetenacum

○ Mamucium

Mona

Condate ○
○ Lindum
Deva ○

Oceanus Hibernicus

Viroconium ○
Letocetum ○
○ Ratae
Venta Icenorum ○

○ Bravonium

Camulodunum ○
Moridunum ○
Blestium ○
○ Glevum
Verulamium ○
Venta Silurum ○
○ Corinium
Isca Augusta ○
Londinium ○
Abonae ○
Pontes ○
Durobrivae ○
○ Rutupiae
Aquae Sulis
○ Calleva
Durovernum ○
○ Dubris

Venta Belgarum ○

Noviomagus ○
Isca Dumnonorium ○
Fretum Gallicum
Vectis

Oceanus Britannicus

N

Orcades

0   50 miles
0   100 km

Britannia

even soldiers—unlike the governors of senatorial provinces. It would not be done to have a senior ranking official, a seasoned soldier, travelling through the empire in military uniform with such power, so this privilege is confined to his role in the province as the emperor's representative.

Unlike the governors of senatorial provinces, appointed for a single year, Julius Severus will be expected to stay in Britannia for however long the emperor chooses. Although most imperial governorships last for about three years, Severus served in Dacia for at least six years, and Agricola was governor of Britannia for a similarly extended period. Whatever the duration, once Julius Severus sets foot on the island he will be expected to stay there until his tour of duty is over: he is not allowed to leave the boundary of his province unless for the purpose of fulfilling a vow; and even then, he must not spend a night away.[3]

RUTUPIAE, GATEWAY TO BRITANNIA

Rutupiae (Richborough), just south of the Isle of Thanet, is the port from which Claudius launched his invasion in AD 43, and in AD 130 it is still the key point of entry to Britannia, representing the shortest crossing from Gesoriacum. It lies on the coast at the centre of the Wantsum Channel, which separates the Isle of Thanet from the British mainland. At the Wantsum Channel's southern mouth is a shingle barrier, which partially closes the channel, with another shingle bank to the north-west, so that Rutupiae provides a large, sheltered anchorage.[*]

Dominating the entrance to the port and the entire surrounding landscape is a gigantic monumental arch. It represents the *accessus Britanniae*, the symbolic gateway to Britannia, sited at the place where terrifying *Oceanus* meets the shore of this remote province. Glistening in Italian marble from the imperial quarries at Carrara,

---

[*] In the twenty-first century, the Wantsum Channel is completely silted up, and the Isle of Thanet is connected to the mainland. The shingle barrier is now known as the Stonar Bank.

and adorned with bronzes and sculptures (and conceivably also an enormous sculpture of a chariot drawn by elephants*), this four-way 'quadrifrons' structure is one of the largest—if not *the* largest—arches in the empire. Its four arches point north, south, east and west, and it aligns with Watling Street, thus connecting with the great network of roads that penetrates the whole province. It was erected by Domitian in about AD 85, just two years after Agricola's defeat of the Caledonians at the Battle of Mons Graupius (near Inverness). This was the victory that completed the conquest of Britain, by reaching the very furthest corners of the earth, or, in the words Tacitus put in Agricola's mouth as he rallied troops before the battle, the place 'where land and nature end'.[4]

Although Dubris (Dover) will soon become the main British naval port and base of the *classis Britannica*, Rutupiae is and will remain an important hub and entry port for goods.[†] Its name in the literary imagination is synonymous with the whole island.[‡] At about 21 hectares, Rutupiae may be small in comparison with the great ports of the Mediterranean, but its theatrical setting and historic importance still make it a splendid place to stage the formal *adventus* or arrival of a new governor. Tacitus may have asserted piously that when Agricola (his father-in-law) arrived as governor, in *c.* AD 77, he elected to get straight down to campaigning in North Wales instead of holding any welcome celebrations, 'choosing work and danger rather than ostentation and ceremony';[5] but

---

* Although there is no direct evidence for this elephant *quadriga* at Richborough, a coin of Domitian dated AD 95 or 96 depicts an arch surmounted by a chariot drawn by elephants. The so-called Torlonia relief, found at the site of Portus in the nineteenth century, depicts a scene from Portus showing the Domitian arch with elephant *quadriga* (and other scenes): it portrays the charioteer holding a sceptre with a human head, a motif found on coins issued during his reign.

† Rutupiae is the only channel crossing mentioned in the third-century Antonine Itinerary, a collection of about 225 routes along the empire's roads.

‡ As the poet Lucan wrote, 'When the tides of Ocean and the Rutupian shore are raging, the waves are not heard by the Caledonians' (*The Civil War*, VI, 67), meaning that when far from events, one cannot be expected to know what is happening—Britannia being as remote as you could get in the Roman world, and the Caledonians being even further away than that.

observances of the *adventus*, such as hanging out garlands or fill-ing the air with incense,[6] are usually to be encouraged. Whatever the scope of the inauguration ceremonies and celebrations for Julius Severus, protocol at least requires that an incoming governor should always arrive at the customary port of entry, 'for provin-cials think maintenance of customs and privileges of this kind very important'.[7]

While for some it is a mark of honour to be part of the official welcoming party for an incoming governor or other senior official, for others it is simply a costly and time-consuming affair. But it is a brave—or foolhardy—man who dares to opt out of such a cer-emony.[8] Emperor Claudius was furious with the people of Ostia when they failed to send boats to meet him on entering the Tiber; he complained bitterly that they had reduced him to the rank of a commoner.[9]

The more judicious—or ambitious—attendee will try to be among the first to greet Julius Severus, perhaps travelling some distance to do so, although those already due to receive him else-where are officially exempt from having to greet him now.[10] For his part, the new governor will need to cut a dash in his military uniform, with his five lictors (ceremonial bodyguards), assigned to him while in office, walking before him: their job is to clear a path, keep order and compel respect. As they process from the quay-side and straight up the steps leading to the victory arch, Severus's party will no doubt be reassured by the size and confidence exuded by the monument. As part of the ceremonial duties surrounding his arrival, Severus will make a sacrifice for a safe passage across *Oceanus* at the religious sanctuary that stands close to the sea, to the south of the arch. A little further to the south-west, on slightly raised ground at the edge of town, lies an amphitheatre, which can seat between 4,000 and 5,000 people.[*]

Conveniently situated a short walk away from the arch, in the north-eastern corner of the port, is the recently rebuilt stone

---

[*] The dating of the amphitheatre is uncertain. It has been suggested that it might be late third century and contemporary with the Saxon Shore fort.

courtyard building that accommodates the official government guesthouse, the *mansio*. Though modest in size, with a small bathhouse, it is decorated and appointed in a way that will be familiar enough, even if it is somewhat basic by Roman and eastern Mediterranean standards. On the table will be imported food, drink and crockery—Spanish olive oil, Greek or Italian wine, and Gallic Samian ware. But the new arrivals might be eager to try the famous local oysters for dinner, which are now farmed along the coast of Cantium (Kent) and highly rated by connoisseurs. Some gastronomes are said to be able to tell 'at the first bite whether an oyster comes from Circei [in Lazio, Italy], or near the cliffs of the Lucrine Lake [Campania, Italy], or from the beds of Rutupiae'.[11]

TO LONDINIUM VIA DUROVERNUM

Julius Severus can choose to continue his journey from Rutupiae to the province's capital, Londinium, by ship; but there is also the option to become better acquainted with his new province by road. He need not worry about any of the logistics himself, as he has his own *strator consularis*, or transport officer, whose job is to make travel arrangements for him.[12] Even for those travelling independently, there will be little difficulty in finding the road to Londinium out of Rutupiae. The gigantic victory arch is aligned directly with Watling Street, which runs all the way to the capital and thereafter continues to Verulamium (St Albans) and up to Viroconium (Wroxeter).

The busy street leading out of town is lined with shops and workshops, including one selling lamps and another offering metal goods made on the premises. A busy port like Rutupiae is also provided with taverns, where people can drink and play games, using dice towers or *pyrgi* which, with their angled slats, prevent people from cheating at throwing the die.

Just south-west of Rutupiae the road forks, with one branch leading south-east to Dubris. Anyone heading to Londinium needs to continue west, to Durovernum Cantiacorum (Canterbury), 11.5

miles (18.5km) away. The Romans have divided Britannia into *civitates*, tribal states, each with their own *civitas* capital, and Durovernum is the *civitas* capital of the Cantiaci.

Before the conquest, the people of this region had long had contact with Rome, and Durovernum was already an important centre in the Iron Age. With its convergence of roads and river networks, all now leading along Watling Street, the town remains a key link in the Roman transport network. A senior official such as Julius Severus will be expected to visit the temple at the heart of the town and to make a sacrifice there.[13] Across the road from the temple is a distinctive Romano-Celtic theatre where religious gatherings also take place. Reminiscent of theatres in Gaul, it is partly an amphitheatre design, with a central arena, but a third of its seating is taken up by a stage.[14]

With the temple enclosure on their right, travellers heading for London will round the corner of the precinct onto what is fast becoming the town's main street, with new roads being laid off it.[15] Once over the River Stour, the road passes through an industrial zone in the north-west quarter of town. Here are brick, tile and pottery kilns, iron-smelting furnaces and bronze-working facilities. It will be a relief to get past this noisy, smoky district, whose fumes must make even the eyes of those in carriages water.

From here, Watling Street passes through easy and pleasant countryside studded with farmsteads in a more or less straight line to Durobrivae (Rochester), just over 25 miles (40km) away. As arguably the most important road in the province, along which all road traffic must progress to Londinium from the south-coast ports, it is extremely busy. Wheeled transport comes in all shapes and sizes. The plodding goods vehicles include the Gaulish *benna*, with basketwork sides; but the most common is the *plaustrum*, a two- or four-wheeled wagon drawn by yoked oxen, or occasionally by mules. One would hope, with Julius Severus and his retinue on the road, that such tediously slow contraptions have been diverted onto minor routes and byways.

For their own transport, senior members of the official party may choose to travel in a *reda*, a large four-wheeled carriage drawn by two or four horses, while for swifter travel there are lighter vehicles, such as the two-wheeled *cisium*. Servants and baggage usually travel in the lumbering, open *petoritum*, and it is to be hoped that both have been sent on ahead in readiness. Julius Severus and his family might well travel in a covered two-wheeled *carpentum*, usually pulled by mules. Such carriages can be luxuriously appointed, with large gabled roofs supported by ornamental columns, and fitted out with every comfort. The heavier four-wheeled *carruca* is also an option; it can be adapted for use as a sleeping wagon (*carruca dormitoria*) on long journeys.

If Severus needs to work while travelling, he can dictate notes to a secretary, who will need to have a steady hand: no amount of plump cushions and plush curtains can disguise the fact that the carriages—with their wooden wheels, iron tyres and lack of springs—make for bone-shaking experiences.[16] This did not stop Emperor Claudius, a gaming addict, from having a game board specially fitted to his chariot so that he could play while driving himself around.[17] However you choose to distract yourself while on the road, there is no getting around the fact that travelling by carriage is uncomfortable and noisy. As Horace puts it, the *streptitus rotarum*—the jarring screeching of wheels—can badly get on your nerves, even after a very short length of time.[18] Travelling in these conditions is immensely tiring, and even if you are fit and well before the start of a journey, it may take its toll after a time.

Severus could choose to ride for parts of the journey, for in the Kent countryside on an early summer's day, he will at least be unlikely to suffer the extremes of heat, dust and insects that colleagues in other parts of the empire must endure.[19] On the contrary, given that this is Britannia, it might still be rather damp and chilly. Those on horseback, lacking the protection of a covered carriage, might well be grateful for their leather travelling cloaks, with the hoods pulled up against the rain.

Twelve miles into the journey, there is a small stopping place called Durolevum.* This may be as far as you would wish to travel in a day. But since it is unlikely to offer much in the way of comfort, then—weather and daylight permitting—it could be advisable to press on to Durobrivae, which lies at a crossing of the River Medway. A *mansio* lies just behind Watling Street.† Typically, *mansiones* are courtyard buildings, and here officials, soldiers, their animals and carriages can be accommodated securely. Travellers can be assured of a bed, a meal and (they will hope) a bath. Those travelling with special permits are able to obtain a change of animal or carriage to take them on to the next stage.

An official transport system, which later became known as the *cursus publicus*, had been established by Augustus as a form of courier service for disseminating news and messages more speedily and efficiently throughout the empire, via a system of basic *stationes*, 'posts', and *mutationes*, 'changing posts'.[20] In theory, the service is carefully regulated; to use it, people need to be issued with a permit or diploma, either signed by the emperor in person or issued by provincial governors (who have a limited number to give out).[21]

In the early post-conquest days, official types of lodging in Britannia were normally attached to forts. As parts of the province became more settled, they began to be found in towns and cities and at convenient stopping places in between, where small roadside settlements sprang up to cater for the needs of the military. The system is now being much improved, and bigger and better accommodation, with separate bath houses, is being built in many parts of the country.

The service is, unfortunately, also open to abuse by the unscrupulous, and it can prove to be a real burden to the locals who are obliged to maintain it, despite many attempts over the years to impose regulations on everything from tipping (not acceptable) to the maximum weight of saddlebags, the size of wagons and the type of whips allowable for use on animals: knotty and very stout clubs are banned, and any soldier found employing them will be demoted

* This is possibly Ospringe, near Faversham.
† The remains of the (conjectural) *mansio* lie under Rochester Cathedral.

(if he is an officer) or deported (if he is a common soldier).[22]

If the travellers rise early the next day, it will be possible to reach Londinium, almost 29 miles (47km) away, in one long day, breaking the journey at Noviomagus (Crayford), about 15 miles (24km) further on. About 8 miles (13km) from Durobrivae, the road runs by the River Ebbsfleet, which joins the Thames just over a mile to the north. Here, at Vagniacae (Springhead), travellers enter a sacred landscape of springs, temples, shrines and ritual pits, including those containing the remains of twenty-three dogs. Pilgrims come here to celebrate the deity of the sacred springs at the head of the river and to gain strength from her healing powers. Within the sacred enclosure lies a late-first-century AD temple, to the north of which is a large rectangular stone-lined pool. Another, smaller temple of more recent date contains within its foundations the remains of four babies ritually murdered, two of them decapitated, and placed at each corner of the building.[23] All in all, it is an interesting place at which to stop—to make an offering at the temples, to take spiritual and physical refreshment from the springs and temple bakery, and to rest in accommodation provided for pilgrims.

For new arrivals in Britannia, this region will appear at least to be peaceful and relatively prosperous, strongly reminiscent of parts of northern Gaul in terms of the style of buildings, the language spoken and the general feel of the place. There are many substantial farms and houses in the surrounding countryside, especially as you get further north. Eleven or more substantial villa estates nestle just to the west of Watling Street, in the broad valley of the navigable River Darent, where lie water meadows and good arable land.* It will probably be more agreeable to stay in one of these villas than to spend another night in an indifferently run *mansio* on a grubby little roadside settlement.

As Julius Severus and his party near their destination, Watling

---

* A Roman 'villa' meant a house in the country, ranging in size from a farm to a vast estate. At this date, villas in Britannia were generally of modest size. Those in the Darent Valley, including Lullingstone, were much aggrandized in the third and fourth centuries, as elsewhere in Britain.

Street takes them onto Shooters Hill. From its west slope they will be treated to a magnificent view of the whole of the Thames basin, as they prepare to make their descent—into Londinium.[24]

CHAPTER V

London, Seat of Power

Londinium... cognomento quidem coloniae non insigne,
sed copia negotiatorum et commeatuum maxime celebre.

London... while not distinguished by the status of 'colony'
is greatly renowned for the large number
of merchants there and the volume of its trade.

TACITUS, *Annals*
(XIV.33)

*

LONDINIUM is like nowhere else in Britannia. The capital of the province, and Britannia's largest and most important city, it attracts trade and commerce from all over the empire. Lying on the boundary of several ancient kingdoms, with the Catuvellauni and Trinovantes to the north and the Atrebates and Cantii to the south, Londinium holds a pivotal position at the head of a tidal river and at the intersection of key routes into the heart of the province.*

The saying that all roads lead to Rome can certainly be adapted and applied to Londinium. Although a network of roads covering the whole province now interconnects all the chief military bases, tribal capitals, ports, towns and administrative centres of Britannia, Londinium is its undoubted epicentre and the place where all major roads—north, south, east and west—pass through or originate. In

---

* There is no epigraphic evidence to indicate London's formal civic status. It seems likely that by the Hadrianic period it was at least a *municipium*, a town which had been granted a charter based on the constitution of Rome itself. It later seems to have been promoted to the highest rank of *colonia*.

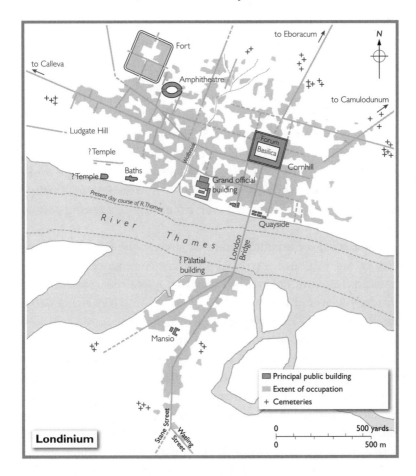

to Eboracum

N

Fort

to Calleva

Amphitheatre

to Camulodunum

Ludgate Hill

?Temple

Forum
Basilica

Cornhill

?Temple

Baths

Grand official
building

Present day course of R. Thames

River

Thames

Quayside

London Bridge

? Palatial
building

Mansio

■ Principal public building
▦ Extent of occupation
+ Cemeteries

0   500 yards
0   500 m

Londinium

Stane Street

Watling
Street

Walbrook

addition to its connections in the south-east with the coastal ports of Rutupiae and Dubris, and with Portus Lemanis (Lympne) on the south coast, Londinium also connects via Durovernum with the iron-working sites on the Weald and the corn-producing areas of the South Downs through which Stane Street passes on its way to Noviomagus Regnensium (Chichester).

Arriving at Londinium from the Kent ports along Watling Street, Severus's party joins Stane Street at bustling Southwark[1] on the south side of the Thames. The area south of the river is really a series of low-lying islands surrounded by marshland. Early on, the Romans set about making this area less prone to flooding so that the sandy islands could be occupied and the main route into Londinium from the south laid across the islands. But in recent decades the river level has sunk, and more land has been reclaimed, leading to further expansion, so that there is now a considerable and increasingly affluent settlement here.[2] Although Southwark has only a modest timber wharf, in contrast to the massive timber quays on the opposite side of the river, it is a bustling commercial centre boasting solid oak warehouses with wooden shingle roofs, a market, many workshops, probably a *mansio* just off Watling Street and numerous temples to serve the needs of its cosmopolitan community.[3]

Amid all these buildings and this activity, the first-time visitor cannot fail to notice a palatial structure commanding a prominent position overlooking the waterfront. Were you to be admitted inside, you would find heated rooms, with interiors richly decorated with expensive materials such as red cinnabar and gold leaf. This lavishness extends to the bath house, whose walls are covered with sophisticated artwork, in which winged Cupids stand enigmatically in the centre of ethereal, festooned pavilions. This is workmanship comparable to any in Italy, commissioned by (or on behalf of) people whose status means that they can demand the sophistication of Rome wherever they might be in the empire. These baths are comparable in size to the public baths over the river at Huggin Hill.[4] Such a large and luxuriously appointed building must surely be the residence of a senior official, perhaps even the imperial procurator himself.* And if that is so, then Maenius Agrippa will one day occupy it.

In order to cross the Thames from the south and proceed directly up to the heart of Londinium, to the forum and basilica, you must go over a narrow wooden bridge, wide enough only for one-way traffic. You might pause to make an offering or to throw a coin into

---

* The palatial building stood on the site of Winchester Palace. It is not known who resided here. The bath house wall-painting depicting the Cupid has been restored and is on display at the Museum of London.

the river at the shrine to Neptune.[5] The river is every bit as busy as the streets of the capital. Barges, fishing boats, merchant ships from Gaul and warships of the fleet can all be seen sailing along it. Some have made long and perilous journeys from across *Oceanus* to serve the demand for imported products from an increasingly prosperous and sophisticated population, which now includes native as well as foreign-born customers.

Looking left, upstream from the bridge, where the mouth of the River Walbrook meets the Thames,* there are extensive quays lined with stone warehouses and jetties. Downstream, east of the bridge, the port is expanding rapidly, with masonry as well as timber-framed stores, warehouses and shops alongside the quay and set back from it. Here, near the south-eastern limits of the city, are deep-water berths where the larger ships, carried up to London on the tidal stream, may dock or ride at anchor on the ebb tides.

The creation of Londinium's port during the Flavian period (between AD 69 and 96) was a major feat of engineering, which involved terracing the steep slopes running down to the north bank of the Thames so that they could be built on. On the lower terrace, which was raised about 2 metres (6.5 feet) above flood level, revetted timber quays were laid out using huge oak timbers, alongside which jetties and landing stages were constructed.

Some goods are being rolled off ships down the gangplanks, but heavier items require cranes and stevedores.[6] The huge wooden barrels of wine imported via the Rhine can carry some 960 litres and weigh in when full at 1.166 tonnes.[7] Pottery—such as the Samian ware shipped annually along the Loire or Gironde, and then through the Bay of Biscay and across the Channel—is, with luck, still intact. More modest quantities of wine from southern Gaul arrive in flat-based amphorae, probably carried along the Rhône and Rhine before being ferried across the Channel.[8]

From Spain and Gallia Narbonensis come jars of olive oil, fish sauce, wine, the grape syrup known as *defrutum* and olives. Each

---

* Just west of Canning Street railway bridge.

legion in the army requires about 1,370 amphorae of olive oil a year, which means that Baetica—the main source of oil for the army of the western provinces—needs to send more than 4,000 amphorae to Britain annually, the produce of more than 43,000 olive trees.[9] Mainland Greece and the island of Rhodes also supply wine, reaching Britannia—as do the many visitors arriving in Londinium—by varied and circuitous routes.

The traffic is not all one way. Waiting to be loaded onto ships heading back to the Continent are consignments of wool, hide, tin and lead. There is also live cargo in the form of slaves, hunting hounds, bears and oysters. Fish is landed live here too, caught at the mouth of the Thames or in the Channel and most likely transported the 40 miles or so upstream in seawater containers. Oysters are traded immediately downstream of the bridge. Brought up from Cantium, some now with the less distorted shells which mark them as being farmed from artificial beds, they too are kept alive in salt water and then dispersed around Britannia, even as far as Hadrian's Wall, while others are sent to the Continent.[*] Up on the Wall, oysters may well be consumed as much for their curative properties as for their taste. When boiled in their shells they are said to be good for colds, and powdered oyster shells relieve sore throats (together with abscesses and hardness in the breast) when mixed with honey. Many soldiers in Britannia this winter, despite the advantages of thick socks in their boots, might be driven to try beaten raw oysters as a cure for chilblains, though it is not clear whether the prescribed mixture is for internal or external use.[10]

While tastes are changing fast, Britannia does not yet produce its own fish sauce, that staple of the Roman larder, so for now the province is reliant on imports from merchants such as Lucius Tettius Africanus, who markets his bottles of *liquamen* to Londoners as 'excellent fish sauce from Antipolis (Antibes)'. The best kind is *garum sociorum*, made from the intestines and offal of mackerel, with its most celebrated centre of production being in Spain at

---

[*] Oysters found at Benwell are thought to have been harvested in southern England.

Carthago Nova—'New Carthage' (Cartagena).[11] But it has a price to match its reputation. All grades of fish sauce are now to be found throughout the province: the legionary base at Deva (Chester) keeps a pungent 'flavoured sauce of fish-tails matured for the larder' in their mess stores.[12]

The banks of the Thames also accommodate shipbuilding and repair yards, and a base for the ships from the *classis Britannica* which are at the disposal of the governor. Perhaps among them is the *Ammilla*, whose ram is in the shape of a dog's head and stempost in the form of the swooping neck of a goose or swan.[*] Making their way slowly up the river are keel-less, flat-bottomed barges of crude design, 16 metres (52 feet) or so long and over 6 metres (20 feet) wide. They have massive timber frames and planks nailed in with huge clench nails according to the technique used in this northern part of the empire. The boats are certainly no beauties, but are built for hard work rather than leisure and need to carry loads of Kentish ragstone from quarries near Maidstone—the nearest supply of good building stone to London—up the River Medway and then along the Thames. Buried under their masts are old coins placed there for luck. One such barge has a coin struck forty years previously, at the time of Domitian, carefully positioned with its reverse uppermost, representing the goddess Fortuna holding a ship's rudder.[14]

LONDINIUM'S BUILDING BOOM

Once the road passes across the bridge onto the north side of the river, it leads straight up to the forum. It is immediately apparent that, as in Rome, the city centre is being transformed by massive public building schemes as well as by smaller-scale works, the latter partly initiated after a devastating fire about five years ago. A much larger forum—nearly four times the size of its predecessor—is being built up around, and upon, the first-century original, with

---

[*] *Ammilla* is the name of a ship found on a miniature bronze prow inscribed 'AMMILLA AUG FELIX', perhaps commemorating a victory in a race.

ranges of rooms and porticoes around its sides. On completion, it will be the largest in the province.* Occupying its north side is a tremendous basilica, built of grey Kentish ragstone.[14] It is enlivened by contrasting red brick courses and red roof tiles, and sections of the portico are plastered and painted.[15] The basilica is the biggest building in Britannia and the largest north of the Alps.† When finished, Londinium's forum and basilica will be the central focus of life for a city which is already 'widely renowned for the number of its merchants and volume of its trade'.[16] If the forum is anything like others across the empire, on completion it will be stocked full of statues of distinguished men,[17] including perhaps the larger than life-sized bronze statue of Hadrian, made to commemorate his visit in AD 122.‡

Governor Julius Severus, on arriving in his new capital city for the first time, will receive further welcoming parties. The most important dignitaries in the city, including members of the city council (*ordo*), will receive him formally in the basilica, which serves as a city hall, a council chamber and a court of law. Here the councillors (*decuriones*), who must first satisfy a property qualification before they are considered for election, discuss local issues, hear petitions, make dedications and organize the dissemination of imperial decrees and regulations, together with news about censuses to be held and legal rulings.§

Members of the provincial council of Britannia will also be anxious to meet the new governor and pay him all due honours. The council's members represent each of the *civitates*, the tribal states,

---

* Evidence from excavations of the Leadenhall Court site was sufficiently detailed to identify many features of a building site, including workers' huts and stores, mortar-mixing pits and hoof prints of pack animals bringing ragstone rubble from the waterfront at the foot of the hill.

† By comparison, St Paul's Cathedral is some 174 metres (574 feet) long, including its portico. Corinium (Cirencester) held the prize for the second-largest basilica in Roman Britain.

‡ It is speculative that the statue of Hadrian was in the forum and that it was made to commemorate the visit, though both scenarios are possible—the head alone survives, which was found in the River Thames.

§ No details about the London council are known.

and are leading figures in their respective communities. Councillors can invite men with powerful connections in Rome to be the province's patron and represent their interests abroad, pleading their cause in Rome if necessary. The council can send its own embassy to Rome to speak before the Senate, or indeed before the emperor himself.[18] As a body, they are entitled to present a vote of thanks—or of censure—to retiring governors, and to deliver it before the emperor. In turn, the emperor may be gracious enough to bestow on them, either as a council or as individuals, the honour of holding special ceremonies, games and gladiatorial shows.[19]

As at Lugdunum and elsewhere in the empire, the provincial council also has a religious function, celebrating the emperor's divine spirit annually at a festival at which they hold sacrifices, games and banquets. Unlike their counterparts in Gaul, however, the British elite do not appear to have the same inclination to compete with each other by erecting splendid monuments.[*20]

On sweeping into Londinium's basilica for the first time, even the most jaded member of Severus's entourage must be surprised, if not impressed, by its size as they stand in its central space: a nave flanked by side aisles, with a raised apse at its marble-lined eastern end. Both the public rooms and the offices, arranged over several floors on the northern side of the nave, are brightly decorated.

Although coloured stone and marble are used sparingly here, in comparison with buildings in Mediterranean cities, many different types from quarries all over the empire are now being imported into Londinium: white Carrara marble from Italy and from the island of Thasos in the northern Aegean; red limestone (*rosso antico*) from Cape Taenaros in the Greek Peloponnese; purple-veined white breccia (*pavonazzetto*) from Docimion in Phrygia;[†] maroon and white breccia from Skyros, together with other coloured marbles

---

* It is unknown if the British centre of the cult's activities was transferred to Londinium, as seems likely, or remained at the original provincial capital and imperial cult centre of Camulodunum (Colchester), whose temple had been sacked and the colony's inhabitants massacred during Boudicca's destruction of the city in AD 60–61.

† In what is now Turkey.

from Euboea in Greece; green and white (*campan vert*) and white and pink (*campan rouge*) breccia from Campan, on the Gallic side of the Pyrenees; and, from the eastern desert of Egypt, rare red porphyry from Gebel Dokhan.

The Greek, Turkish, Italian and Egyptian stones all come from imperially owned quarries. Most likely they are shipped to Britannia via Rome, on a consignment of 'marble for public building works', rather than being ordered individually and transported directly from the quarries themselves. The French stone from the High Pyrenees, which is brought to Britannia in greater quantities than the others, is more likely to be imported directly from the south-west of France, possibly via Burdigala.[21]

The roads being laid out around the forum have attracted new buildings, workshops and commercial premises, and the area is still a semi-permanent building site, with workers' huts, stores for building materials and pits for mixing mortar. Once the official visit is out of the way, an endless line of pack animals will resume their labours up the hill from the river bearing the ragstone rubble from Kent. Weighed down by their loads, the pack horses' hooves press so heavily into the ground that their imprint remains to tell the story of their toil.*

In contrast to the exotic marbles, the brick used for public building works is made locally. Those bricks destined for official use bear the stamps 'P. PR. BR' or 'P. P. BR', often followed by 'LON' for Londinium. The abbreviations stand for *Procurator Provinciae Britanniae Londinii*, roughly 'property of the procurator of the province of Britannia at London'. Bored but literate brickies or tile makers around the capital scratch graffiti on their work to pass the time and have some fun. One inscription, written in a breezy rhyming couplet on a freshly made, still-soft building tile, records cryptically that 'Austalis has been wandering off on his own every day for 13 days.'[22] Perhaps it is an in-joke passed around the yard for Austalis's mates to snigger at.

---

* After two millennia, the hoofprints were excavated in Leadenhall.

GREAT FIRES OF LONDINIUM

Despite all the building work and the flashy new forum and basilica, Londinium remains, if truth be told, a poor comparison with Rome. For anyone coming from the empire's capital or the great Mediterranean cities, Londinium must seem tiny and irredeemably provincial. Rome squeezes around a million people into a city that stretches for about 8 square miles. By contrast, Londinium now covers a mere 330 acres (138 hectares), a fraction of the size of even Rome's Campus Martius, and has just 20,000 inhabitants—and that by a generous reckoning.* Where Rome is built on seven hills, London is built on two, on the north bank of the Thames and separated by the River Walbrook.†

Sophisticated newcomers passing through Londinium on their way to remoter parts of Britannia may be alarmed to hear that this is the most recognizably Roman of all the cities in Britannia, with the most cosmopolitan population and more well-appointed and richly decorated buildings than anywhere else in the province. Although many public buildings in Londinium are built of stone, the majority of shops, houses and warehouses are still wooden, including the bridge across the Thames. While Rome has an impressive system of aqueducts to quench its thirst, Londinium instead relies on wells that draw on a (thankfully) endless supply of natural springs.

Where many of Rome's buildings are ancient—or at least built and aggrandised on ancient foundations—London is a thoroughly modern city, with no building pre-dating AD 60–61. This is where Boudicca, Queen of the Iceni, having sacked Camulodunum, also wreaked vengeance on Londinium, burning the young city to the ground and massacring those of its inhabitants too weak or too reluctant to flee her merciless war bands.[23]

Just recently, no earlier than AD 125, the city has been devastated

---

* That said, this figure represents a density of population that was not reached again for a thousand years.

† The western hill corresponds to modern Ludgate Hill, with St Paul's Cathedral on top of it, and the eastern hill to Cornhill, topped by Leadenhall Market.

once again—by fire. It began west of the River Walbrook and spread eastwards, fanned by a westerly wind and devouring at least 65 acres—a much bigger area than was ravaged during Boudicca's destruction. This most recent fire spread rapidly, possibly from near the quayside south of the forum, although the forum basilica itself escaped unscathed. It badly damaged, however, the area to its immediate east and a large number of timber and clay houses to the west. Although in AD 130 some places have not yet recovered, or are operating on a reduced scale in comparison with their pre-fire days, most areas have been quick to pick up the pieces. Some prime commercial sites have already been redeveloped.*

Fires are a constant hazard in cities, especially as all heat and light requires a flame to be kindled, whether in the form of oil lamps, candles, braziers, open fires, under-floor heating or ovens. In Rome it is one of the duties of the prefect of the city guard to keep fires under control, with the help of the 500-plus trained *vigiles urbani*, or city guards. The prefect has the authority to punish people who are careless, by flogging them if necessary, and everyone is obliged to keep a supply of water at the ready in an upstairs room.[24] Prudent householders are also advised to keep vinegar to hand to douse fires, as well as siphons, poles, ladders and buckets.[25]

Londinium, though, probably lacks any trained fire-fighters. There is considerable caution about the formation of fire brigades in Rome's more distant provinces. When the younger Pliny asked Trajan for permission to found a fire brigade in the city of Nicomedia in Bithynia (in northwestern Asia Minor), *c.* AD 112, the emperor refused his request, fearing that the citizens might use it to form a political club; instead Trajan advocated the provision of fire-fighting equipment that individual property-owners could make use of.[26] Following the fire in Londinium, the governor of Britannia must have been concerned to make adequate provision against future outbreaks. But given that Britannia is such a troublesome place, Hadrian may well have been as unenthusiastic as

---

* In the vicinity of Newgate Street.

Trajan was in allowing the formation of fire-fighting organizations.

The London fire does not seem to have dented confidence unduly, though, and recent post-fire buildings are noticeably smarter than their predecessors. Although still mainly built of timber and unfired clay, they are better made and more expensively decorated, with more mosaic floors and wall veneers of Continental marble on show; some even now have their own bath suites. Close to the waterfront, one new house sports a small bath house complete with a mosaic-lined plunge bath and separate latrine.[27] Even modest shops and workshops are now enhanced by reception rooms with painted walls and cement floors, unheard of for this status of building before the fire, or in towns elsewhere in Britain at present.

LONDINIUM, SEAT OF GOVERNMENT

As governor, Julius Severus and his family will reside in Londinium, as will his imperial procurator,* judicial legate, close advisers and a modest staff of military men, freedmen and slaves to help deal with the vast amount of administration that comes with running the province. Soldiers especially attached to the governor's staff, including his horseguard, are billeted at the fort in the northwest of the city.

At the top of the province's pecking order is, of course, Severus. As the emperor's personally appointed representative, he answers directly to Hadrian. He comes to Britannia with definite orders and specific imperial instructions, and he will correspond regularly with the emperor, keeping him up to speed through detailed reports and consulting him about potentially tricky matters before taking action.[28] The governor is also the only person in Britannia charged with the power to pronounce capital punishment on Roman citizens.[29] In short, he is in supreme charge of both civilian and military life in the country.

---

* The identity of the imperial procurator is unknown for the period AD 130–133.

Britannia hosts a very large number of soldiers, and its governorship is one of the two most senior posts available in the empire.* Usually, governors of provinces need only to have served as praetors first, a senior position in the career path for men of senatorial rank that is known as the *cursus honorum*. Governors of Britannia, however, are drawn only from men who have served in the very highest rank of senators: as consuls. Although four or five governorships along the northern frontiers are also assigned to ex-consuls, together with the plum job of governing Hispania Citerior (Tarraconensis), perhaps only Syria is considered more important for a military man.[30]

But to have an experienced ex-consul governing an imperial and highly militarized province is a potentially risky scenario for an emperor who himself holds the rank of proconsul for almost every province in the empire.† This may be why the British job is officially classified as 'propraetorian', even though those appointed to it are proconsuls. The governor's title is thus *legatus Augusti pro praetore*, 'the legate of Augustus with propraetorian rank', in charge as the emperor's deputy. Holding supreme command of the army stationed here, as well as of the government and the judiciary, any governor of Britannia needs to be both an able administrator and an effective military commander: both skills are ones at which Julius Severus excels.

Also in the gift of the emperor is the procuratorship, the most senior post in Britannia available to an *eques*, or member of the equestrian order—and it will be one that will fall to Maenius Agrippa, after his service as prefect of the *classis Britannica*. The main duty of the procurator of an imperial province is to oversee the collection of revenues on behalf of the *Fiscus* (the emperor's personal treasury). The procurator has his own staff, some of

---

* Later, the province was divided into two, at around the end of the second century AD, and into four in the fourth century.

† The emperor was technically appointed by the Senate and people of Rome as proconsul of nearly every province, except those peaceful provinces of long standing that did not need a strong military presence.

them brought with him and others already working in the province. As well as supervising the collection of taxes, the procurator oversees the pay of the military and the administration of imperial property, such as estates and mines.[31]

The relationship between procurator and governor is, though, a notoriously tense one, not least because the procurator is expected to keep a check on the province's finances while being subordinate to the provincial governor. Although both men are appointees of the emperor, they are of different social rank and on different pay scales (the governor being a senatorial posting and the procurator an equestrian one). They are also appointed at different times, so one always has the advantage of having settled into a province before the other.[32]

Although the highest-ranking positions in the administration are now reserved for men of equestrian rank, especially after Hadrian's reorganization of the imperial secretariat,[33] freedmen still hold many posts, including less important procuratorships.[34] Within the hierarchy of administration in Britannia are many sub-groups, including whole social structures of slaves. Take, for example, the imperial slave Montanus, who works in London and employs an assistant slave called Vegetus. Vegetus can afford to pay 600 *denarii*—the equivalent of two years' gross salary of a comparatively well-paid legionary soldier—for a slave girl from Gaul known as 'Fortunata', a girl recorded as being 'in good health and with no history of running away'. Work, even for a slave within the imperial administration in Britannia, is clearly lucrative.[35] Slaves are commodities—to be bought and sold, and on which tax must be paid. If you need the money, then you can always sell them on again: 'take due care to turn that girl into cash', is the advice given to one inhabitant of Londinium.[36]

An important duty of a governor is to head the judiciary and to hear legal cases. But with the north of Britannia effectively under martial law and periodic violence flaring up, governors spend a considerable amount of their time on military matters rather than on civilian ones. For this reason Julius Severus will have an imperial judicial legate (*legatus augusti iuridicus*) to assist him, a post first appointed under the Flavian emperors. This is also a very senior position, being assigned to someone of senatorial rank who has already served as a legionary legate and who will expect to go on to govern a province. If necessary, he will be able to deputize for the governor. As the title suggests, his primary duty is to preside over legal cases, such as those concerning inheritance and property disputes.[37] One such *legatus iuridicus* is Marcus Vettius Valens,* seemingly well respected, who will agree to become 'patron of the province'—a title conferred on him by Britannia's provincial council, who look on him to defend their interests in the wider empire.[38]

Some of the most imposing offices for imperial staff are located in an impressive stone building overlooking the river, to the west of the bridge over the Thames.† The procurator's staff will consist of a greater proportion of imperial freedmen and slaves[39]—men such as Montanus and Vegetus—in addition to soldiers seconded from auxiliary regiments in the army. Some are skilled in short-hand (*exceptores*), others at financial accounts or tax collection. They scribble away, sometimes on expensive imported papyrus, but mainly writing and filing memos on official-issue wooden tablets bearing stamps from their respective offices along the lines of: 'issued by the imperial procurators of the province of Britain'.‡ Secretaries take notes on wooden tablets made of thin rectangles of imported silver fir, which are coated in wax and written on with a stylus.[40] These can be reused by warming the wax or erasing the letters with the flat end of the stylus. More permanent records are made on specially prepared wooden tablets, written upon with bronze quill or reed pens with split nibs. At their desks the secretaries and clerks keep small metal or pottery pots containing ink made from the pigment lamp-black. Letters and memos are dictated, so secretaries need to be able to write quickly and on the

---

* He was serving in the early 130s, possibly under Julius Severus.

† On the site of Cannon Street station. It was clearly an important building, but its exact status is conjectural.

‡ Only a few fibres of Roman papyrus have survived in damp Britain.

hoof if necessary. Unsurprisingly, if working in a rushed or noisy environment they may sometimes mishear the odd word or phrase, or anticipate incorrectly. Was that *et hiem* (and winter) or *etiam* (even)?[41]

Records are kept scrupulously and there is a mass of filing to do in vast archives. Every governor is expected to keep records of his work, not only in correspondence with the emperor but also in the form of *commentarii*—accounts of day-to-day operations and observations on events and individuals—and *acta*, the records of official decisions and directives. For their work, governors, procurators and *iuridices* need reference libraries containing law books, regulations, records of military promotions, works on tactics, *itineraria* and maps. (Certainly, while governor in Bithynia, Pliny the Younger found he had to go through the edicts and letters of Augustus, Vespasian, Titus and Domitian.[42]) Papyrus letters are docketed upon receipt with the day, month and year listed in full, with single letters being glued together to make a roll for filing. Official legal documents are written on wooden wax tablets (*tabulae*) before being duly signed and sealed.[43]

The governor, who has an estimated 200 men working in his office,[44] is served by legionaries seconded to him from elsewhere in Britain. They act not just in military roles or as bodyguards, but in administration.[45] Some men from auxiliary units are seconded to London to serve as *singulares*, men 'singled out' as the governor's bodyguards in the form of horse and foot guards. They are 'the governor's own', who take part in official ceremonies in the capital. Others have policing roles (*speculatores*), whose duties include executing condemned criminals,[46] while the *beneficiarii consularis* (beneficiaries of the governor) are legionaries with a status just below the rank of a centurion, possibly about 180 in number.[47] These troops are dispatched on special duties outside the capital and are to be found all over the province.[48] The *stratores consularis*, or grooms of the governor, have the job of provisioning the army with horses rather than just looking after them. They are auxiliaries, as are the actual grooms (*equisiones*) for the governor's horses.[49]

The thousand or so soldiers on duty in London are housed in a large stone fort in the north-west of the city, built in the early years of the century. Apart from the headquarters of the *classis Britannica* in Dubris, it is probably the only permanent fort in the south of the province.* Its four gates, each with entrance towers, enclose an area of about 12 acres. It is therefore much smaller than, for example, the legionary fortresses at Isca Augusta (Caerleon, at 50 acres) or Deva (Chester, at 56 acres), and more in keeping with the largest auxiliary forts.

LONDINIUM AT LEISURE

Adjacent to the fort lies the amphitheatre, which has also bene-fited from the burst of activity generated by Hadrian's visit eight years ago. Like the fort, it has been rebuilt in stone. Hadrian, who is passionate about both hunting and the military, knows how to use gladiatorial weapons and frequently attends shows, 'in almost every city erecting some building and giving public games'.[50] He may well have presided over ones in Londinium in AD 122. In his beloved Athens, a few years ago, he staged a spectacular hunt (*venatio*) involving a thousand wild beasts,[51] and in Rome's Circus he has provided many shows involving wild animals, often includ-ing a hundred lions.[52]

London's arena may not see many lions but, unlike amphithe-atres elsewhere in the province, which are often peculiarly British in form, it is typical of others throughout the empire. It reflects the city's status as a provincial capital with a cosmopolitan population. Its decoration is, though, somewhat less flamboyant than some of its Continental counterparts: its walls do not boast the elaborate scenes of animals, gods and fights that characterize amphithea-tres of Mediterranean towns, or the magnificently elaborate stucco work of Rome's Colosseum. Londinium's arena is, instead, plas-tered and painted with a rather more modest fake-marble effect,

---

* These are the only two known permanent forts for the period.

and the wall is topped by iron railings.

Unless there are pressing military matters up north, it will do Julius Severus no harm soon after his arrival to host shows and games. Surrounded by his senior staff and guests, he will be able to preside over the games from a box (*tribunal*) situated over the amphitheatre's south gate, the more elaborate of the four entrances.[53] Other VIP seats are accorded to the city magistrates and the sponsors of particular games. These high-ranking spectators will ensure that they have good seats reserved at the ringside in the widest part of the arena (on the line of the short axis). In Londinium there might also be special covered seating available on the north side, opposite the governor's box. It is important to be seen in the right seats wherever in the empire you are. When German envoys in Rome during Claudius's time saw the Parthian and Armenian envoys sitting among the senators, they caused a stir (showing 'naive self confidence', according to Suetonius) by moving from their seats among the common people to which they had been shown. In protesting that their merits and rank were not in any way inferior to those of other emissaries, their chutzpah paid off and Claudius allowed them to sit among the VIPs.[54]

While Rome's Colosseum has an estimated capacity of 50,000— some say more—Londinium's amphitheatre, which is 100 metres (330 feet) wide at its maximum extent, can hold about 7,000 spectators, the majority of whom sit on wooden seats. Hadrian, attempting to instil a sense of public morality (as his idol Augustus had done more than a century before), has decreed that men and women should be segregated in the theatre and circuses.[55] Augustus, who had stopped men and women sitting together at shows, had apparently relegated women to the back rows and excluded them altogether from athletic contests, perhaps because the athletes performed naked, in the Greek habit.[56] The women of Londinium attend the performances nonetheless, losing hairpins and jewellery in the process through being jostled in the crowds—or possibly from jumping up and down with excitement.[57]

The majority of spectators throng through the east entrance, passing temporary wooden stalls erected outside the amphitheatre, some of which tempt with hot snacks cooked in ceramic portable ovens (*clibani*),[58] others with souvenirs of the show. Samian-ware cups depicting scenes from the arena are popular. One shows a man with a ridiculously tiny rectangular shield facing a charging bull, surrounded by three lifeless bodies: possibly it depicts prisoners condemned to the beasts.[59] Inside the arena, such brutal scenes are played out for real.* While the crowds in Rome are treated to lavish shows with hundreds of exotic beasts, native-born animals such as bears, stags and the bull depicted on the cup are the staple fare in Britannia. The animals arrive at the amphitheatre in crates, driven or wheeled into the beast pens (*carceres*) situated at the entrance passages into the arena (on the long axes of the amphitheatre). When their turn comes, they are released into the arena through the vertical sliding trapdoors.[60]

While everyone looks forward to an exciting show with plenty of action, safety measures are in place to keep crazed animals and desperate combatants from climbing over the walls of the arena and into the laps of the front-row VIPs. In Rome's 48-metre-high Colosseum, there is about a 4-metre (13-foot) drop between the front-row seating and the arena floor. Additional protection for spectators is available in some places in the form of ivory inlaid rollers around the arena walls, as well as additional fences laid inside the arena, with netting across them.[61]

So that animals and humans in the show can move about easily, the surface of Londinium's arena is hard, made of rammed gravel mixed with pink mortar. But it is covered with a layer of sand, which provides a cushioning layer for falls, not to mention its utility for the mopping up of blood and gore. Appearing on the programme might be armed men fighting animals, or different sorts of beasts pitted against each other. Sometimes the latter

---

* Archaeological finds from a timber drain in the arena include the remains of a bull. The distal humerus of a brown bear was also found, together with the remains of deer, horses and dogs. Human bone has been located too, but it is not clear whether this is associated with activity in the amphitheatre.

are in 'amusingly' odd combinations, such as a bear and a python, or a lion and a crocodile—in those parts of the empire with better access to such exotica. More common in Britannia are a bull and a bear, the latter brought down from Scotland and the far north of England. The animals are tethered together by means of an iron ring in the centre of the arena.[62]

Criminals condemned to the punishment known as *damnatio ad bestias* (condemnation to the wild beasts) might also form part of the day's entertainment. To add to the amusement, prisoners are sometimes forced to participate in little tableaux, occasionally with elaborate props and machinery. In the first century AD the poet Martial pictured a scene in the Roman arena, in which a Caledonian bear was brought on to attack a condemned criminal—all part of a re-enactment of a popular story about the robber Laureolus, who was devoured by a bear while being crucified.[63] In Apuleius's fiction *Metamorphoses* (*The Golden Ass*), a woman who has poisoned members of her family is condemned to the beasts and forced to have sex with an ass on a large bed in the centre of the arena. The ass—really a man turned into a beast by magic— elsewhere has no qualms about making love to women in his animal form; but he is unable to bear the shame of being exposed in the arena in this public 'marriage', not to mention fearful of being torn apart by a wild animal while *in flagrante,* and so he escapes. Martial, describing games and shows in the Colosseum, also urged his audience to believe the story of the legendary Pasiphaë, wife of King Minos of Crete, who lusted after a bull by whom she conceived the minotaur: 'whatever story you've heard about, you can see it in the arena—the old legends here gain credibility'.[64]

If the beast shows in Londinium's amphitheatre are not entertaining enough for you, then there are other amusements to be had. Bored soldiers use animals grazing in the open pasture on the edge of the city as target practice, and there is good hunting in the surrounding woods and fields.* The city also boasts several

---

* An ox tibia found with an iron *ballista* (catapult) bolt shot through it is evidently the work of a soldier manning the defences of late Roman Londinium, on the site of what

public baths, all sited by the natural springs that provide them with a ready water supply. An old baths complex, first built around AD 70–90 and terraced into the steep hillside, is now being extensively remodelled: a further *caldarium* (hot steam room) is being built, the underfloor heating system is being redesigned and new timber-lined drains are being inserted, while the interior decoration is also being updated with imported marble. Accessible directly from the river, and a short stroll away from the government offices, the baths afford pleasant views overlooking the Thames.* Here, too, men and women might have to bathe separately—another of Hadrian's efforts to improve public morality.

At the baths—or simply strolling around the streets—more Latin will be heard in Londinium than elsewhere in the province, where Brittonic, the native Celtic language, is the norm. But you will also hear many other languages, such as the Gaulish of the not-so Fortunata slave-girl or Greek from the lips of men such as Aulus Alfidus Olussa, born in Athens.[65] The port of London is the place of arrival for people from diverse lands, who will make the city and the wider province their base. They may be travelling on business or serving in the army, and their stay may be temporary or last many years. They may come from elsewhere in Britannia too, drawn to the capital by the opportunities to trade or serve the imperial cause. Everyone can obtain food and drink to appeal to their native palates, and everyone can worship their native gods in the many temples in the city.

The cosmopolitan nature of London and its multicultural appeal is nowhere better demonstrated than in the dedication by a certain Tiberinius Celerianus, a merchant shipper, in the precinct of a temple in Southwark. It is made on marble imported from north-western Turkey and dedicated to Mars Camulos and the Imperial Spirits— Mars Camulos being a hybrid deity formed from the great Roman god of war, Mars, conflated with the Celtic deity Camulos, much

---

became the Tower of London.
* The baths were sited on what is now Upper Thames Street.

worshipped in northern Gaul, from where the merchant originates.* Despite his Roman names (although 'Tiberinius' is a bit of a concoction), Celerianus is from the Bellovaci, a Celtic tribe, and his inscription uses colloquial Celtic rather than the standard Classical Latin to describe his profession: *moritix*, or merchant seafarer.†

But the most striking part of his dedication is the fact that Celerianus declares boldly that he is *Londoniensium primus*—'first of the Londoners'. It is not clear what he has been the first to do, yet this, the earliest surviving inscription to describe Londoners, is created by a man who—despite his Gallic origins—counts himself proudly as one of them.[66]

---

* Around modern Beauvais.

† *Mor* means 'sea' in modern Welsh.

CHAPTER VI

Westwards to Silchester

Deo qui vias et semitas commentus est
T(itus) Irdas s(ummus) c(urator) f(ecit) v(otum) l(aetus) l(ibens)
m(erito) Q(uintus) Varius Vitalis b(ene)f(icarius) co(n)s(ularis) aram
sacram restituit Aproniano et Bradua co(n)s(ulibus).

To the god who invented roads and pathways,
Titus Irdas, chief supply officer, gladly, willingly and deservedly
fulfilled this vow. Quintus Varius Vitalis, the governor's
special duty officer, restored this sacred altar in the consulship
of Apronianus and Bradua.

LOST ALTAR FROM CATARACTONIUM
(Catterick)[1]

*

LONDINIUM is as much a place to pass through as to live in permanently. If circumstances are not too pressing in the north, where military matters must be Julius Severus's principal concern, the new governor will be able to tour his province, once he has acquainted himself with the workings of his new capital. After all, it is part of his responsibility ultimately to ensure that the whole infrastructure of the province is sound and that the extensive network of roads, harbours, bridges and public buildings is maintained.

The direct road north is the one which Minicius Natalis will take to join the Legion VI Victrix. It leads straight out of Londinium's forum,* up to the *colonia* of Lindum (Lincoln) and from there to

---

* Later known as Ermine Street, it left the city at modern Bishopsgate.

Eboracum. But Severus on his tour of duty can choose a more circuitous route, inspecting the bases of all three legions based in Britannia. Travelling west out of Londinium, he can take in the fortress of the Legion II Augusta at Isca (Caerleon) in Wales, and then proceed north via the base of the Legion XX Augusta at Deva on his way up to the Wall, stopping at Eboracum on the way back down south—should he choose not to sail back down Britannia's east coast. On his way to the north-west, he will be able to visit the great temple complex and sacred waters at Aquae Sulis (Bath) and two important *civitas* capitals: Calleva Atrebatum (Silchester) and Viroconium Cornoviorum (Wroxeter).

The main east–west thoroughfare through Londinium lies immediately south of the forum.[*] Just before the city's boundary it meets an impressive monument built of Bath stone,[2] before crossing the road over the River Fleet and—immediately outside the city—passing through a cemetery. The road leads to Calleva Atrebatum, just over 44 miles (71km) away, and from there to the whole of the west of Britannia.[†]

A short way beyond the city's boundary, the road comes to a junction, where Watling Street West[3] branches north to Verulamium (St Albans), 22 miles (35km) away.[‡] This is the *civitas* capital of the Catuvellauni who, at the time of the conquest, occupied one of the biggest and most prosperous territories in the province. Surrounded by rich arable land and pasture, Verulamium has the status of *municipium*, the second rank of chartered towns, inferior only to a *colonia*.[4] It lies slightly above the River Ver on the south-west side of the river valley, and forms the junction of three major routes.[§]

---

[*] The road left Londinium at Newgate, south of modern Smithfield and St Bartholomew's Hospital. Later in the second century the city was bounded by a defensive wall.

[†] The road west out of Londinium followed the line of modern Oxford Street. Calleva's importance on the road network is indicated in the Antonine Itinerary: after Londinium, it is the town that crops up most frequently.

[‡] The junction with Watling Street West is at today's Marble Arch, where Edgware Road picks up the Roman route that is still in use all the way to the outskirts of St Albans (see Margary, 1973, p. 171).

[§] The Roman town was situated about two-thirds of a mile to the west of what would become the medieval town.

From here, Watling Street continues north through Durocobrivis (Dunstable) and up to Viroconium and Deva; travellers can also pick up a route to the east from Verulamium to Camulodunum, as well as others leading south-west.

But Julius Severus instead continues westwards.[*] Where the road rises (at Notting Hill), there is a fine view, whereupon the road continues south-west. Unlike Rome, with its miles of urban sprawl, immediately beyond the city of London lies open pasture, with woods and grassland where you might find woodcock, owls, golden plover and red kites, or even—along the river from Southwark to the Thames basin—white-tailed sea eagles. It is an easy journey to Brentford, which lies about 10 miles (16km) from the heart of the capital, at the point where the road passes along the northernmost edge of the bend in the Thames, at the crossing of the River Brent. Here, a small roadside settlement provides the opportunity for official travellers to change horses if necessary and for those in less of a hurry to rest and find refreshment.

The Thames is not crossed for another 9 miles (14.5km), until reaching Pontes—or Pontibus, 'at the Bridges' (Staines).[5] Here the road runs through the centre of town, which is built on one of five gravel 'islands' where the River Colne meets the Thames. Alder grows in abundance in the wetlands between these islands. Shops and houses hug each side of the road, clinging to the highest portions of ground and raised a little above the rest of this flood-prone area.

Pontibus is flourishing, and many of its timber-framed buildings are being embellished with painted wall plaster, mosaics and window glass.[†] As a halfway point on the journey to Calleva, some 22 miles (35km) further west, it is a convenient place to stop.[6] Severus's entourage and any other travellers will have access to all sorts of goods and services here, including smiths, who are kept busy

---

[*] Along what is now Bayswater Road.

[†] This period represented the high point of the town's prosperity, for it went into decline by the end of the second century and remained in the doldrums for the whole of the third century, possibly because of problems with flooding.

with repairs. Some are replacing loose or lost linchpins on carriage wheels, or seeing to broken harnesses, while others are putting new iron tyres onto carts. While they are at work, the travellers will be glad to stretch their legs and take refreshment, tucking into beef, pork or a bit of widgeon.[7]

Although the town is surrounded by rich grass and arable land, beyond that lies heath and woodland, and as the road proceeds further west it passes through long stretches of lonely, underpopulated country.[8] Milestones punctuate the route, one after every thousand paces (*mille passus*) or 5,000 *pedes* (feet): a Roman mile (1.48km).[9] The road then changes alignment (at Bagshot Park, in Berkshire) and runs almost due west for most of the remaining 17 miles (27km) to Calleva.*

At this point the road is about 6.8 metres wide. But, as Julius Severus will discover on his tour of duty around Britannia, there is no such thing as a set standard in size or construction in the province's extensive road network, and not all the roads are dead straight. Road width varies greatly, from about 5 metres (16.5 feet) to more than 10 metres (33 feet). Few roads outside towns are paved, most being surfaced with gravel and small pebbles, sometimes mixed with a layer of sand or silt, and densely crushed together. In terms of 'standard' road construction, typically a road consists of a main raised *agger* (bank), flanked by two sets of parallel drainage ditches. Between the outer and inner ditches on either side of the *agger* run two 'side roads' which are usually unmetalled. The *agger* is built up of layers of stone or gravel, depending on what materials are available locally, and on soft ground it might be built over piles of timber and layers of brushwood. Some streets in towns and at forts are paved, while others are cobbled.

Unmetalled side roads provide easier going for horses being ridden at a canter, for Roman horses, being unshod, find hard surfaces and stony roads wearing on their hooves.[10] Not all roads have flanking lanes, though, and different solutions have to be found

---

* This stretch of road is still visible and is popularly known as The Devil's Highway'.

to building roads over difficult terrain. On some steep roads, for example, parallel lanes at different levels are cut into the hillside.[11] Julius Severus and his entourage should be able to enjoy an unhindered journey along the roads, for it is unthinkable that his party will be held up by goods traffic in lumbering wagons, or by animals driven on foot. It is to be hoped that outriders will have been sent in advance to clear the way and instruct people to take secondary routes to their destinations. Soldiers on the move clearly expect people to get out of their way on the roads, and many are those who have felt the force of a hobnailed boot, when they have failed to move fast enough. In all events, *cisiarii* (waggoners) are expected to exercise due caution when driving. According to Roman law they are deemed liable if, while overtaking another vehicle, they overturn the wagon or damage property, including slaves.[12]

CALLEVA ATREBATUM—ECHOES OF THE IRON AGE

Calleva Atrebatum (Silchester), the administrative centre of the Atrebates tribe, is the first major town west of Londinium. Standing in an open landscape surrounded by pasture, hay meadows and heathland, Calleva stands at the junction of main roads leading to other significant towns in all directions. Built on a spur of gravel about 90 metres (295 feet) above sea level, Calleva, whose Celtic name signifies a wooded place, has commanding views to the east and south, extending over about 40 hectares.* Despite the town's distance from a river, it has a ready supply of water from the many springs that are easily accessible via shallow wells.

Calleva is also a place with a singular history. It is thought to have been settled by newcomers to the island, refugee members of the Atrebates tribe in northern Gaul (near Arras). They had fled to Britain in about 52 BC with their leader, Commius, who had turned against Julius Caesar and consequently become one of

---

* This is the extent of the late-second-century walled city. The Iron Age settlement covered some 32 hectares.

Calleva Atrebatum

Rome's 'most wanted' in Gaul. Calleva seems to have been built as a planned settlement, perhaps as early as 40 BC, and it became one of the most sophisticated in Iron Age Britain, open to Roman influence in the form of goods from northern Gaul and the wider Roman Empire.[*]

Three British leaders—Tincomarus, Eppillus and Verica—all claimed to be sons of Commius and might have ruled from Calleva. In a dizzying sequence of fraternal feuding, Tincomarus was ousted by Eppillus and by AD 7 had fled to Rome. Eppillus, who styled himself *rex* (king), issued coins carrying the marks of 'CALLE' or 'CALLEV'. He was in turn overthrown by Verica, who

---

[*] It was an *oppidum*, an extensive system of linear earthworks defining a settlement or territory in the late Iron Age, most of which were high status—and some of which have the characteristics of later towns.

ruled until the early AD 40s, when he was forced to leave Britain, probably by Caratacus, who had gained much territory from the Atrebates, possibly including Calleva itself.[13] It was Verica's flight to Rome that provided Claudius with the pretext to invade Britain in AD 43.

Under the Romans, power in the region was recalibrated, and Calleva became part of the kingdom of Cogidubnus: he was assigned leadership of some tribes after the Roman conquest, and might also have been a prince of the Atrebatic house.[14] Calleva clearly retained high status within his kingdom.[15] On Cogidubnus's death, Calleva was established as a *civitas* capital of the Atrebates.[*]

Today, travellers approaching Calleva from Londinium first pass an amphitheatre on their right, built on a sloping site on the outskirts of town. It was constructed at some time between AD 55 and AD 75.[16] Its circular arena is enclosed by a wooden wall, behind which are circular banks and metre-wide terraces formed out of the excavated soil. With an estimated capacity of 7,250 standing specta- tors, this huge earthwork—using the same building techniques and skills as the great, late Iron Age ditches that, until recently, encircled the town—must seem peculiar to anyone from Rome or the Med- iterranean. Conventional Roman amphitheatres are, almost with- out exception, elliptical, with the best seats in the boxes that face the short axis. By contrast, Calleva's, now over seventy years old and beginning to show signs of wear, is not only circular and lacks seats, but has no carefully organized entrance passages to chan- nel the crowds into their places. Instead, spectators must climb up ramps or stairs built against the outside of the amphitheatre. It is to be hoped that marshals are on hand before a gathering, to prevent a scrum to get a ringside position.

Although small and plain by Roman standards, Calleva's amphi- theatre still represents a huge undertaking: a large area of land must have been needed to provide sufficient turf to revet its outside wall,

---

[*] Although the area assigned to the Atrebates comprised a fraction of their earlier territory it still extended across land that would later form Berkshire, north Hamp- shire, south Oxfordshire, Surrey and Wiltshire.

as well as 68 acres of woodland to provide sufficient timber.[17] Here is a structure whose resolutely circular form may suggest that it was used by the locals not so much for Roman-style entertainments but as a place for open-air meetings and (perhaps) somewhere to observe the old traditions and customs. Displays of horsemanship take place here and, when the building was first constructed, the remains of a horse, including a skull, were ritually buried to ensure protection for the site. But its rather neglected, not to say dilapidated, appearance indicates that in the normal scheme of things the amphitheatre is not frequently used.

Perhaps the arrival of Britannia's governor will provide an excuse to mount a show—Julius Severus might even fund one to commemorate his visit. He can certainly be assured of a large welcoming party as he proceeds on to the forum, passing a religious precinct at the town's eastern edge, where Romano-Celtic temples are brightly painted with red stucco exteriors.[18] While Severus is formally received, other, considerably less elevated visitors will have to make it a priority to organize accommodation for their masters. The *mansio* is situated near the south gate and the road to Noviomagus. It is a large compound, occupying most of an entire street block (*insula* VIII) but set nearly 100 metres (330 feet) back from the road, tucked behind other properties.

The *mansio*'s principal accommodation is arranged around three sides of a porticoed courtyard and consists of suites of rooms on offer to higher-ranking officials only; the lower-ranking soldiers and officials will need to rely on being billeted elsewhere in the town.[*] Although spacious, none of the suites is provided with central heating from hypocausts, instead relying on charcoal-burning braziers for warmth.[19]

After a room is secured, a bath will be welcome, and the well-appointed *mansio* bath house is situated in a second open courtyard. If you are important enough to stay in the *mansio*, your slave will accompany you, carrying towels, oil and strigil (for scraping

---

[*] This exclusive arrangement for the *mansio* applied to this period.

dirt and dead skin off your body, after anointing you with the oil). If you do not have such status, you will still be able to make use of the public baths south-east of Calleva's forum: these were among the first Roman buildings to appear in the town in the AD 50s, and they have undergone alterations over time.

Thus refreshed, newcomers to Calleva can explore their surroundings. To the west of the baths is a Romano-Celtic temple, which nonetheless has distinctly Roman dedications to Peace, Victory and Mars by a *collegium peregrinorum consistentium Callevae* ('guild of resident aliens at Calleva'). The *collegium* represents a provincial version of the smart temple guilds to which Hadrian and Minicius Natalis belong in Rome.[20]

The first-time visitor should make for the forum basilica at the town's heart, which makes a natural starting point for a tour of the town. Here, a new structure in Bath limestone—the nearest source of stone to Calleva—is being erected around its wooden predecessor, dating from about AD 85. While the timber basilica had been perfectly aligned with the road east to Londinium, the challenge of erecting this new stone building around the wooden one has led to a two-degree shift in orientation away from the street grid.

Anyone with an eye for architectural detail, and who has travelled in Germania, may notice a familiarity in the style of the Corinthian capitals. They bear the hallmark of work by sculptors from the Rhineland, suggesting perhaps that the stonemasons working on the project trained in the legions.

The single-aisled stone basilica at Calleva is curious in that it has opposing apses at either end of the hall. The contemporary forum basilicas at Viroconium and Venta Silurum (Caerwent) have rectangular rooms at each end, while Londinium's basilica has an apse at one end of the hall; only Calleva has two. What lies behind this decision? Have the Callevans decided to outdo Londinium? Whatever the reason, the novel design will not prove very long-lasting.*

The forum basilica—or at least the site of it—may hold

---

* Around AD 150, an arrangement more in keeping with basilicas elsewhere was adopted, with three rectangular rooms at either end.

significance for the Callevans that long pre-dates the arrival of the Romans. It stands at the old Iron Age centre of Calleva, and buried here in that earlier time was the articulated skeleton of a raven. It is a bird that has symbolic associations for Celts, and which is ritualistically buried elsewhere in Britannia: ravens are messengers from the Otherworld, an association perhaps stemming from the birds' black plumage and their diet of carrion.[21]

A SUBTERRANEAN MAGICAL WORLD

Calleva's air of ancient mystery is not limited to buried ravens. All over the town, hidden in pits and wells, and under floors or patches of ground, is a whole magical world that has its roots in Celtic Iron Age belief. Underneath a room in the forum, for example, are the skulls of four dogs, spurs from gamecocks and the blade of a small knife. In two pits between the north side of the forum and the main east–west street are thirty-nine necks of flasks or bottles; in another pit, almost 2 metres (6 feet) below the ground, are a small bronze figure, possibly of the infant Hercules, some fragments of pottery and an iron screw. Among several ritual deposits in *insula* ix, there is a pottery vessel containing the complete skeleton of a rare small dog, two or three years old, carefully laid to rest as though it were still alive. It too dates from the late Iron Age.

In one part of town (*insula* xxii) a concoction of mallow, hemlock and nettle seeds—a regular witch's brew—may be found in one pot inside a well; a little further down the shaft are two more pottery vessels, containing elder. A pit in another street block (*insula* xxvii) has three pots containing, among other plants, hemlock, elder, thistle, deadly nightshade, self-heal, purple dead nettle, Good-King-Henry, dock and hazel. Yet another pit in the same area reveals hemlock, elder, dead nettle, cat's valerian and white bryony. Hemlock and deadly nightshade are poisons that stupefy and dull the senses, and hazel and elder are held sacred, while white bryony is associated with the mandrake, that most magical of plants.*

In the southern part of town, along the road leading towards Noviomagus, are several pits and wells containing pots and animal skeletons. A complete skeleton of a cockerel can be found here, along with three goose bones, while one pit has the bones from at least five dogs.[22] Indeed, among the particular curiosities buried at Calleva are fifty complete dog skulls, found around the town.[23] The significance of burying dog skeletons is unclear, although it is a practice not entirely unfamiliar to Romans. Columella, a first-century authority on agriculture, related how on 25 April the blood and guts of unweaned puppies were offered to the goddess Robigo ('mildew') in the hope that she would safeguard the new season's crops. Dogs are also associated with Celtic gods such as Sequanna, who presides over the source of the Seine at her shrine of Fontes Sequanae, near Dijon, and who has a dog as a companion. There, tourists can buy little statuettes of pilgrims holding small dogs in their arms, which they deposit at the shrine. Elsewhere, such as at Epidaurus in Greece, the injured and afflicted can have their wounds licked better by sacred dogs.[24]

SOME PROVINCIAL PECULIARITIES

One curious fact regarding the dog skeletons at Calleva is that young dogs, and especially female ones, seem to have been skinned before being deposited, perhaps because their soft fur was put to other uses.[25] Diodorus Siculus, in the first century BC, wrote of how Gauls dined on the ground, using dog or wolf skins as coverings; in a memorable passage he described how the the men got food and drink entangled in their lavish moustaches as they ate.[26]

Times and habits have changed, certainly as regards dining

---

* Many of the plants and trees contained in these deposits continued to have significance in later magical belief long after the Romans. The elder was closely connected with burial rituals and was held sacred among Germanic peoples; St Patrick is said to have driven the snakes out of Ireland with a wand made of hazel—another tree held sacred. White bryony came to be known as the 'English mandrake'. De Cleene and Lejeune (Ghent, 2004), Vols I and II.

etiquette. In the smarter *triclinia* (dining rooms) of Calleva, you can now lean on couches rather than carouse on puppy-skin rugs; but having room to lie prone while eating takes up a great deal of space, and so is only an option for those who can afford big houses. By contrast, most people—here as in Italy—sit up to eat.* The dining rooms of the better-off boast Samian ware from central Gaul, together with other fine tableware from the Rhineland and Gallia Belgica.[27] This is the exception rather than the rule, however, for most pottery is now produced in the province: Black Burnished ware from the Poole Harbour kilns, and fine grey ware and white ware from Oxfordshire. There is the odd *mortarium* (mixing bowl) from Isca Augusta and other bits and pieces from Verulamium, Camulodunum and the Nene Valley (in Cambridgeshire). But the main suppliers of coarseware pottery to Calleva are local.†

As for the food and drink consumed, the inhabitants of Calleva enjoy a varied diet. Their slight preference for mutton and goat reveals their Celtic origins, although they also consume pork, together with occasional meals of venison, hare and domestic fowl. For vegetables, they eat peas and cabbage, and they season their dishes with coriander, dill and mustard. Native fruits such as plums and blackberries are supplemented, for those who can afford it, by the more exotic imports of figs, grapes and mulberries.[28] Callevans consume Spanish olive oil and the *garum* (fish sauce) imported in amphorae from Gades (Cadiz) and southern Spain; they can also obtain Gallic wine. As you might expect in a provincial town far to the west, such imports are found in proportionally smaller quantities than in Londinium.

Dietary habits are not the only customs that seem to have changed over time. Whatever the state of their facial hair, the Callevans' love of personal grooming suggests that they keep themselves

---

* Paintings at Pompeii show people sitting at tables in bars and restaurants. The *triclinia* habit never really caught on in the north-western provinces, and it seems that in the later empire the north-western preference for sitting up to eat prevailed.
† Most pottery in Calleva comes from the Hampshire kilns producing Alice Holt grey-ware.

tidier than did the Gauls of old. Here, as in other British towns, the people are keen on cleaning their nails, and they are very attached to their distinctive personal grooming sets, of a type found only in Britannia, which include scoops for cleaning out ears.[29] Visitors interested in women's hairstyles might also notice that in contrast with the practice in other British towns, very few bone hairpins are used in Calleva.[30] There are some rather stylish metal ones to be spotted, though, including one depicting an elegant (right) hand complete with bracelets, daintily picking up a piece of fruit.[*]

This sense of a local identity might also—to the observant traveller—be discerned in the style of Calleva's houses. Some have elaborate entrance porches with flanking columns or piers on the street side, of a type found only in this place. Some of these, which are connected to the main houses by long porticoes, have small rooms attached, occasionally even heated by a hypocaust. They might be used as reception rooms or places to hold meetings outside the main dwelling.[31]

Even though, all over town, timber buildings are being replaced by ones in flint and tile, the old Iron Age orientation of buildings and street pattern is being respected. In one of the most central street blocks (*insula* IX), close to the forum, stand two substantial brick-and-flint houses and a further timber building, set diagonally to the street grid and thus on a completely different alignment to the surrounding houses. They are all the more noticeable given the prominent position they hold in the town centre. But if truth be told, they might first come to the visitor's attention because of the smell and the sight of flies buzzing around: a latrine belonging to the buildings is situated right at the intersection of the streets, with a rubbish dump just to its south.

Private property-owners are responsible for keeping the street front immediately outside their houses free of rubbish, and there are also efforts—in Rome at least—to keep the streets clean.[32] But what happens inside people's houses is a different matter, and

---

[*] It is a design also found in the jewellery boxes of women in the north of Britannia, at Coria (Corbridge) and can be seen at the museum there.

prudent landlords are careful to draw up contracts to ensure they are legally covered if their properties are not left in good order when vacated. House leases from Egypt specify that rooms should be 'cleansed of excrements and every kind of filth' at the end of the contract period.[33] Peering over the wooden fence that surrounds the three buildings in Calleva, the passerby is greeted by a more salubrious sight than the smell suggests: an ornamental garden with clipped box and holly bushes and honey bees buzzing round.

These houses in Calleva are of modest appearance, in keeping with the generally small size of British town houses.[*] The larger of the two has three rooms on the ground floor, with a surrounding corridor on three sides; it is a design that can be found in both town and country houses in Britannia and Gaul at this time. The second house is more unusual. Of a square plan, its footprint completely encompasses an earlier circular building, a roundhouse, which lies beneath it, and its layout seems to have been partly determined by its predecessor. The owners of these houses—whom we must presume are related—clearly honour their ancestors and perpetuate the traditions of their forebears, not only in respecting the plan of former buildings, but also in terms of the ritual offerings they make on site, some of which are already of great age when deposited.

Perhaps unsurprisingly, in light of the rubbish dump, some of the householders here suffer from the parasitic whipworm, which causes an irritation of the bowel. The afflicted will, though, almost certainly be ignorant of the cause of their troubles: the roundworm *Trichuris trichiura*. They will have little idea of how to prevent it through improved hygiene.[34] Another scourge are the flies attracted to human or animal waste, which help to spread trachoma, an eye disease, prevalent all over the empire from damp Britannia to dusty Egypt. While little is understood about preventing the disease, there are many people who claim to be able to treat it. Because eye infections spread quickly in close quarters, such as in barracks or onboard ship, the *classis Britannia* has its own specialist

---

[*] In the subsequent fifty years or so, town houses and villas expanded greatly in size and ambition.

opthalmikos, or eye doctor. Indeed, the great medical writer Galen mentions such a man attached to the fleet and describes the ingredients of his eye ointment: copper, zinc hydroxide, zinc carbonate, opium and mercuric sulphide.[35]

Infections are also easily spread in the steamy intimacy of bath houses, especially if the water is rarely changed. Independent doctors and quacks can often be found in these establishments, peddling their advice and their jars of eye ointment, or *collyria*. Pilgrims also often visit temples seeking relief from such complaints and leave votive eyes made of metal, plaster or even gold in thanks for any cure—which they attribute to the gods rather than to the quacks.

It is to be hoped that Julius Severus and his party will remain immune from the health hazards of bath houses, for the next stop on the itinerary is the place where bathing and religion is most spectacularly combined in Britannia and whose mysterious hot springs have a most dramatic connection to the sacred world: Aquae Sulis (Bath), some 58 miles (93km) to the west of Calleva.

CHAPTER VII

Bath, a Tourist Hotspot

In quo spatio magna et multa flumina, fons calidi
opiparo exculti apparatu ad usus mortalium:
quibus fontibus praesul est Minervae numen, in cuius
aede perpetui ignes numquam canescunt in favillas,
sed ubi ignis tabuit vertit in globos saxeos.

In [Britain] there are many great rivers, and warm springs
sumptuously appointed for the use of mortals.
The presiding spirit of these is Minerva,
in whose temple the eternal flames never whiten
into ash, but when the fire dies away, it turns
into stony spheres (embers).

SOLINUS, *Collection of Curiosities*
(22.10)

*

AT CALLEVA Atrebatum, two main roads leave from the western side of town. One heads south-west towards Durnovaria (Dorchester) and Isca Dumnoniorum (Exeter), while the other runs north-west to the *colonia* of Glevum (Gloucester), former base of the Legion II Augusta. Julius Severus and his party will want to take the latter route if their next destination is Aquae Sulis (Bath), travelling on it for some 12 miles (19km) as far as Spinae (Speen, near Newbury).

Just beyond Spinae, the road to Aquae Sulis branches off (south of Wickham¹) and continues for 15.5 miles (25km) west to Cunetio (Mildenhall).* Cunetio possesses a regular street plan and public

---

* Spinae is named on the Antonine Itinerary, suggesting that in the third century AD, at least, there was a posting station here. Cunetio is also mentioned in the Itinerary.

buildings, including a twenty-four-roomed *mansio* in the town centre,[2] but its origins pre-date the Romans. It lies on the southern bank of the River Kennet and at a pivotal crossroads, where several major roads converge on the river crossing. Narrow barges make their way slowly along the water, carrying grain downstream towards the Thames, into which the Kennet ultimately flows. Wheat and barley grow on the well-drained soils of the surrounding chalk downs, whose slopes are dotted with still-modest villas.[3] To the south and west the open downland gives way to the rolling hills, dense with oak trees, of the Savernake Forest. Pottery is made in this area; the forest provides a plentiful supply of firewood and charcoal for the potters' kilns.

Just past Cunetio, the main route west crosses the road that connects Venta Belgarum (Winchester) with Corinium (Cirencester) and continues across sarsen-strewn Overton Down.* Here, the high chalk downland grasses provide pasture for sheep. The area is also home to the farmers of pre-Roman settlements near to ancient trackways such as the Ridgeway, over which the road now passes.[4] In places, the old field layout has been reorganized, and irregular 'Celtic' fields of the Iron Age have been overlaid with rectangular fields laid out from double lynchetted trackways—trackways running between fields with embankments (lynchets) formed by the soil slippage from many years of ploughing.[5] Following the River Kennet to its source, west of Cunetio, the governor's entourage will enter an extraordinary prehistoric landscape full of ancient monuments charged with ritualistic significance. The road proceeds straight from the site (at West Kennet) of a huge longbarrow, built in about 3,500 BC, to the foot of the great Neolithic monument of Silbury Hill, which was used as a sighting point in laying out the road west.[6] This hill is still revered as a religious site, and ritual shafts lie in an arc around its base.[7] Its peak—should you care to climb it—offers a fine view to the north, towards the massive

---

* The route passed through modern Marlborough. The sarsen stones were later known popularly as the 'grey wethers', being likened to a flock of grazing sheep.

henge at Avebury, constructed in 2,500 BC.* Most sacred among the streams and springs in the locality is the Swallowhead spring, regarded as the source of the Kennet. Passing through the roadside settlement at Silbury Hill, which has an inn to accommodate both pilgrims and passing travellers,⁸ the road crosses the downland to just south of Verlucio (Sandy Lane), a market centre surrounded by villas and settlements, which lies roughly midway between Cunetio and Aquae Sulis.† Here, travellers can rest and seek refreshment, mustering their energy for the final 14 or so miles of the journey.

Lying in the crook of the River Avon, at a crossing point where several major roads converge, Aquae Sulis occupies the centre of an area rich in corn, wool and quarry stone, and boasts a nascent pewter industry. West of here, the road from Calleva continues to the port of Abonae (Sea Mills) at the mouth of the Avon. An ancient track, running south-east to an Iron Age port (Hamworthy, on Poole Harbour), also crosses the Avon at this point. Here the road meets the great Fosse Way, which cuts diagonally across Britannia, connecting Isca Dumnoniorum (Exeter) in the south-west to Lindum Colonia (Lincoln) at its north-eastern terminus.‡ The Fosse Way marked the initial western frontier of Roman rule in Britain after the conquest, a neat division between the more pliant and (to an extent) Romanized south and east and the unknown and decidedly non-compliant north and west of the island.

A fort was probably established here at the time of the conquest, and a small settlement grew up at the crossroads, initially to serve the soldiers, although the military soon moved on. But Aquae Sulis has always been more than a crossing point on a river. With its phenomenal natural hot springs, held sacred since prehistoric times, it became a cult centre and is now the biggest tourist attraction in Roman Britain. Today, people come here to worship the goddess and to bathe in the thermal waters that issue from the sacred spring.

---

* Roman coins have been found on the summit, recorded by the antiquarian William Stukeley in the eighteenth century.
† Its status as a market centre is conjectural.
‡ The road from Calleva meets the Fosse Way at Batheastern.

Its temple and adjoining baths are dedicated to Sulis Minerva—a
union of the Celtic deity Sulis with the Roman goddess Minerva.

BRITANNIA'S NO. 1 TOURIST HOTSPOT

Throughout the empire, temples, shrines and sanctuaries are places
of pilgrimage and simultaneously centres of tourism. People visit
them not solely to worship the deity associated with them, but also
to participate in all sorts of related activities, such as buying souvenirs and admiring the paintings, tapestries and sculptures that are
displayed in and about the temples and their precincts.

It is true that in today's empire the principal tourist destinations,
apart from the coastal resorts around the Bay of Naples, are Greece
and Egypt: the latter can offer, among its numerous attractions, the
Valley of the Kings and the pyramids[9], and you can even visit Croc-
odilopolis (Arsinoe) to watch the sacred crocodile being fed and
having its teeth brushed.[10] (This year while in Egypt, Hadrian and
his wife Sabina will be visiting the talking statue at Thebes, believed
to be Memnon, child of the goddess of Dawn, the King of the Ethi-
opians who had died at the hands of Achilles at Troy.[11])

Local beauty spots also draw the crowds, such as the source of
the River Clitumnus, just off the Via Flaminia in Italy.* In addition
to its beauty, this site also boasts an ancient temple to the river god
Clitumnus, who issues prophetic oracles from his shrine, as well as
boat rides, swimming, public baths and tourist hotels.[12] While Britain cannot offer the magnificent and ancient architecture of Greece,
Egypt or Italy (perhaps excepting Stonehenge), there is Aquae Sulis
and its ancient and wonderful spring—far more dramatic and unusual, in fact, than the gently meandering source of the Clitumnus.†

The hot water that bubbles up from the ground at Aquae Sulis

---

* Between Spoleto and Trevi in Umbria.

† Stonehenge was visited in the Roman period, although we have no record of what
anyone thought about it. The sacred waters and temple of Minerva at Aquae Sulis
are among the few features of Britannia to be mentioned by the third-century writer
Solinus in his *Collection of Curiosities*.

was once rainwater that fell over the Mendip Hills to the south and gradually percolated deep into the ground through carboniferous limestone, flowing north beneath the Somerset coal field to a depth of between 2,700 (8,860 feet) and 4,300 metres (14,100 feet). Here, the earth's heat raises the water's temperature to between 64 and 96 degrees Centigrade. Under pressure, it then rises to the surface through fissures and faults in the Jurassic rocks under Aquae Sulis to emerge in the form of three hot springs.

The force and volume of water created by the largest spring (the King's Bath stream), where it bursts out of the ground, created a valley between two small hills before running down to the Avon. The springs were known to Mesolithic hunters who once camped among them. At the time of the Roman conquest, the area lay in the territory of the Dobunni, who held the waters to be sacred. For pre-Roman pilgrims the experience must have been deeply awe-inspiring, for they would have approached the bright green, bubbling waters (as hot as 46 degrees Centigrade) through a swamp of alders, along a rubble and gravel causeway edged with small stakes. The mystery of the waters was enhanced by the steamy mist rising from them and the lurid orange-red stains from the iron salts around the edge of the pool. Here the Dobunni worshipped Sulis, goddess of the spring, and made offerings to her. As did the Romans at Clitumnus, the Dobunni threw coins into the waters as gifts to their deity.[*]

The scene today, however, would be unrecognizable to the ancient Dobunni. Since Boudicca's rebellion, the whole site has been thoroughly and spectacularly transformed, very possibly as part of a policy of reconstruction and active 'Romanization' following the devastation wrought by the British queen. Tough Suetonius Paulinus, who won the decisive victory against Boudicca, was replaced as governor soon afterwards by Petronius Turpilianus, a man who—according to Tacitus—'they hoped would be more merciful and readier to forgive offences to which he was a stranger.'[13]

---

[*] Eighteen coins have been discovered, most minted locally.

His successor, M. Trebellius Maximus, governor from AD 63 to 69, was apparently also someone who ruled with *comitas*, or civility. Under him the native Britons 'learned like any Romans to condone seductive vices', a policy pursued by Agricola during his governorship from AD 77. As Tacitus described it, 'temples, market buildings and houses were built and by means of porticoes, baths and elegant banquets the Britons gradually succumbed to the blandishments of vice and enslaved themselves in the name of civilization'.[14]

Whoever was responsible for developing Aquae Sulis as a religious centre and tourist attraction, the site has received a thoroughly Roman treatment, including the waters themselves, which have been channelled in a brilliant piece of engineering.* In order to build over and around the spring, the flow of over a million litres (250,000 gallons) of water a day needed to be properly contained. Highly skilled surveyors and engineers, undoubtedly seconded from the army, constructed a huge drainage system to remove the excess water. They did it with characteristic thoroughness and foresight, blocking the natural stream, which drained away from the spring to the Avon, and building a new drain lined with stone to channel the huge volumes of continuously flowing water away to the east. This ensured that the main drain did not run under any major buildings of what would be the temple complex but could be accessed from rectangular manholes in the street. The drain is big enough for a slave to walk along with a shovel to clear away any built-up sediment; it is the sort of job that a convicted criminal is condemned to perform.[15]

With ruthless efficiency, the Roman engineers consolidated the swampy ground around the spring by driving oak piles deep into the mud. They next enclosed the ground with a two-metre-high wall, which they waterproofed with clay and massive sheets of lead from mines in the Mendips, each sheet weighing nearly half a ton. This caused the hot springwater rising through the underlying rock to fill this container, its sandy sediment settling at the bottom of

---

* The system was so well built that the spring water still enters the Great Bath through the Roman channels in the twenty-first century.

the tank so that only clear water was channelled through to the baths. This reservoir could be flushed clear of sediment whenever necessary by opening the sluice and allowing a great rush of water through it. As soon as the sacred Celtic spring was tamed by the power of Roman engineering, building work could begin on the large temple and baths complex adjoining the spring.

Visitors to the sacred spring now enter the huge temple precinct by the east gate, first having to battle, no doubt, with the touts and dodgy guides who plague tourist sites across the empire. They are notorious for rushing up and offering to explain everything, however obvious, in ways that are exaggerated or simply wrong.[16] They may well drive pilgrims to pray to Minerva to protect them, as tourists elsewhere in the empire have implored: 'Zeus protect me from your guides at Olympia and you, Athena, from yours at Athens!'[17]

As at other tourist sites, there is doubtless plenty of merchandise on offer.[18] If you are a pilgrim you can buy silver offerings for the goddess, such as fine silver pans, their handles decorated with tendrils, leaves and flowers, and with 'D.SULI' ('for the goddess Sulis') picked out in dots on a panel. Or you might plump for bronze pans with brightly coloured enamelled decoration in red, blue and apple-green. This distinctively British style can also be found in the souvenir cups and dishes made for soldiers on Hadrian's Wall. Attractive enamel brooches are popular too; they come in the form of horses and riders, or hares, and can be found at many places in the province.[19]

The cups or dishes dedicated to Sulis Minerva are used to pour libations to the goddess before being thrown into the spring. Pilgrims may opt, of course, to make offerings to other gods at temples around the town—the dedicatory panels on the offerings are left blank, so that they can be inscribed with the name of the chosen deity on purchase. There is something to suit all tastes and pockets: portable altars, miniature lamps and pots, and large leaves or feathers of silver (or gold or bronze) to be hung up or displayed near the cult image. As this is a centre to Minerva, the merchandise is rather less obscene than the pottery on sale around the temple that houses the renowned nude statue of Aphrodite on the island of Cnidus: there, you can also get attendants to unlock a back door for a better view of the goddess's celebrated bottom.[20]

Having got past the stalls at Aquae Sulis, and either eluded the guides (or even engaged one), you will pass through the main entrance in the precinct's eastern wall. Here the Lex Sacra (Sacred Law) is usually posted, informing visitors of temple etiquette and providing such details as which offerings are appropriate and at what time of day certain rituals should be carried out. On entering the precinct, you are confronted by a great sacrificial altar, which lies between the entrance and the temple and is directly aligned with both. The spring and its reservoir lie open to the elements, enclosed by a low balustrade, in the south-east corner of the large courtyard.[21] The inner precinct—the area in front of the temple and around the main altar—is paved with massive limestone slabs, while the surrounding area is gravelled.*

Immediately to the west of the altar is the temple of Sulis Minerva, set on a high concrete podium and approached up a steep flight of steps. If its massive entrance doors are open, you will be able to espy the glittering cult statue within the temple. The four 8-metre-high Corinthian columns of its entrance porch support an ornate triangular pediment. It is a dramatic and curious piece of sculpture, and it has as its central decoration a circular shield, bordered by oak wreaths, which is held up by two winged figures of victory each lunging towards it from globes. The wreaths signify the civic crown for courage awarded to emperors since the time of Augustus, and the shield held by the Victories is a clear signal of Roman power and domination over the world. Here is a work symbolizing power and martial triumph, and any Roman guide might convincingly interpret it in this way.

---

* Later in the second century there were radical alterations. The temple, altar and spring were enclosed by a colonnade; access was restricted to the spring, which was roofed with a massive vaulted chamber; and the temple was remodelled and doubled in size.

In the corners of the pediment are figures of Tritons,* and beneath the shield in the spaces between the Victories and the lower edge of the pediment are two helmets, one in the form of a dolphin's head and the other with an owl perched on top of it. Both owl and dolphin are attributes of Minerva. Moreover, the association of martial Minerva with a Gorgon's-head breastplate will cause no surprise to visitors familiar with Classical iconography. But the head depicted is not the female Gorgon of Classical mythology but that of a frowning man with a swirling moustache, wild hair and staring eyes—unmistakably Celtic in appearance. His hair, streaming out in all directions—as if he were floating on his back in water—coils all around his head and merges into wings and serpents. Is it evoking the powers of Sulis, Celtic goddess of the spring?

AWAY WITH THE DRUIDS

A Romano-British guide might well read the Gorgon's head differently. For the Celts, the sun and sky gods are linked not just with heaven but with water and the underworld too. And both sun and water are related to healing. So a Celt with no Classical training who is looking at the pediment might see a depiction of the sun and of the water in the form of the sea snakes and the dolphin. The owl, too, might have connections with the underworld in Celtic belief. And the oak leaves would not necessarily signify a victory crown so much as they suggest an oak grove, associated with the Druids.

The Druids were priests who, according to the elder Pliny, cut mistletoe from oak trees with golden sickles as part of their ritual.[22] They had a high status in Celtic society as teachers and judges and, according to Julius Caesar, they were philosophers and astronomers who taught that the soul was immortal.[23] The Druidic doctrine was said to have originated in Britain, and people in Caesar's day who wished to study it more deeply travelled to the island to do so. Yet

---

* Too little is left of these figures to be absolutely certain that they are Tritons.

the Romans disapproved of the Druids heartily, and abhorred their practice of human sacrifice—in their sacred groves 'no woodland nymphs found a home, nor Pan, but savage rites and barbarous worship, repellent altars erected on massive stones; and every tree made sacred with men's blood'.[24] Claudius is said to have 'utterly abolished the cruel and inhuman religion of the Druids in Gaul'.[25]

Although the Romans subject criminals to all sorts of exquisite deaths in the arena, they make a fine distinction between the execution of criminals according to the law and blood sacrifice to the gods. Any creature that is sacrificed for religious purposes must be brought 'willingly' to slaughter. From a political point of view the Druids were also deeply suspect because they were absolute judges in all aspects of life, with the authority of life and death over those brought before them, a privilege in the Roman Empire accorded only to those specially invested with it by the emperor. They were also, in their own society, 'exempt from paying taxes and military service'.[26]

In sum, the Druids were completely and utterly independent of everything that Roman authority imposed on its subjects. They were thus dangerously subversive, having everything to lose and nothing to gain from Roman rule. Rome therefore sought to extinguish them.

The Druids in Britannia made their last stand on the island of Mona (Anglesey), which the governor Suetonius Paulinus attacked just before the outbreak of Boudicca's revolt. As his troops approached, they were confronted by 'a motley battleline, densely armed standing on the shore, among whom were brazen-faced women shouting curses, their dress wild and their hair loose as though they were Furies; and also Druids, their hands held high, fulminating their angry prayers to heaven'. This disconcerting scene initially made the soldiers freeze to the spot, until Suetonius managed to snap them out of it by telling them not to be scared of a bunch of fanatical women.[27] Thereupon the soldiers conquered their fear and the island and destroyed the sacred groves 'devoted to Mona's barbarous superstition'.

Nowadays at Aquae Sulis, a temple guide (depending on the nature of his audience) might point out that just as the Romans contained the forces of the Druids and their native religion, so Romans had also contained the forces of nature in the sacred spring. There is other potential symbolism and allusion too. The six-point star burst atop the pediment could be a pun on Sulis/Solis (the Latin for sun being *sol*; genitive: *solis*), or it might invoke the imperial cult. But were our temple guide to warm to his Druid theme, he might allude to the fact that the Romans had first brought light into what the poet Lucan described as a sacred 'grove which from the earliest time no hand of man had dared to violate; its chilly nooks hidden from the sun; its tangled, matted branches imprisoning the air within'.[28] The Druids worshipped their gods in sacred groves, just as Sulis had been worshipped, before the Romans came, in her mysterious alder-fringed pool.

As for the pediment's breastplate, it was the tradition for Roman generals to dedicate weapons taken from their enemies, as when Marcus Vettius Bolanus dedicated a breastplate 'torn off a British king' when governing Britannia in AD 69–71.[29] Might the temple pediment proclaim that the Romans have conquered the native priests, by displaying the head of a Celt on the shield of the Roman martial goddess Minerva, just as they have tamed the sacred spring now contained in its great pool?

Firmly contained within the walls of the temple, at the end of the single *cella* (chamber) beyond the porch, stands the life-sized cult statue of Sulis Minerva. When the temple doors are open, she can watch over the sacrifice being made in her honour at her altar outside. Made of gilded bronze and clothed in martial dress, wearing a breastplate with the Gorgon's-head mask,[*] she glitters in the light of the perpetual flame tended by the priests who serve her, the lumps of burning coal never being allowed to whiten into ashes.[30] The light also catches dozens of pairs of eyes made from glinting coloured glass, which are embedded in the tin, bronze and perhaps

---

[*] Her gilded bronze head was discovered in 1727. A relief carving of Minerva found in the Great Bath shows her wearing a breastplate in the form of a Gorgon's-head mask.

even silver masks pinned up as votive offerings, on walls in and around the temple.*

Shining, too, is the regalia of the priests, their crowns, diadems and masks enhancing their mystery and that of the goddess they tend. In processions, and when officiating at certain ceremonies, they carry sceptres—symbols of their authority and status which, like wands, are invested with special powers. Most British sceptres are wooden shafts, with strips of copper alloy wound in spirals around them, and crowned with terminals depicting gods, animals, birds or even emperors.† While men recruited from the curial or governing classes serve as part-time priests, to enhance their social status, others are 'career' priests. One of the latter was G. Calpurnius Receptus, whose freedwoman and dutiful wife, Calpurnia Trifosa, erected a monument in his honour, when he died at the age of seventy-five, in the cemetery on the other side of the river.[31]

MAKING A SACRIFICE

After the flickering intensity of the temple interior, the natural light will seem staggeringly bright to anyone emerging into it. Directly in front of the temple, the great sacrificial altar, 2.4 metres square, has a slightly dipped surface made shiny from the viscera of sacrificed animals. At each corner of its base are depicted resolutely Classical gods, among whom are Bacchus holding a thyrsus (wand) and pouring a drink for a panther squatting at his feet; Hercules Bibax (Hercules 'the drinker') sporting his lion-skin cape, the lion's paws knotted around his chest, and holding a large drinking vessel

---

* A tin mask found in the sacred spring has hollowed-out eyes, thought to be for coloured glass, and six nail holes: two on top, and two on each side. See Cunliffe (1988).

† Sceptres were also made of iron or copper alloy. Minerva's priests at Aquae Sulis might have had sceptres terminating in a bust of the goddess, such as the one with an iron core found at Stonea in the east of England. It is not known to what extent 'British' and Celtic customs, in terms of crowns and sceptres, were used in apparently 'establishment' centres like Aquae Sulis in the Hadrianic period.

in one hand and a knobbed club in the other; and Jupiter, with a trident in his hand and an eagle at his feet.*

Aquae Sulis's importance as a religious centre is underlined by the distinguished presence of a *haruspex*, a specially trained priest who can divine meaning from the entrails of sacrificed animals. The existence of such a personage here is a clear indication of the status of the site, for otherwise such a man is unheard of in the province. Whereas an *augur* interprets the movement of birds' flights and the meaning of dreams, a *haruspex* possesses even more arcane knowledge, which enables him to read marks on an animal's liver, understanding the connection that each part of the organ's surface has to a particular god. It is an extremely powerful job, and it is one that demands the greatest amount of tact and intuition, for a *haruspex* will need to be able to divine the mood of the person— be it Julius Severus on an official visit, or some other high-ranking official or prosperous merchant—who has paid for the sacrifice and wishes validation for his future actions.

Hadrian, as emperor, is the *pontifex maximus* (chief priest), and Julius Severus—as Hadrian's representative in Britannia—will be expected to officiate at religious ceremonies as part of his duties. Just as he is ultimately responsible for ensuring that the correct procedures are carried out according to the law in civic society, so Severus must preside over religious rites with the same sort of care. To be neglectful and fail to observe the correct proprieties risks causing offence to both men and gods. While Severus cannot do much to prevent natural disasters or unforeseen catastrophes, he must ensure that none of them can ever be ascribed to his disregard for religious observance.

A sacrifice is conducted according to elaborate ritual. The spilling of the animal's blood must be expiated by rigorous observance of certain rites, and the ceremony is fraught with the danger of ill omen. On major feast days, and to mark special occasions such as the visit of the provincial governor, a heifer will be sacrificed for

---

* The fourth god is too weathered to identify.

Minerva: a female animal offered to a female deity. It is a carefully orchestrated spectacle, in which everything and everyone must play their due part. Centre stage is the sacrificial victim, wreathed with garlands, its horns gilded, perhaps. It must be led calmly to the altar, so that it meets its doom 'willingly'. Flute players accompany the procession to drown out any sounds that might be interpreted as unpropitious, and the effect might well create a soothing atmosphere for the animal's last moments. Incense lies on the air, burning on the main altar and on numerous smaller votive altars in the precinct.

Julius Severus, officiating, will greet the processional group with his toga pulled over his head to keep out any sights or sounds that may be deemed unlucky and jeopardize the sacrifice. *Mola salsa*, flour mixed with salt, is sprinkled between the cow's horns, and a couple of its hairs are cut to symbolize purification. Other participants in the sacrifice will also have ritually cleansed themselves before the ceremony.

Now an attendant fells the animal with a pole-axe, stunning it before the knife is plunged into the beast. (Some axes are partly modelled in the form of the animal they are about to slay.[32]) The heifer's liver is removed for the *haruspex* to interpret. The heart and viscera are also extracted—to be declared, it is hoped, uncorrupt—and burnt, with the prized thigh fat and wine poured as a libation. After the gods have been given their due, the remains of the animal will be taken away to be roasted, then returned to the sacred enclosure for a celebratory feast.

All around the temple courtyard are numerous smaller altars and statues decorated with flowers, their dedicatory inscriptions picked out in red paint. Some of the altars are smoking with incense, others still shining from the gore of sacrifice. A statue to the goddess Sulis, dedicated by Lucius Marcius Memor, a *haruspex*, stands near the great altar.[33] Two small altars in memory of retired centurion Marcus Aufidius Maximus have been erected by the slaves whom he had set free,[34] while Priscus, son of Toutius, a stonemason of the Carnutes, from around Autricum (Chartres, in northern France), has set up an inscription to the goddess.[35] He may have come here as a tourist, or on a business trip to buy stone from the Bath quarries, or perhaps to work on a building project here.

Another stonemason, called Sulinus, son of Brucetius,[36] whose name recalls the goddess Sulis, has dedicated his altar to a collection of local deities, the Suleviae. Perhaps he, too, was on business here. He came from Corinium, some 30 miles (48km) to the north, where he dedicated another altar to the Suleviae.[37] Pilgrims wishing to buy altars to dedicate to their favourite deities are able to get them ready-made from men like Sulinus, who manufacture them in bulk but leave a space for personalized inscriptions.

THE JOY OF WARM BATHS

The baths of Aquae Sulis lie immediately south of the temple. Constructed in the late first century AD they are now being altered.* Their unique feature is the sequence of thermal swimming baths, fed by the sacred spring, which are contained in a monumental aisled hall, more than 33 metres (108 feet) long by almost 20.5 metres (67 feet) wide. The simple grandeur and careful design put them on a par with anything west of Rome—or arguably within Rome itself. The building is cleverly conceived, so that the whole focus of the main hall's interior is the view of the sacred spring and altar beyond: these can be seen through three large windows in its north wall. Additional light comes from a clerestory, or high-level tier of windows, under a pitched timber roof.[38] The walls of the hall are plastered with thick red mortar and painted in blocks of colour. In the centre of the hall is a large pool (the Great Bath) containing the naturally warm spring water, with a smaller pool beyond it. Heated swimming pools, especially ones as large as this, are extremely rare, for heating water is a very costly exercise. Pools that are naturally heated by thermal waters are unique in Britain

---

* They underwent further changes over time, remaining in use until the late fourth or fifth century.

and uncommon elsewhere—their existence is regarded as truly miraculous.

Broad-pillared arcades, paved with huge slabs of white lias limestone, run around the side of the hall. Alcoves are set into the walls, three on each side. Here, you can sit and gaze upon the waters. In other baths it may be common to play games, eat and drink, conduct business, flirt and gossip, or even have your armpits or other body hair plucked. But since this is part of a sacred zone, the activities carried out immediately around the pool are likely to be of a more religious or contemplative nature. There might be a sanctuary or shrine in the north-west corner of the main baths, and there are other small votive shrines and statues in and around the pools. Priests and perhaps even doctors are in attendance. (Oculists and other purveyors of potions and remedies operate elsewhere in the town.)

The Great Bath occupies almost the whole central area of the hall.* All four sides descend, in four steps, into the water, and the entire pool (including steps) is waterproofed with sheets of lead. In the middle of its north side there is a fountain, fed by a lead pipe from the sacred spring.† The bath itself is supplied by a pipe that links directly to the reservoir of the spring. Water from here also feeds the other pools, and the excess is removed through a drain in the north-east corner. The water level is maintained in the bath through a bronze sluice.

In addition to the thermal pools, you will also be able to enjoy more conventional baths. The original entrance hall and baths suite to the west of the pool have recently been adapted to accommodate an additional, large, cold plunge pool and sauna. After changing in the new *apodyterium* (changing room) and perhaps taking exercise in this part of the baths, you can gradually acclimatize to the increasing levels of heat in a warm room (*tepidarium*). Before proceeding to the very hottest rooms, your attendant will rub you with oils. Then, it is on into the *caldarium* (the hot steam room) and the

---

* Its dimensions being 22 metres by 8.8 metres, and 1.5 metres deep (72 × 29 × 5 feet).
† This was later replaced by the smaller fountain that is still visible today.

laconicum (hot dry room) to work up a good sweat. Having had the oil scraped off with strigils, you will be ready to descend the massive stone steps and plunge into the cold waters of the large circular bath.[*]

At the other (east) end of the baths, the smallest and narrowest of the three pools has recently been replaced by a new suite of baths, which has its own separate changing room. Such an arrangement might allow men and women to use the baths at the same time. The men no doubt are given access to the larger western suite and main bath, while the women use the eastern baths and smaller thermal pool.[†] It was, after all, Hadrian's decree (following Augustus's example) that the sexes should bathe separately ('*lavacra pro sexibus separavit*'), and in places where there are no separate facilities, they will need to bathe at different times.[39]

The Roman attitude to nudity and to mixed bathing is complex, and opinions have changed from generation to generation. In the days of the republic, Romans were shocked by the Greek habit of exercising naked and were averse to being seen naked in public, to the extent that (according to Plutarch) Cato the Elder refused to bathe with his son.[40] But that anecdote is making a point of describing an exceptionally austere and old-fashioned character, and Augustus's subsequent attempts to segregate male and female bathers may have been a reaction to an over-enthusiastic public acceptance of nudity. This is the age, after all, in which the poet Martial wrote: 'The gymnasium, the baths, the stadium is in this part: get back! We have taken off our clothes, spare us the sight of naked men!'[41]

While there are plenty of salacious references to women being at the baths at the same time as men and revealing their bodies, it is rarely clear what this means in practice. When writers criticise women for being naked, they may not necessarily mean that they have taken off every stitch of clothing. It might mean that

---

[*] Measuring 9 metres (30 feet) in diameter and 1.2 metres (4 feet) deep.
[†] The idea that this might represent separate changing rooms and have been so devised for the separation of the sexes is purely conjectural.

the women are simply wearing very little. For exercising, women wear a form of bikini;[42] leather ones can be bought in Londinium.[43] Perhaps, to conservative folk who expect 'respectable' women to cover up from head to toe, anyone wearing such a skimpy item may as well be 'naked'.[44] Quintilian, writing in the AD 90s, wondered whether a woman bathing with men could be taken as a sign of adultery, while Juvenal described a woman 'who goes to the baths at night, bossing around her slaves with perfume jars, all because she delights to sweat among the crowds'. Having exercised with heavy weights, the woman enjoys a massage with a happy ending, the masseur 'forcing a cry from his mistress, as he strokes the surface of her thigh'.[45] Salacious satires these might be—but they are only amusing because there is some truth in them, and because they send up familiar characters and situations.

CUTPURSES AND CURSES

As with inns or taverns—or anywhere, in fact, where strangers mix—unsavoury characters lurk, ready to exploit those away from home and in a vulnerable situation. In Aquae Sulis, as you take to the waters you are inevitably separated from your clothes and personal possessions by your state of undress.* Bath thieves (*fures balnearii*) are a hazard of all bath houses, and Aquae Sulis is unfortunately no exception. It is advisable to bring your own slave to guard your possessions while bathing, or failing that to try to hire an attendant from the baths (who might be able to offer other pleasurable services as well).[46] But if you are too poor to do either, you will have to take a risk. Although anyone caught stealing is punishable under Roman law and may end up condemned to the mines, plenty of thieves get away with their crimes.

If you are the unlucky victim of an elusive thief, then your only

---

* References to sets of clothes for the baths could mean either bathing costumes or robes worn after a bath. A curse tablet found at Aquae Sulis refers to *paxsa(m) ba(ln) earum et [pal]leum*, 'my bathing tunic and cloak', which has evidently been stolen from the baths.

recourse may be to magic.[47] Among the many offerings thrown into the sacred spring are curses (*defixiones*), in which the wronged seek justice from Sulis. In sometimes dubious and often extremely vivid Latin, prayers entreat the goddess to bring down terrible vengeance on the thieves of cloaks, sandals, rings and petty cash. They are written on small sheets of lead or pewter, tightly rolled up and consigned to the waters, testament to countless incidents of theft and petty squabbles experienced by the more humble visitors to Aquae Sulis.[48]

Throughout the Greek and Roman world, curse tablets are used in quite specific ways. They can be devised with ease. All you need to do is, as one set of instructions directs, '*take lead from a cold-water pipe, make a tablet and write on it with a bronze pen…*'[49] Using pseudo-legal language, as if pursuing a claim in court, curse tablets express a contract with the deity, whereby the victim promises to give the god something in return for punishing the offender. As such, the lowly curse tablet reflects the *quid pro quo* deals that, in many ways, characterize Romans' relationships with their gods. It is the sort of relationship implied on votive altars too, with their common shorthand 'VSLLM' (*Votum Solvit Laetus Libens Merito*), 'fulfilling his/her vow gladly and freely as it is merited', and its variants.[50]

Curse tablets are written all over the empire, but no other province has quite such an obsession as Britannia with cursing people over theft and property rights. Elsewhere, passions are more likely to be raised and curses meted out to rival lovers and opposing teams in chariot races.* Some of the British curses are quite chilling. One, from a rural shrine (at Uley in Gloucestershire), north of Aquae Sulis, vividly implores Mercury to punish an embezzler with lack of sleep, unknown diseases and ailments; for good measure, his whole family is also to be rendered *seminudi, edentuli, tremuli, podagrici sine cuiusque hominis misericordia*, 'half naked, toothless, tremulous, gouty, beyond human pity'.[51]

---

* Only twenty of around 1,300 known curse tablets elsewhere in the Roman world are concerned with theft. But in Britannia only one paltry *possible* love charm from Old Harlow has been found, and not a single curse on a sportsman.

Every single curse text from Aquae Sulis is unique, despite the formulaic nature of curses.[52] They are written in shaky capital letters by the barely literate, or in nonsense language, or in mirror text, or in anagrams, or in Latin using Greek letters.[53] But in one respect there is a theme: in contrast to the names of Roman citizens that appear on the altars and inscriptions in stone at Aquae Sulis, the curse tablets are predominantly populated with Celtic names. Although some of these people are evidently used to writing and have a stylish hand,[54] the spelling and choice of words in the tablets reflects the novel way that Britons pronounce and use Latin.[55]

The humble curse tablets are in striking contrast to the more valuable objects thrown into the spring, including a bag with thirty-three engraved gemstones, the items of silver, the pewter and enamelled bronze cups, and brooches, as well as tens of thousands of coins. Curiously, votive deposits depicting parts of the body are largely absent from the waters of Aquae Sulis, suggesting that people do not come here primarily to secure a cure from the goddess.[56]

BEYOND THE SANCTUARY

Having bathed, sacrificed and feasted, you will find there is plenty to see outside the confines of the sanctuary. Beyond the precinct, to the north of the baths, is a monumental theatre built on the same axis as the temple. Such a building is fairly rare in Britannia but is found in this sort of relationship to large temples in northern Gaul. Judging by the workmanship, it may well have been built with the help of Gaulish craftsmen such as the aforementioned Priscus. The theatre is twice the size of the temple, and visitors from warmer climes may note wryly the larger-than-life-sized gargoyles, which disperse the rainwater that accumulates in the gutter cut into the cornice.[*]

Most extraordinary of all is a huge and elaborately worked *tholos*, a Greek style of temple consisting of a circular inner *cella* encircled

---

[*] Knowledge of buildings in Aquae Sulis beyond the temple and baths is very incomplete. The identification of this monumental building as a theatre is conjectural. Most of it lies unexcavated under Bath Abbey.

by a colonnade. It is highly unexpected in a north-western province, and in Britannia is little short of astonishing. It stands on the same axis as the temple of Sulis Minerva, exactly mirroring its proportions. The building is new, and it surely reflects the influence of the emperor himself. After all, it would have been unusual for Hadrian not to visit Britannia's premier tourist destination during his tour in AD 122; perhaps it amused him to commission a Greek-style building in such an outlandish place, and so to spread his craze for all things Greek even to the north-western boundaries of his empire. Hadrian was certainly in the mood for commissioning building projects at the time, for on leaving Britannia and crossing to Gaul he built a basilica 'of marvellous workmanship' at Nîmes, in honour of Plotina, Trajan's widow and Hadrian's adoptive mother.[57]

Beyond the sanctuary, there are also two other natural hot springs, situated in the south-west quarter of the town. One (Cross Bath) is an open pool contained within a large, oval, walled enclosure. Immediately south of the other spring (Hot Bath), into which pilgrims like to throw coins, is a large and elaborate suite of baths.*

Although visitors have been travelling from far and wide to the Romanized springs for decades, and there are more splendid and extraordinary buildings here than in the average Romano-British town, Aquae Sulis remains much smaller than any *civitas* capital. The whole focus of Aquae Sulis is on the temple and baths complex, and the place remains undeveloped as a town, without a formal street grid. The town's resident population, the lesser temple and baths staff, the tourist guides, craftsmen and shopkeepers all probably live on the level dry ground to the north, along the Fosse Way in the direction of the ford, and across the river. The spa is popular with the military, and many soldiers choose to spend their leave or even retire here. Some die here: Gaius Murrius Modestus of the Second Adiutrix from Forum Julii (Fréjus, in the south of France) did not live long enough to become a veteran, dying here aged twenty-five. Julius Vitalis of the XXth Legion, recruited in

* Both springs might have had small temples attached to them.

Gallia Belgica and based at Deva, died at the age of twenty-nine, after only nine years' service. His funeral costs were paid by the guild of armourers, to which he belonged. It is not clear whether fifty-eight-year-old Rusonia Aventina of the Mediomatrici (a tribe centred on Metz, in eastern Gaul) died here while on holiday or after having made Aquae Sulis her home. Peregrinus, son of Secundus, was a Treveran (from the area around Trier) and, perhaps feeling homesick, he offered an altar to Mars Loucetius and Nemetona, gods from his native eastern Gaul. Tactfully, he placed it outside Minerva's precinct.

Having exercised all due diplomacy themselves by making the appropriate religious observances and bathing in the sacred waters, our travellers must take to the road again, heading north-west out of Aquae Sulis—and into Wales.

CHAPTER VIII

The Fortress and Amphitheatre at Caerleon

Νέμεσι πτερόεσσα, βίου ῥοπά, / κυανῶπι θεα, θύγατερ Δικας, /
ἃ κοῦφα φρυάγματα θνατῶν / ἐπέχεις ἀδάμαντι χαλινῷ, / ἔχθουσα
δ'ὕβριν ὀλοὰν βροτῶν / μελανα φθονον ἐκτὸς ἐλαύνεις. / ὑπὸ σὸν
τροχὸν ἄστατον, ἀστιβῆ / χαροπὰ μερόπων στρέφεται τύχα...

Winged Nemesis, holding life in the balance, / dark-eyed goddess,
daughter of Justice / who checks the pointless whinnying of mortals
with her adamantine bit, / she hates the deadly hubris of men
driving out dark envy. / On her ever-turning wheel
restless steel grey Fortune rotates...

From a *Hymn to Nemesis* by MESOMODES OF CRETE,
Hadrian's court musician[1]

*

HEADING out of Aquae Sulis towards the port of Abonae, at the
mouth of the River Avon, the road taken by Severus's party will
keep the Avon on the left, climbing steeply over Kelston Round Hill
and then onto the *statio* of Trajectus,* almost 6 miles away.[2] Here,
the travellers might welcome a break after the steep climb, even
after such a short distance. A route from the Mendip Hills leading
southwards joins the main road west (at Willsbridge), which then
runs over Durdham Down. Abonae lies some 3 miles (5km) to the
west, where it is joined by another road running north direct to
Glevum (Gloucester).[3]

The main settlement of Abonae is situated on a small plateau
above the river, and it is enjoying modest prosperity, despite a

---

* Trajectus is probably on the site of today's Bitton.

recent fire. Some of its buildings boast painted wall plaster and mosaics. With its access to the Bristol Channel and its location at the junction of the roads to Glevum and Aquae Sulis, Abonae serves as a market town for several small agricultural settlements in the area.[4] Samian ware from south and central Gaul, olive oil and fish sauce from Spain, and wine from southern Gaul are all available here, possibly obtained from ships on their way from the Continent to the legionary fortress at Isca Augusta, just across the Bristol Channel.

From Abonae, officials and soldiers can sail across to Isca Augusta, which has its own port about four miles up the coast from the mouth of the River Usk. Another short ferry crossing, a little further north—where the estuary of the River Sabrina (Severn)[5] is at its narrowest, only about a mile across—takes passengers directly to the *civitas* capital of the Silures tribe at Venta Silurum (Caerwent).[6] However short the journey, many travellers still take care to toss coins or offerings into the waters in thanks to the river goddess for their safe passage.

On crossing the Severn Julius Severus will be entering the territory of the Silures. Their land extends over much of south-eastern Wales (over what will approximate to Gwent, the Glamorgans, southern Powys and Monmouthshire). Visitors who have read up a little beforehand might feel some trepidation on entering this country for the first time, for the Silures—who are said to have originated in the Iberian peninsula—are supposedly fierce, with dark faces and curly hair, the inhabitants of a harsh landscape.[7]

Before the Roman conquest, the Silures lived in predominantly fortified settlements on coastal promontories (such as Sudbrook), or in hillforts (such as Llanmelin and Lodge Hill Camp near Isca), although they also had dwellings on the often flooded Gwent Levels. They depended on farming for their livelihood and do not seem to have had any sort of tribal capital, probably living in clans and extended family groups. After the invasion of Britain, the defeated Caratacus sought refuge among them and, inspired by Caratacus's heroic reputation, the loosely knit Silures rallied around him. Even after his final defeat in North Wales, in the Ordovices' territory, the Silurians, who 'could not be dissuaded from fighting by either savagery or clemency',[8] kept up the war in the south, seriously harassing the Romans with their guerrilla tactics, using their knowledge of the difficult terrain. In one of their most devastating attacks they managed to surround a group of legionary cohorts who had been left to build forts: they killed the camp prefect, eight centurions and some of the best men in the company, and the remainder were only saved from being massacred when the garrisons of nearby forts got wind of their plight and came to the rescue.[9]

The country around here, with its hills, dense forests and boggy ground, is ideally suited to guerrilla warfare and to ambushes in mountain passes and marshes. This helped the Silures to give the Romans, who find such terrain hard to negotiate, a run for their money for more than thirty years and earned them a reputation for being exceptionally tenacious, *'ac praecipua Silurum pervicacia'*.[10] This was a struggle to the death, for the Roman commander during the early years of conquest in Wales had vowed that the very name of the Silures should be utterly extinguished. But the Silures managed to persuade other tribes to join their insurgency by lavishing gifts of booty and prisoners upon them,[11] and it was only in AD 75, under the governorship of Sextus Julius Frontinus, that the Silures were finally subdued. Even then, in defeat, they were accorded a rare tribute from Tacitus as 'the strong and warlike Silures, a brave enemy who live in difficult terrain'.[12]

SAILING UP THE USK

Visitors to the legionary fortress at Isca sail up the mouth of the Usk to a substantial harbour just south-west of the fortress. It is provided with a quay and landing stages, wharves, warehouses and offices, so that ships can sail right up to the fortress from the sea. This excellent arrangement means that the supplies and ships enjoy the protection of the legionaries, and neither provisions nor men are dependent on overland routes through the difficult terrain and amidst people who, within living memory, have been sworn enemies.

Frontinus could not have chosen a better spot for the fortress. It is sited on a gently elevated plateau, on the right bank of the Usk and at the river's lowest bridging point before it enters the Severn Estuary. It also sits clear of the Usk's flood plain to the east and south, yet is protected by a broad loop of the river, which forms a natural boundary to the south, with a small tributary, the Afon Lwyd, flanking its eastern side.[13] This strategy of siting legionary fortresses on rivers that are readily accessible from the sea is also evident at Deva, at the mouth of the River Dee, and at Eboracum, which sits on the navigable Ouse, whose mouth is at the Humber Estuary. Isca encloses fifty acres of land, and unsurprisingly, given its location, its name derives ultimately from the British word for river water.[14]

As Julius Severus and his entourage travel up-river, a whole cluster of imposing and unmistakably official buildings looms into view. Dominating the riverside and the adjacent port facilities is a huge courtyard building, covering over two acres.[15] It is not quite Portus, but nonetheless it looks imposing and efficient. Even here, approaching the extreme western fringe of the known world, visitors can experience the full embrace of imperial Rome.

The port serves not just Isca and its immediate environs, but also auxiliary forts further upstream. Isca lies on the road that, to the east, ultimately leads to the former legionary bases at Glevum and Viroconium, and to the west, Moridunum (Carmarthen), tribal capital of the Demetae, which is reached via an auxiliary fort at Cardiff.* But right now the whole place looks rather sleepy. The unpaved courtyard, which is big enough to contain thousands of men, together with their equipment and packhorses, is all but empty, and the warehouses and depots further along the quay look quiet too.† Since construction of Hadrian's Wall began in AD 122,

---

* The fort might have been called Tamium, but that is not certain.
† The River Usk was, in the Roman period, much further east than it is now. The quay, wharf and warehouses are all conjectural.

large numbers of men—from at least seven out of ten cohorts, maybe more—have been deployed in the north during the more clement months of the year.* Occasionally vexillations† of the legion are also sent abroad, including men such as Tadius Exuperatus who died, aged thirty-seven years, 'on the German expedition' and whose sister erected a tombstone at Isca in memory of him.[16]

Some people always need to remain at the base, of course, and the place is by no means deserted. There are representatives from each cohort, maintaining a presence, welcoming and training recruits, and supervising soldiers who are rejoining their unit or waiting for assignment. Just dealing with the upkeep of this vast place is a huge job, and day-to-day administration takes up considerable time. A mountain of correspondence is produced each day. Daily rosters detailing (for example) which men need to collect timber for building work,[17] receipts for rations and supplies, records of pay, and more, are all filed neatly on wooden tablets, with relevant copies if necessary. Records are maintained of all personnel and equipment, specifying who is on leave and where men are posted. Every day reports also need to be written up, recording the daily password, which could be—for example—the name of one of the seven known planets.[18] Troops are also on hand to police the area, to maintain contact with the surrounding auxiliary forts, and generally to keep the system running smoothly.

They must ensure too that valuable materials being exported from Wales such as iron, lead and gold are transported under guard and are fully accounted for when they leave the area. A fort‡ in Carmarthenshire guards the Dolaucothi gold mine. The only one in the province, it is very modest in contrast with the gold mines of Dacia and the 230-plus gold mines of Asturia,[19] Galicia and Lusitania, which provide over 20,000 pounds in weight of gold a year.[20]

---

* Possibly all ten cohorts were serving on the Wall, but inscriptions attesting their presence have been found from only seven of them. It might be that they returned to Isca during the winter months.

† From the Latin for the *vexillum*, or banner, under which detachments of soldiers served and fought.

‡ At Pumpsaint—it was perhaps called Luentinum.

Lead, however, is a very different matter. Whereas in Spain and Gaul it is extracted 'with considerable effort', in Britain lead is said 'to lie so abundantly within the upper layers of the earth, that there is a law limiting the scale of its extraction'.[21] Lead is extracted in many places in Britannia—in Flintshire and the border country (between Montgomery and Shropshire), from mines at Lutudarum (near Wirksworth, Derbyshire[22]), from sources in the North Pennines and from the Mendips, near Aquae Sulis. Lead from North Wales and Shropshire is also exported from ports near Deva, while lead from Derbyshire and Yorkshire is loaded onto ships in the Humber (at Petuaria, Brough-on-Humber).[23] Cast into 'pigs', or ingots, and stamped as '(Property) of the Emperor Caesar Hadrian Augustus',[24] lead is used to make pipes, in sheets to line tanks, fountains and baths, for securing iron clamps in building blocks, in official seals on documents and packages, and even as a material for manufacturing votive statues. It also has medical uses—to diminish scars, ulcers and haemorrhoids, and even to suppress libido: when lead plates are applied to the loins and kidneys, they are believed to restrain sexual passion and prevent wet dreams.[25]

FORTRESS ISCA AUGUSTA

The fortress at Isca Augusta was built by legionaries—the men of the II Augusta, a legion so named because the Emperor Augustus either raised or reformed it. The legion first arrived in Britain from the Rhine frontier (at Strasbourg) during the conquest of AD 43 and served with distinction under its commander and future emperor, Titus Flavius Vespasianus. During his time in Britain, Vespasian 'smashed the power of two extremely strong tribes, over twenty *oppida* and the Isle of Wight'.[26] Vespasian had probably left Britannia by AD 47, but the legion remained, and from about AD 55 was stationed at Isca Dumnoniorum.

When Vespasian made a successful bid for power during the civil war (AD 68–69) that followed Nero's death, the troops in Britain were inclined to support him because of his earlier command of the II Augusta and his distinguished service there. Soon after taking power, Vespasian, the first emperor of the new Flavian dynasty, began the successful push into the north of Britannia led by the province's new governor, Petillius Cerialis, in AD 71–74. With Frontinus's governorship (AD 74–78) and the conquest of the Silures, construction of Isca Augusta began.

The fortress lies north of the river. To its west is an amphitheatre, and Julius Severus may be pleasantly surprised to see a handsome porticoed courtyard building adjoining it, of a type often found next to theatres and amphitheatres in Roman cities and containing gardens and fountains.[27] Visitors entering the fortress from the river do so through the south gate, the *porta praetoria*. From here, the *via praetoria* leads to the centre of the fortress, where it

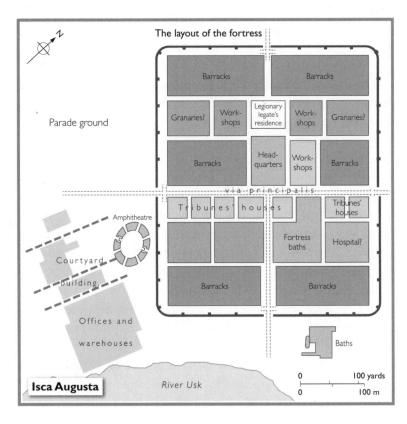

The layout of the fortress

Parade ground

Barracks   Barracks

Granaries?   Work-shops   Legionary legate's residence   Work-shops   Granaries?

Barracks   Head-quarters   Work-shops   Barracks

via principalis

Amphitheatre

Tribunes' houses   Tribunes' houses

Courtyard building

Fortress baths   Hospital?

Barracks   Barracks

Offices and warehouses

Baths

0   100 yards
0   100 m

Isca Augusta   River Usk

intersects with the main east–west road, the *via principalis*, in front of the *principia*, or headquarters building. Just as the main road into a Roman town runs straight to the forum basilica at its heart, so in legionary fortresses the main roads converge on the camp's central focus, the headquarters. Once inside a fortress, a soldier, whether he comes fresh from Africa, Dacia or the Rhineland, will be able to orientate himself very soon, for the main streets and general layout of all the principal buildings are much the same across the empire.

Towering over the surrounding buildings of the fortress, and covering just over 2.5 acres, is the baths complex, a massive construction of stone and concrete. It could easily accommodate the entire garrison, together with their concubines and children. The vaulted ceiling of its baths suite rises, at its highest point, to more than 15 metres (50 feet), with a span of more than 12 metres (40 feet). In scale and form, these structures can hold their own with any in the empire.[28]

The fortress baths, in common with others all over the empire, are also gyms and social clubs. Here, in remote Isca, there might be no access to (or little demand for) Greek and Latin libraries, unlike at the major baths in Rome. The only art on display here might well be the sculptural group in the *nymphaeum* (fountain house) and the odd statue of Fortuna in the changing rooms. Nevertheless, this vast building is a central focus of the legion's social scene. Here the soldiers swim, bathe, take exercise, play board games (perhaps *ludus duodecimo scriptorium*, akin to backgammon) and chat to friends. They also enjoy snacks here—munching olives, slurping shellfish and chewing on mutton chops, chicken pieces, pigs' trotters and pork ribs.[29]

At Isca, the open-air pool is larger in area than the Great Bath at Aquae Sulis and an excellent place to swim.* It is a little over a metre and a half (5 feet) at the deep end, shelving to just over a metre (4 feet) at the shallow end, and its floor is lined with flagstones. The

---

* Its length was 41 metres (135 feet).

pool is fed by lead pipes, through which a continuous flow of water brings in the 365,000 litres (some 80,250 gallons) needed to fill it. The attractive *nymphaeum* stands at one end of the pool. Its apse is painted with a colourful aquatic scene, and it frames the sculptural group in which a dolphin spurts water out of its mouth to cascade down a flight of steps clad in Purbeck marble. Charming though this is, the fountain house's days are numbered as it is suffering from subsidence and will be demolished within the next decade.[*] The baths buildings themselves sport an *apodyterium* and a vast *frigidarium*.[30] In the triple recesses at the end of the hall is a cold plunge-bath, flanked by two large round basins, also carved from Purbeck marble.[31]

Women and children have access to the baths, though in the disciplined era of Hadrian they might well have to use them at different times to the soldiers. The baths' patrons leave a legacy of lost property: hair pins and jewellery; children's milk teeth (and adults' teeth from mouths riddled with gum disease[32]); a handsome strigil inlaid with silver, gold and brass, depicting the twelve labours of Hercules and inscribed with the cheery inscription in Greek '*kalws elouse*' ('it washed nicely');[33] and a multitude of engraved gemstones of amethyst, cornelian and jasper, loosened from signet rings in the moist heat of the baths and trapped in the drains.[†]

A SPACE FOR SPECTACLE

The baths provide one form of recreational activity for the troops, the amphitheatre another.[‡] It was built in about AD 90, in a rather tight space outside the fort's walls near the porticoed courtyard building. Its eight barrel-vaulted entrances, built of tufa and banded with tile and stone, allow up to 6,000 spectators to make their way up to their wooden seats in the grandstand: room enough

---

[*] When the pool was also shortened to 25.5 metres (84 feet) in length.
[†] A total of eighty-eight gemstones have been found in the drain.
[‡] Caerleon has the most complete and thoroughly excavated legionary amphitheatre in Britain.

to accommodate the entire legion, plus guests. The interior wall of the arena is plain, even more so than Londinium's, although its exterior walls are rendered and picked out with false ashlar joints, highlighted in red paint. The coping stones for the parapets of the arena wall and for the top of the open entrances are of fine oolitic limestone from the quarries near Aquae Sulis.

Being so close to the fortress and adjoining the parade ground, the amphitheatre might well also provide a culmination to military parades and a setting for major festivals and ceremonies in the army's calendar, such as *honesta missio* (demobilisation) on 7 January and the celebrations attached to the *rosaliae signorum*, the festival of the standards. At this ceremony, traditionally held in May, the legionary standards are taken out of the shrine in the *principia* and garlanded with roses, the occasion also being marked with religious ceremonies and sacrifice.[34] The legion celebrates its birthday on 23 September (the date of its founder Augustus's birthday), and this is also a time of parades, shows and sacrifices—as is Hadrian's birthday on 24 January.

The amphitheatre is one of the very few types of building that the Romans can claim to have invented—most other familiar Roman structures, such as the theatre, forum, basilica and circus, being indebted to Greek prototypes. Developing during the late Republic, the amphitheatre found its full expression under imperial rule. Equally Roman, too, are the gladiatorial contests—although arguably these originated in Campania—which began as games held as part of funeral ceremonies held in honour of the dead. The first known reference to such a display in connection with a funeral in Rome is in 264 BC.[35] Such *munera*, a word which originally meant works, public offices or duty, also began to be applied specifically to these funeral honours. The rich families of Rome seized on the political capital that could be gained from financing and mounting such expensive entertainments, and they hired increasing numbers of gladiators for the purpose. In time, the *munera* became forms of show for the entertainment of the populace and to enhance the standing or popularity of the host, without necessarily requiring the justification of a funeral.

It is through the arena, and the shows and ceremonies that are enacted here, that Rome's supremacy and role in establishing order in the world is acted out in brutal showmanship. Here Rome can demonstrate her mastery over nature, through the hunting down and slaughtering of wild beasts, and the supremacy of her laws, in inflicting capital punishment and sending convicted men and women to their deaths in the arena. It is in the amphitheatre that Rome can afford its citizens that extra *frisson* of superiority over barbarian forces, condemning prisoners of war to fight to the death and to take part in celebratory tableaux after Roman victory. The gladiators are part of this process, displaying thoroughly un-Roman methods of combat. Some types of fighter are even known by the names of foreign peoples, such as the popular *thraeces*, 'Thracians', who carry curved, dagger-like swords and small shields.

Some desperadoes volunteer as gladiators, but most are recruited from among prisoners of war, the criminals *damnati ad ludum* ('condemned to the show') and slaves, although Hadrian has recently made it illegal for anyone who owns male or female slaves to sell them to either pimps or gladiator trainers without giving good reason.[36] Gladiators operate on the fringes of society, like prostitutes and actors (the latter notorious for moonlighting as the former). They are 'infamous' in the original sense of suffering *infamia*, or public disgrace, because of what they do. Anyone who has been a gladiator is barred from holding political office in local government, from serving on juries or from becoming a soldier; they also lose another privilege of Roman citizenship—freedom from physical assault—and on being recruited into a gladiator training school they must swear to bind themselves body and soul to their *lanista*, or manager.[37] The people who freely hire themselves out as gladiators are known as *auctorati* (bondsmen), and in this shady pecking order they hold a higher status than the slave gladiators, who in turn are rated more highly than the *venatores*, or hunters, and the stagehands who bring on the prisoners and the beasts.

Many gladiators are highly trained fighters, who are first and foremost expected to put on a great show. The best of them command a huge following and can be hired out for large amounts of money. As far as the most skilled fighters are concerned, it is in their managers' best interests to keep them in tip-top condition and ensure that they stay alive. Doctors are provided to treat injured gladiators: this is how the famous medical writer Galen started his career, trying to work out how to reinsert the intestines hanging out of gladiators' gaping wounds.[38]

FIT GLADIATORS, FICKLE GODS

There are plenty of salacious digs about women's attraction to gladiators. Juvenal satirizes the predilection in his misogynistic Satire VI, relating the story of Eppia, the senator's wife, who abandons her family and her wealth to run off to Egypt with an ugly old gladiator well past his prime. He concludes that 'it's the sword that they love' (*ferrum est quod amant*), 'sword' (*ferrum*) being very likely a vulgar pun. Juicy gladiator gossip never loses its appeal.* Gladiators are only too happy to promulgate their ladykiller status: 'Celadus, the Thracian makes the girls pant' (*suspirium puellarum Celadus Tr(ax)*), to quote just one boast scrawled in graffiti by the gladiators of Pompeii.[39]

The poets might joke, and gladiators might boast, but to be a gladiator is to enter not just a different social class but a different state of existence—one that hovers even more precariously between life and death than that of the average person, and one that many find both ignominious and terrifying. It is so disgraceful a prospect that, on one occasion, twenty-nine prisoners strangled each other to death rather than submit to the arena. In the first century AD, a German prisoner of war condemned to fight as a hunter in a beast show made an excuse to slip to the lavatory before the performance and rammed a sponge down his throat, choking himself rather

---

* Towards the end of the second century, rumours abounded that the Emperor Commodus was the product of his mother Faustina's affair with a gladiator rather than the natural son of Marcus Aurelius.

than suffering the horrible fate that awaited him.[*]

The fact is that, however carefully a *lanista* has his gladiators' wounds tended, spectators at the arena expect to see people die, and anyone who foots the bill for a show—be it an emperor or a local magistrate—will gain kudos from the perception that he is rich enough to pay for the deaths of numerous men and beasts. As an inscription from a provincial town in Italy boasts so brutally of one such patron, 'over four days he put on 11 pairs and of these he had 11 of the best gladiators in Campania killed and also 10 bears cruelly killed'.[40] Emperors spend extraordinary money on shows. To celebrate his conquest of Dacia, Hadrian's predecessor Trajan spent millions of *sestertii*, providing 4,941 pairs of gladiators and 10,000 beasts, both tame and wild, during games that lasted more than 120 days.[41] Roman emperors, of course, have the best resources available, including the imperial gladiator schools in Rome, of which the Ludus Magnus, as its name suggests, is the largest and is situated conveniently near the Colosseum. They also have the provincial procurators and army at their disposal to help capture and transport beasts from all over the empire. One centurion of the Legion I Minervia based in Bonna (Bonn) boasts of having caught fifty bears for the arena in the space of six months. Britannia also exports bears and stags, while soldiers serving in northern Britannia are probably charged with procuring bears for imperially sponsored shows, possibly hunting them north of the Wall.[42]

For your average provincial magistrate, however, putting on a gladiatorial show is hugely expensive and fraught with logistical problems.[†] What do you do if, having advertised gladiatorial games

---

[*] The source is Seneca (*Letters*) LXX1, 9–21.23. This is, incidentally, one of the very few references in literature to the Romans using sponges on sticks to wipe their bottoms. Such sponges would have had to be imported into Britannia, and there is no convincing material evidence to suggest that anyone ever bothered to do so; they more probably used moss and rags as substitutes. For another rare sponge-on-stick reference, see Martial (*Epigrams*) XII, 48.

[†] By AD 177 such was the consternation about the expense of mounting provincial gladiator shows that Emperor Marcus Aurelius abolished the tax on the sale of gladiators and tried to fix a scale of prices for putting on shows.

to win political favour, you are faced with a nasty surprise, such as that mass suicide of prisoners on the eve of your show, or the loss of your consignment of bears in a shipwreck? And what if the animals you do have are too mangy and lethargic after a traumatic journey to provide much drama in the arena?[43]

The aristocracy in Britannia, however, appear to be singularly untroubled by such problems. For whatever reasons, they seem reluctant to pay for gladiators, bears or public works of any description, and they do not indulge in the sort of competitive public munificence displayed elsewhere in the empire. As a rule, privately sponsored games featuring gladiators in non-military amphitheatres are unheard of.[44] The schools of gladiators that appear in Britannia and on international tours of Gaul, Spain and Germany do so under the surveillance of an imperial procurator, indicating they are funded by the state.[45]

Despite the apparent reluctance of private individuals in Britannia to foot the bill for gladiators outside the legionary forts, images of gladiators are found everywhere—decorating wall-paintings, mosaics, vases, glassware, ceramics, sculpture, penknives and oil lamps, and catering to all pockets and tastes. Fights are depicted, but also popular is the theme of the dying gladiator: the moment at which he lies defeated, poised between life and death, is often rendered with a combination of brutality and sentimentality. Winged cupids acting out the roles of gladiators on mosaics appeal to similarly mixed sentiments.[46]

Large numbers of glass cups from Gaul showing gladiators may be found the length and breadth of Britannia.[47] But local craftsmen also cater for the demand. The Camulodunum potters have a whole range of gladiator motifs in the moulds they use,[48] and the potters from around Durobrivae (Water Newton, near Peterborough), who specialize in drinking cups with hunting scenes, also produce cups depicting gladiators.[49] Clasp-knives with gladiator terminals and blades that fold into their handles, like penknives, are also perennially popular. Probably imported from Gaul, they are made in copper alloy, bone or ivory.[50]

As in Londinium, on show days at Isca there are stalls outside the main entrance to the amphitheatre that sell drinks, snacks and souvenirs such as glass cups bearing scenes of chariot-racing. In the amphitheatre, spectators show their support for their favourite fighters by carving graffiti. One supporter of the 'net men' (*retiarii*) —those gladiators who, clad only in a loin cloth, wield a large wide-mesh net and a trident—indicates their favour by drawing a trident between two images of the distinctive shoulder guard (*galerus*) worn on the left arm of a *retiarius*, as well as a palm frond denoting victory.[51]

Different types of fighters have their own following. There are the fans of the 'small shields', who are nicknamed *parmularii* (after the *parmula* used by Thracian fighters), or there are the *scutarii*, the 'big shields' (after the *scutum* used by *secutores*).[52] A *secutor* wears a helmet that covers his whole face leaving just two small holes for his eyes. He thus has very limited vision and needs to get close to his opponent—extremely hazardous if he is fighting against a *retiarius*, who can cast his 3-metre-wide net to ensnare him. By way of compensation, the *secutor* is armed with a sword as well as his large shield.[53]

A gladiator called Lucius who has somehow or other ended up in Ratae Corieltauvorum (Leicester) seems to have had at least one fan, a woman called Verecunda.[54] Verecunda is a *ludia* (literally 'show girl'), an actress or performer—or a gladiator's moll, which is how Juvenal uses the word when he asks how the senator's wife Eppia could possibly have run off with a gladiator: 'What does she see in him that it's worth enduring the label *ludia*?'[55] Are Lucius and Verecunda members of a professional troupe on tour in the provinces? Does Verecunda love her Lucius as passionately as Eppia had her lover? If Juvenal's sneering words are to be believed, the allure of gladiators is strong enough to make a woman abandon her family, her home and her country.[56]

One thing is certain: if you are married to a gladiator you can look forward to an early widowhood, as happened to Aurelia in Verona, who buried her husband Glauco after he 'fought 7 fights, died on the eighth, lived 23 years and 5 days'.[57] Inscribed on his tombstone is the advice: 'I warn you not to put your trust in Nemesis. That is how I was deceived. Hail and Farewell'. It is Nemesis, that 'winged balancer of life, dark-faced goddess, daughter of Justice', who is the deity most closely associated with amphitheatres.[58] Nemesis, who is sometimes equated with Fortuna and depicted with her attributes of wheel and rudder, can distribute good or bad fortune, success or failure, life or death. Shrines to Nemesis are found around amphitheatres throughout the empire.[59] Nemesis is also associated with the huntress goddess Diana, appearing together especially in the context of the amphitheatres' hunts (*venationes*). A temple dedicated to Diana is situated near the amphitheatre.[60]

People also ask Nemesis to help them regain their stolen goods and to take vengeance on the thief. Whoever has left a lead curse tablet at her shrine at Isca's amphitheatre promising 'Lady Nemesis, I give thee a cloak and a pair of Gallic sandals; let him who took them not redeem them (unless) with his own blood'[61] is evidently less of a skilled negotiator than the visitor to Londinium's amphitheatre who promised: 'I give Diana my headgear and scarf, less one third. If anyone has done this, I give him, and through me let him be unable to live.'[62]

Mercury, too, is honoured at Isca's amphitheatre. One of the most popular gods in Britannia, he is commonly associated with merchants and travellers, but he is also connected with the dead through his Greek incarnation as Hermes, who—as Hermes Psychopompus—conducts the souls of the dead to the underworld. In some places, masked attendants dressed as Mercury, with his winged cap, brandish a burning hot model of his *cadeuceus,* or wand, to check if those who appear to be dead truly are: 'We have laughed at the sport of your midday game of the gods, when Father Pluto, Jove's own brother, drags away, hammer in hand, the remains of the gladiators; when Mercury, with his winged cap and heated wand, tests by branding whether the bodies were really lifeless or only feigning death.'[63]

VENTA SILURUM, THE SILURIAN CAPITAL

The legionaries who sit in the arena can on the whole expect to live longer than the gladiators whose performances they watch. Soldiers such as Julius Valens, who is buried at one of the cemeteries that lie along the roads leading from the fortress, lived to be a hundred years old. He, like many of his comrades who were able to enjoy their retirement, settled in the *canabae*, or civilian settlements that have grown up around the fortress. Here, the veterans congregate at the taverns, where they drink out of cheap, locally made beakers while snacking off shellfish such as oysters, mussels, limpets and cockles.

Julius Severus and his party will ride through these outlying *canabae* as they take up the next stage of their journey—towards Viroconium Cornoviorum (Wroxeter). This was once the site of a legionary fortress that spearheaded the conquest of North Wales. Now, with the region long subdued, Viroconium is a flourishing *civitas* capital and the legionary base there has been transferred further north, to Deva (Chester).

The party will pick up the main road north, Watling Street West, at Blestium (Monmouth). Although the most direct route north from Isca is the busy road through Burrium (Usk), a high official on a tour of the province will no doubt be expected to visit the local *civitas* capital at Venta Silurum (Caerwent). It lies across the River Usk, about 8 miles east of the fortress. The main settlement in the area around the fort lies in the lowlands of the Vale of Glamorgan and Monmouthshire, where there is good farmland for growing cereals and rearing cattle. The easily flooded Gwent Levels have been drained, a task possibly involving the local soldiers, and the land now provides pasture for horses, cattle and sheep.

Venta Silurum was founded within a very few years of the Silures' final defeat. Despite the Roman threats during the early years of the campaign in Wales, it was not in their best interests to punish the Silures too savagely for giving them such a hard time for so many years. Besides, their defeat came at the advent of Agricola's governorship in AD 75, as he pursued his policy of 'Romanizing' the defeated tribes. It is unlikely that the Silures remained *dediticii*, or without political status or rights, for long. They were evidently granted, under the watchful eye of the nearby legionaries at Isca, land, a form of self-government with their own council, and help with building their town centre, the forum and basilica. They may have had to hand over hostages for a period—perhaps the sons of high-ranking families, who could be sent to a more civilized place to acquire a little Roman polish.[64]

It is also possible that Venta Silurum was populated with veterans from Isca and elsewhere. There are certainly clues that the legionaries helped out with building and planning the town, providing cranes and other lifting devices, together with sculptors to carve the capitals of the forum basilica's fine (30-foot-high) Corinithian columns from local sandstone. The town is near enough to Isca to be a destination for the soldiers and an alternative to the *canabae* outside the fortress as a place to spend their cash when on leave.

At about 44 acres, Venta is one of the smallest tribal capitals in Britannia and covers a smaller area than the 50 acres of nearby Isca.[65] Although divided into twenty street blocks or *insulae*, there are many open spaces within the street grid, and it is really not much more than a straggle of buildings along the main road to Isca.* Shop fronts open out onto the main street, with their workshops and living quarters behind. Some houses are surrounded by yards, paddocks and agricultural buildings, and town quickly blurs into country, with farms on its very fringes.

Visitors enter the forum through an archway on the north side of the main street. It occupies the whole of the central block (*insula* VIII),[66] with shops on the ground floor, each of them a single room with a large open front that can be secured with wooden shutters at closing time; there is also a shellfish snack bar in the north-east corner. The basilica, where the town council sits, is a single long hall with an office at one end and is small compared with those of

---

* Even in the third and fourth centuries, the population numbered only between 2,400 and 3,800 inhabitants.

other *civitas* capitals.[67] Across the road from the forum are the public baths (*insula* XIII) and an adjacent temple (*insula* XII). Visiting officials and dignitaries can stay in a newish *mansio* in the southwest corner of town, set back from the street. Consisting of a courtyard house with a large basin fountain at its centre and a separate baths building, the *mansio* is comfortably appointed, with identical suites of rooms in its north and south ranges and a dining room and kitchen. But as yet it has no central heating, and the rooms are warmed with braziers. The house only seems to cater for officers and officials—those of lesser rank must find accommodation elsewhere in town.[68]

Having passed through Venta, Julius Severus and those accompanying him must now make for the crossroads at Chepstow, where there is a bridge over the River Wye and a road leading east to the *colonia* of Glevum (Gloucester), a former legionary base. Severus, however, follows a direct, though hilly, route north to Blestium, a distance of 12.5 miles (20km). The road keeps to the high ground to the west of the spectacular Wye gorge and much of it affords splendid views over the surrounding countryside. On leaving Blestium, where the road is joined by the busy direct route from Isca, there is a long ascent through a narrow valley—the first stage of a 40-mile stretch to the small roadside settlement of Branogenium (Leintwardine), at the crossing of the River Teme. The journey must be broken somewhere, and one possibility is to make a small diversion to Magnis (Kenchester, near Hereford), a market town for the Dobunni tribe, which has a *mansio*. At Branogenium, officials and military men can stay at the *mansio* outside the fort that lies a short distance to the south-west (at Buckton). They will be among the last visitors to stay here, as the fort is very soon to be vacated.[69]

Throughout his tour, Julius Severus will not have to worry about any of the logistics of travel himself, as he has his own *strator consularis* (transport officer) to depend on, as well as the insights of people with local knowledge; but, as a military man, he will expect to have access to detailed plans of the whole region. A good leader must know not only the distances by the number of paces but also the quality of the roads, the shortest routes and all the by-roads, and detailed information about mountains and rivers. The best-prepared officers have maps containing both annotations and drawings, to enable them to see the best route 'in front of their very eyes'.[70]

For everyday use, civilian travellers are more likely to have a type of route planner, showing the main roads depicted as a series of continuous lines, with the distance between various places written below in numerals, and mainly in Roman miles. (Although in parts of Gaul distances are traditionally measured in leagues, 1 *leuga* or league being equivalent to 1.5 Roman miles.[71]) Symbols on the route planner depict what is on offer at various places. In addition to showing the large harbours, lighthouses, mountains and major rivers, there are bird's-eye views of towns and the different sorts of facilities available *en route*: spas (*aquae*), inns with stabling, and major temples. The maps, produced in sheets in papyrus form, can be wound on two wooden cylinders, or rollers, and packed in luggage. Route planners also exist as lists, giving the start and finish of each itinerary, the total mileage, together with stopping places and distances between them. Maritime routes are available in this form too, listing journeys by sea along the same lines and mainly measured in *stadia*.[*]

Were he to consult his maps, Julius Severus would see that from Branogenium to his next main destination, Viroconium, is a distance of 24.5 miles (39km). The road, which makes its way through the hilly country of the Strettons, keeps to high ground above the valleys, with decent views where possible and maintaining a direct course for long distances.[72] The town the new imperial governor is making for is a substantial one—the *civitas* capital of the Cornovii. For Viroconium Cornoviorum, AD 130 is a significant year.

---

[*] As in the Antonine Itinerary. Although the subject of much discussion regarding its purpose and discrepancies within it, this third-century itinerary no doubt had earlier equivalents, which would have provided a useful reference source for a journey to Britain in AD 130.

CHAPTER IX

A New Forum at Wroxeter, Capital of Cattle Country

Si in aliam quam celebrem civitatem vel provinciae caput advenerit,
pati debet commendari sibi civitatem laudesque suas non gravate audire,
cum honori suo provinciales id vindicent; et ferias secundum
mores et consuetudinem quae retro optinuit dare.

When the Proconsul enters any other city which is not a populous one
or the capital of the province, he should permit it to be placed
under his protection and listen to the compliments bestowed upon
him without showing any discontent, since the people
of the province do this in his honour; and he should appoint
festivals in accordance with the manners and customs
which have previously been observed.

ULPIAN, *On the Duties of a Proconsul,*
Book II (*Digest* 1.16.7)

*

AS THE TRAVELLERS draw near to Viroconium they find themselves in cattle country, the territory of the Cornovii (encompassing
much of Cheshire and Shropshire). Sitting in a landscape of mixed
arable and pastoral farms, Viroconium Cornoviorum is protected
by the River Severn snaking around it to the west, and by the valleys of small streams to the north and south. There are fine uninter-
rupted views over the countryside towards the surrounding hills,
where a large number of former Cornovii hillforts are situated.

Prominent among these hillforts to the east is the Wrekin, from
which the town may derive its name.[1] The link with the Wrekin

clearly remains important, because a road runs directly to it from the town's east gate. Along this track, at the highest and most exposed point of the town—and adjacent to the place where the town's water supply, carried by an aqueduct, empties into a huge cistern—is a large, walled compound. This is the town's important livestock market, or *forum boarium*.

Viroconium is built on the site of a legionary fortress established here in the late AD 50s as the base of the Legion XIV Gemina and then the Legion XX Valeria Victrix. Here, on the higher east bank of the Severn at a place where there is a major ford, the army had control to the west and south and a convenient base for attacking Wales and for penetrating further north. By AD 90, however, the XX Valeria Victrix had been transferred to Deva. The fortress's defences were levelled and, with the street grid of the fortress at its core, the town was founded. The extent of the Cornovians' input or enthusiasm for the construction of their new *civitas* capital is unknown; but given their general lack of materialism, it is likely that a considerable amount of backing was needed from the Roman state—plus an influx of veterans—to get the place up and running.

On approaching Viroconium, Julius Severus should be able to enjoy roads cleared of heavy goods traffic in anticipation of his arrival. While the visit of a high-ranking official, and especially that of a new provincial governor, should be a cause for celebration in the town, it is also a source of consternation, particularly among the town's ruling class. It is they who have the responsibility of receiving this elevated personage, greeting him in the appropriate way in Latin, and putting him and his entourage up in at least something approaching the manner to which they are accustomed.

As the *mansio*, just south of the new building site for the baths, is not large enough to accommodate the governor and his entire retinue, some members of his party will have to lodge in private houses. Decorating the town will be another headache. Sufficient coloured flags and garlands of flowers from the surrounding countryside must be obtained, and the banners from any guilds and colleges, together with images of gods and goddesses, will all need to be displayed along the official processional route if the townspeople are going to give the governor the sort of welcome he might expect elsewhere. The town will need to lay on music too, even if it means that the few proficient musicians who can be mustered have to take sneaky shortcuts, dashing through back streets to greet the visitors at various points on the route.[2]

This year, the new forum at Viroconium will be officially dedicated to Hadrian, as an extremely handsome, freshly cut inscription set proudly over its entrance testifies. For a British provincial town, the lettering is exceptionally good, the creation of a master stonecutter who is evidently used to working on monuments of the highest quality.[3] The project could have been initiated almost a decade before by the emperor on his visit to the province. Now, in the summer of AD 130, Julius Severus will officiate at its inauguration.[*] It is one of his duties as governor to ensure that all public monuments and temples are in good condition and properly cared for, so he is charged with inspecting them, assessing whether they need repairs and ensuring that they are mended properly by appointing 'with the proper formalities' reliable superintendents, as well as assigning soldiers to assist if necessary.[4] Good governors take these duties seriously, knowing how important it is to maintain and promote the imperial public image—and that includes making sure that letters are cut properly on public monuments.[†]

---

[*] The inscription is dated to between winter AD 129 and autumn AD 130. If Julius Severus began his tour soon after arriving in Britannia in early July, he could well have presided over the inauguration in August/September that year.

[†] When Arrian, governor of Cappadocia, made his tour of inspection in Trapezus (Trabzon, Turkey) between AD 131 and AD 138, he was appalled that the inscriptions on two altars of 'coarse rough stone' were indistinct and incorrect 'as is common among barbarous people', and erected marble altars with 'well marked and distinct characters' instead. Arrian (*Circumnavigation of the Euxine Sea*) 2, 2.

MIND YOUR LATIN

Severus and his entourage enter Viroconium from across a ford over the Severn, at the town's south-west corner, and proceed along Watling Street to the brand-new forum. Its porticoed entrance opens out onto a large courtyard, on the far side of which is a basilica housing the council chamber, archives and offices of the two annually elected magistrates.[5] Another basilica, identical in size and design and 18 metres (59 feet) high at its apex, will be built as the centrepiece of an imposing baths complex across the street, although at present this is merely an ambitious plan on the ground.[*] Having been formally received, and having carried out his inspection of the forum, Julius Severus will sacrifice an ox (or heifer, if the town's presiding deity is female).[†] Once he has examined its entrails and performed libations upon it and any other animals sacrificed, he will offer prayers to the emperor.

During the course of his visit, Julius Severus will also hear petitions and lawsuits, pronouncing judgement in public from a *tribunal*, or stage, set up in the forum or in the new basilica.[6] He is charged with giving all citizens, rich or poor, a fair hearing. It is his duty to ensure that people of higher rank who can afford the best lawyers are not favoured over those of moderate means, 'who have no one to appear for them or who have had to employ advocates of small experience or no standing who may not be able to present their claims properly'.[7]

In general, as long as they do not happen too regularly or last too long, official visits, though fraught for the hosts and expensive at the time, may prove worthwhile, and a successful inspection can result in more than a few new statues from the emperor. Furthermore, a well-argued petition made to the governor in person can bring enhanced status and privileges for both the town and for the speechmaker.

---

[*] It took the best part of the next twenty years to complete.

[†] The identity of the city's presiding deity is not known. The town's major civic temple seems to lie beneath the Victorian model farm to the north of the forum.

Before they get any payback, however, they will need to put on a good show in Latin. The Romans are sensitive to the correct usage of their language and are as appreciative of an elegant turn of phrase as they are contemptuous of grammatical errors or rusticisms. A person's reputation can be damaged by committing such errors. The poet Martial mocks someone who remains deaf to his verse as a person with 'a Batavian ear'.[8] There is even a story doing the rounds, unlikely though it seems, that the young Hadrian was laughed at in the Senate for a rustic turn of phrase in a speech, with the result that he worked at his Latin until he had reached the utmost facility in it.[9] As Hadrian was born in Rome, it is not clear whether this is a dig at some provincialisms he picked up during his teenage years on his family's estates in Italica (in Spain), or on account of his love for all things Greek. If emperors brought up in the most elevated circles are teased for their use of Latin, then it must be all the harder for the people of the north-western provinces to acquire fluency in the language.

However good your Latin, you can be forgiven for feeling a little nervous when speaking on behalf of the community in front of such a high-ranking official as the governor. As you address the emperor's deputy, it may feel almost as nerve-wracking as speaking to the emperor in person: 'It is no easy business to ask the emperor of the whole world for a favour for oneself; to put on a bold front before the aspect of such great majesty, to compose one's features, to shore up one's spirits to choose the right words and utter them fearlessly, stopping at the right moment to wait for a reply'.[10] It is true that in this example, the polished Gallic orator's admission of reticence and modesty is really an elegant commonplace and a means of winning over his audience; but many town councillors in provincial Britain must be 'not unaware of how inferior our abilities are to the Romans', because 'speaking in Latin and well is inborn in them but laboriously acquired in us and if by chance we say something elegantly our imitation derives from that font and source of eloquence'.[11]

The children of the British aristocracy have been educated in the liberal arts at least since the governorship of Agricola in the late 70s. Rating their natural facility in Latin more highly than the Gauls, he observed how anxious they were to speak Latin elegantly.[12] The British upper classes are still every bit as keen to speak correct Latin in the second century as they were in the first. Visitors to the island are struck by the way in which they speak textbook style Latin, with an old-fashioned pronunciation and rather affected vowel sounds.[13]

It is possible that high-status Britons now speak Latin among themselves and in 'polite society' while continuing to address their servants in the British tongue. The British language (Brittonic, or Brythonic), as spoken at the time of the Roman conquest, was a form of Celtic similar to languages spoken in Gaul. Some British tribes, such as the Atrebates, which were branches of those on the Continent, would have spoken an almost identical language to Gaulish. But since the Romans arrived, the language has changed, and the British have adopted many Latin words into their vocabulary to describe aspects of daily life and administration for which there was no existing equivalent.* As British is an entirely oral language, anyone who needs to write does so in Latin, however crudely—even tradespeople in towns who may barely be able to speak it.

To have real facility in the language and to have the confidence to address formally a high official, it is important to work at Latin from early childhood, laboriously copying out lines from the great literary works such as Virgil's *Aeneid*: you want to avoid your teacher scrawling the crushing '*seg*' across your work (from *segniter*, meaning 'weak' or 'slack') or, worse, giving you a good thrashing.[14] In order to help provincials perfect their Latin, there are bilingual textbooks, which, for an aspiring Roman gentleman from the distant land of the Cornovii, might also contain useful hints on how to behave in certain social situations—and at the very least how to boss your slave around effectively in Latin. When at

---

* Evidence for this comes from the hundreds of Latin loan words present in the descendants of Brittonic—Welsh, Cornish and Breton.

the baths, for example, you need to know how to say '*expolia me, discalcia me, compone vestimenta, cooperi, serva bene; ne addormias propter fures*' ('undress me, take off my shoes, tidy up my clothes, cover them up, look after them well; don't fall asleep on account of thieves'). At the end of the bathing session your slave can be instructed to '*terge mihi caput et pedes. Da caligulas, calcia me. Porrige amiculum, pallam, dalmaticam. Collige vestimenta et omnia nostra. Sequimini ad domum*' ('dry my head and feet, give me my shoes and put them on, hold out my cloak and tunic, collect my clothes and all my things and follow me home').[15]

ROMAN REFINEMENTS, CORNOVIAN CUSTOMS —AND CATTLE

Such phrases as these will no doubt come in handy when Viroconium's state-of-the-art baths are completed. The fact that the town has managed to erect a forum in less than a decade, and is about to start on this luxurious new baths complex, suggests that it has had more than a little official help. The legionaries probably had a hand in designing and building the forum, although their involvement on Hadrian's Wall will have meant only intermittent help—perhaps the reason for the baths project lagging so far behind. When finished, it will be closely related in design to the legionary baths at nearby Deva.

The town's inhabitants might well also be receiving financial support in the form of special tax relief to help fund the project. If the baths were instigated by Hadrian, as part of an official scheme, then money from imperial revenues could also be forthcoming. The British aristocracy, who never quite see the point of spending large amounts of money on public monuments for their own aggrandisement, generally prefer to invest in private property and land instead. Public works are a permanent burden whoever foots the bill for their construction, for once they are finished the expense of maintaining them falls on the local council. Its members have to raise money from local taxation—for example, from rents from stallholders and other vendors who operate in and around the baths, the *macellum* (official meat market) and the forum. If such revenues are insufficient, then Julius Severus might still need to call upon the emperor to provide whatever the provincials cannot be relied upon to supply. This can include not just funds but also quite specific orders for items such as statues.*

Julius Severus could find that he needs to order rather a lot of Roman artwork, for the Cornovii on the whole show very little interest in such refinements: conspicuously unmaterialistic in Iron Age times, even now few people in the surrounding countryside display any eagerness to adopt a Roman lifestyle or acquire Roman goods. Unlike other tribes of southern Britain at the time of the conquest, the cattle-rearing Cornovii neither produced nor used coinage, nor even any pottery except that which they needed for transporting salt from brine springs in their territory (at Nantwich, Middlewich and Northwich).

The arrival of thousands of troops in Britain, and in the very heart of the Cornovii lands, changed that situation profoundly. The Romans stormed and set fire to the hillfort on the Wrekin in about AD 47, planted military installations throughout the territory and propelled those who lived in the vicinity of the legionary fortress into a world of coins, pottery and unheard-of consumer goods. The army created hugely increased demand not just for meat and wool, but also for leather goods and all the by-products of cattle, with army contractors dealing in bulk and consignments of hundreds of hides paid for with large amounts of cash.[16]

Cattle can certainly be big business, and punishments for stealing them, are as severe as for stealing horses. Professional cattle or horse thieves can be condemned *ad gladium*, 'to the sword'—execution in the arena. For serious cases involving armed cattle rustlers, being thrown to the wild beasts is considered to be a justifiable

---

* In Trapezus, Arrian, on finding a statue of Hadrian to be a poor copy of the original, asked the emperor to 'send a statue fit to be called yours' and begged for a better image of Mercury 'no more than five feet high' for the temple. Arrian (*Circumnavigation of the Euxine Sea*), 3.

sentence. Other miscreants can be sent to the mines or put to unappealing work in the service of the state, such as cleaning out public baths and latrines. (For the theft of smaller animals, such as sheep, pigs or goats, there are lesser sentences, while anyone who takes a stray horse or ox will be classified merely as a common thief.)[17]

Cattle are valued for their meat—beef is preferred to pork in the north-western provinces, unlike elsewhere in the empire—but also for much else besides, including that healthy trade in hides. Bullocks are used in harness for pulling carts or the plough; cows for their milk. Even after cattle have been slaughtered, no part of their carcases are wasted. Marrow fat is extracted from their bones on an industrial scale, and the bones themselves are used to make items such as hairpins, needles and combs, while the sinew is used for thread and bowstrings.[18] Both beef and mutton fat are used to make soap and tallow candles—much the most common fuel for lighting in Britain, as oil lamps require expensive imported olive oil.

The increased demand for livestock has created jobs all along the line, from rearing the cattle to butchering and processing the carcases and tanning the hides. The messy, smelly trades of the tanners and fullers (who finish and launder wool cloth) take place in their own districts of town.* Both industries need a good water supply, and the fullers require copious amounts of urine: they collect it from both animals and humans, in some places leaving large pots on street corners, where people can relieve themselves, and which will later be collected when full.[19]

CHANGING FASHIONS

The fullers will have been hard at work in the run-up to Julius Severus's appearance in town, as local dignitaries prepare their outfits for the visit. The British upper classes, it seems, took up wearing the toga enthusiastically decades ago.[20] A Roman gentleman is judged on his creases—and a white toga, worn on formal occasions, needs

---

* This is not conclusive at Wroxeter, though it is possible.

to be super-clean and pressed with sharp folds. Election candidates need to scrub up particularly well, and their togas are rubbed with a special type of fuller's earth to make them shine.[21] The work done by the fullers must meet these high expectations. They treat the cloth by treading it in tubs containing a solution of water and urine (or fuller's earth) and then rinse it in running water. Some whites are also bleached with sulphur. The clothing is then pressed in large screw presses.[22]

It is not clear how much store the majority of Cornovii lay by such matters as dress and personal appearance. Elsewhere in the empire, fashion-conscious men sport beards like the emperor; women who have the chance to spy the Empress Sabina, either in the flesh on her travels or on a bust or coin, might (if they have a competent maidservant) attempt to copy her hairstyle with its elaborately piled braids. But most men and women in Britannia lack the means or the inclination to follow the empire's fashion. Women like Vedica, a Cornovian who went to live at Verbeia (Ilkley in Yorkshire), stick to a more traditional form of native dress.* Vedica wears her hair down in two long thick plaits, every inch the down-to-earth cowgirl and looking impossibly primitive, no doubt, to the sophisticated ladies of Alexandria, Athens or Marseilles.[23] Country dwellers are unlikely to adopt Roman dress, the men continuing instead to wear the traditional costume of checked trousers, tunic and a short cloak. Romans still view trousers with suspicion—in the first century, Martial referred disparagingly to Lydia's backside being as broad 'as the old breeches of a pauper Briton'.[24]

Indeed, anyone coming from the Mediterranean, and especially from places like Egypt and Syria in the east, will be struck by the plainness of British clothes. It is true that cloth is dyed—red with imported madder (*rubia tinctorum*) or bedstraw, purple with local lichens, blue with woad (glastum or *Isatis tinctoria*), yellow with weld (*Reseda luteola*) and red-purple from whelks found along the Atlantic coast of Gaul.[25] But there are none of the fancy weaves,

---

* The identification of Verbeia as the Roman name is conjectured.

brocades or elaborate tapestries to be found further east. In these damp islands people adopt, instead, eminently sensible—and excellent-quality—medium-weight diamond, herringbone and plain 2/2 twill cloths. In the streets, men and women wear variants on loose-fitting woollen tunics, with or without short wide sleeves, which men wear at calf length and women down to their ankles. Over this, men wear a hooded cape, the *caracalla* or *birrus*, which is fastened down the front. Women sport a less voluminous rectangular cloak draped in various ways, according to fashion.

While there are those, of course, who wear imported damask silks (in Kent) and gold thread (in Essex), for the most part diamond twill and checks remain the distinctively north-west European Celtic look.[26] British wool is highly regarded abroad, and the province's blankets and cloaks, which have an excellent reputation for quality, make acceptable presents for high officials and are presented to members of the governor's staff on retirement from their posts.[27]

After decades of Roman presence, Viroconium's population is now a mixed one. Milling around the forum will be local Cornovii, perhaps traders whose families moved here generations ago to take advantage of opportunities offered by the cash-rich legionaries and army veterans who have settled in the area. Retiring soldiers, usually in their early to mid-forties, are presented with discharge tablets at the ceremony of *honesta missio* (demobilization) on completion of twenty-five years' service, when they and any children they might have are granted the much-prized Roman citizenship. Mansuetus, a cavalryman from the second cohort of Dalmatians who has retired here from Hadrian's Wall, will leave to posterity a copy of his own inscribed bronze discharge tablet, lodged in Viroconium's record office in the forum basilica.* Veterans such as Mansuetus will have lump sums to invest—the compulsory savings deducted from their wages over the years—and, immune from

---

* The cohort was originally raised in Croatia, and at this time was serving on Hadrian's Wall. Mansuetus's discharge certificate is dated 14 April AD 135 and was found in the basilica, so this is one explanation for how it could have come to be there.

taxation, will be sufficiently well off to become town councillors, serving alongside other former soldiers and members of the local tribal aristocracy.

Affluent members of Viroconium society live in large, comfortable houses in town, which require a large amount of cheap labour to build.* But some materials, such as stone, are relatively expensive, and even the most prosperous inhabitants of Viroconium have to make economies while keeping up appearances: among the 'stone' columns of their street-facing porticoes are some formed from tree trunks and painted to imitate marble. As well as Roman-style architecture, the houses also now display Roman-style taste in the form of large sculpted phalli attached to the exterior walls. The *Fascinus*, or spirit of the phallus, offers protection for the household against the evil eye. In one example a winged phallus, combined with a hand making a *mano fica* gesture (thumb clasped by fingers)—which is aimed against evil powers in general—pulls a cart. Perhaps its owner hopes to raise a smile from passers-by while warding off the evil eye in the process.

Overall, and in contrast with many images, graffiti and objects found elsewhere in the empire, the British seem to be remarkably reticent, uninterested or backward as regards the obscene and the sexually explicit.† While there are vague references to 'buggers' in some places (Farningham, Kent,[28] Colchester and Silchester[29]), and an observation written in red on white wall plaster (in Alresford, Essex) that 'you are shitting' (*cacas*),[30] it is left to Ratae (Leicester) to take the prize as the rudest place in Britannia. Here, scratched onto the painted wall plaster of an early second-century courtyard fallen into disrepair, is a whole series of insults, ranging from *cinae[de]* (catamite) to *culo*, which means 'arse' in the dative or ablative case, leaving it to the viewer's imagination as to whether it

---

* There were over a hundred such houses at the town's height later in the century.
† This conclusion is based on the tiny number of obscene references to survive in Britain. By contrast a potter in Bordeaux wrote on a plate before firing it: 'I will sodomise 3 times anyone who reads this—go on, read it and find the person who wishes you this unhappiness…'

should be preceded by 'to', 'for', 'by', 'with' or 'from'.[31] As you might expect, the most cocksure graffiti comes from showy Londinium, where a stone tablet boasts of [M]ENTULARUM [...]XI NONI—the '11 (or more) pricks of Nonius'.[32]

The good people of Viroconium will no doubt pray that on the occasion of Julius Severus's first visit to their city no insult will be given, and no offence taken; that the evil eye will be diverted, the Latin speeches will pass muster and the omens will be propitious for the dedication of the new forum; and that Julius Severus and his retinue will soon pass safely and with all due ceremony on their way again—north to Deva, and beyond that to the Wall.

CHAPTER X

To the Wall

Murum lo[ngi] operis... non [mul]to diutius exstrucxistis quam
caespite exstruitur... Vos lapid[ibus] grandibus, gravibus, inaequalibus,
quos neque vehere n[e]que attollere, neque locare quis possit nisi ut
inaequa[lita]tes inter se compareant. Fossam glaria duram scabram
recte percussistis et radendo levem reddidistis. Opere pr[o]bato
introgressi castra raptim et cibum et arma cepistis equitem
emissum secuti magno clamore revertentem...

You have built a long wall... in not much more time than if it were
made of turf... You built with big, heavy, uneven stones which no one
can carry, lift or lay without their unevenness becoming evident...
You dug a hard, rough ditch correctly through the earth and by
scraping it made it level. Your work approved, you quickly entered
camp, took your food and weapons and followed the cavalry
which had been sent out, with a great shout
as they came back...[1]

Extract from HADRIAN's address
to the troops at Lambaesis, Numidia,
North Africa, AD 128

*

ON LEAVING Viroconium and heading north for Deva (Chester),
a little over 38 miles (61km) away, Julius Severus can make first for
Mediolanum (Whitchurch), about 24 miles (39km) hence. There,
at the junction of several roads, there is a *mansio* and small market. Although this is still in Cornovian territory, the countryside is
beginning to change. More cereal crops are in evidence here, and
while there are still settlements with their great ditched enclosures for livestock, the landscape now also reveals solitary roundhouses, surrounded by enclosed arable fields with pasture beyond.[2]

Although some farms have been settled by veteran soldiers who employ Roman methods of agriculture, there are few recognizable villas.

After crossing a bridge over the River Dee,[3] the travellers enter Deva. Here is the legionary fortress and adjacent amphitheatre, which loom over the river, commanding the attention of everyone arriving either by road or up-river from the Irish Sea. But the garrison is even more depleted than at Isca. Most of the troops (and those from surrounding auxiliary forts) have gone up to the Wall, and many buildings, including some of the barrack blocks and the amphitheatre, have been abandoned.[4] The main military base in the north is now the legionary fortress at Eboracum, under the command of Minicius Natalis.

With little to detain them at Deva, the travellers soon move on, taking the road north-east towards Eboracum as far as the auxiliary fort at Mamucium (Manchester), some 34 miles (55km) away. The route passes through a flourishing industrialized landscape where vital supplies for the soldiers of the north-west garrisons are produced. The area is an important centre of brine extraction. Salt is a vital commodity, not only for preserving meat but also for tanning leather and making cheese, and the abundance of brine here has encouraged leather-working and shoe-making.[5] At Condate (Northwich), a stopping place almost 19 miles (30km) from Deva, at the confluence of the rivers Dane and Weaver, there is a connecting road south to Salinae (Middlewich), whose name means 'Salt Works': here there is a brine extraction plant in the *vicus* (village settlement) attached to the auxiliary fort. North of Condate is the industrial centre of Wilderspool (between Widnes and Warrington) on the south shore of the River Mersey,[6] where there is extensive iron-working[7] and a centre for producing mixing bowls (*mortaria*), which are supplied to military sites throughout the north-west.[*]

---

[*] Some of the potters at Wilderspool migrated to Luguvalium on the western part of Hadrian's Wall later in the century so that they could produce their *mortaria* closer to their core market of some 13,800 men stationed on the Wall and in York.

Julius Severus continues, however, along the main road from Deva to Eboracum. He will not continue east across the Pennines any further than the auxiliary fort at Mamucium, from where he can take the road north to Bremetenacum Veteranorum (Ribchester), 26.5 miles (43km) away in the lovely valley of the River Ribble. Before descending into the valley, any travellers on this route will be treated to a magnificent view from the ridge of Ramsgreave (west of Blackburn), with Pendle (Hill) to their north-east and ahead of them, to the north and across the Ribble, Longridge Fell—and a taste of the mountains and moorlands that lie beyond.

Approaching Bremetenacum, this route crosses the river at a ford a little to the east of the fort, which is garrisoned by the *ala* II Asturum, a cavalry unit of 500 men originally raised in Asturia (in Spain).[8] A cavalry *ala* is the most prestigious and best-paid type of auxiliary unit. Bremetenacum itself is cocooned in the gentle valley with its meandering river and rich pasture land, surrounded by a flourishing *vicus*. Here, any travellers can find rest as well as refreshment and relaxation in a respectable enough little bath house by the river. Here, too, is a significant junction, with routes east to Eboracum (via Skipton, Ilkley and Tadcaster) and west to the Fylde on the Lancashire coast.

Travellers heading north of here could, if they wish, choose an adventurous route north across the fells, beginning with an ascent over Longridge Fell, where the road climbs to just below 290 metres (950 feet) short of the summit. It rewards anyone who makes it to the top with a view (on a clear day) of the Irish Sea to the west, the mass of Bowland fells ahead, and the promise of much wilder and more difficult terrain yet to come. This route would eventually take you to Luguvalium (Carlisle), some 80 fairly challenging miles away, via the rain-soaked fort at Low Borrow Bridge (near Tebay), at the head of the Lune Valley,[9] and 18 or so miles beyond that, Brocavum Fort (Brougham, near Penrith), which nestles in the gentle crook of the River Eden.

While this rugged route through wild and underpopulated country is significant from a military point of view, it is not the logical first choice for a provincial governor on tour unless he has a particular reason for wishing to test it out. There is an easier alternative to the west, along much flatter terrain. Quite apart from the physical rigours that would be entailed in the route over the hills, any group of travellers—military or civilian, and of whatever rank—needs to be vigilant while on the road and avoid unnecessary risk. While harsh terrain and bad weather are hazards of nature, there are also plenty of man-made threats, attested to throughout the empire by the numerous tombstones to those unfortunate individuals who have been *interfectus a latronibus*—killed by bandits, who are regarded as little more than terrorists. In the western provinces, there are specially designated officials charged with 'guarding against bandits'.[10] As governor, Julius Severus must keep the peace and flush out such men. If bandits are causing trouble in the province, he might well already have appointed a trusted *praefectus* to try to deal with them.[11]

Travellers wearing or carrying valuables need to take special precautions. Women and girls are warned to keep their jewellery out of sight—the gravestone of one unfortunate ten-year-old girl from Spalatum (Split), who was murdered *causa ornamentorum* (because of her jewellery), offers a salutary lesson.[12] Bandits have no respect for gender, age or rank. Even the commander of the army in Africa, M. Valerius Etruscus, was left naked and wounded after being attacked *en route* to Saldae (near Béjaïa, Algeria); he was lucky to escape with his companions.[13] Attacks can occur on even the busiest roads. Pliny the Younger recalled how someone he knew vanished without trace from the Via Flaminia together with his slaves, and 'no one knows whether he was killed by his slaves or along with them'.[14] It is notable that Jesus's Parable of the Good Samaritan, in which a man is attacked and left half dead to be ignored by one and all, is set not on some obscure byway but on the main road between Jerusalem to Jericho.[15] Chillingly, the cruel wounds inflicted by bandits are listed with those of gladiators and soldiers in battle as offering curious doctors the opportunity of studying the position, arrangement and shape of the internal organs of living patients.[16]

Bearing all these factors in mind (and Britannia, after all, has a reputation as a restless and violent place, especially in the north), an easier, flatter and potentially safer route to the west, which skirts the fells, is a more practical choice for Julius Severus and his entourage.* From Bremetenacum, Julius Severus now rides west along the Ribble Valley for 6 or 7 miles (11km), before picking up the road north from Coccium (Wigan).[17] An easy, direct road now leads them to Lancaster, 21 miles (34km) away.† Here, there is a *mansio* outside the north gate of the auxiliary fort, which commands the surrounding area from its hilltop position above the River Lune.[18] Outside the *vicus* attached to the fort, Severus and his party will pass through a cemetery containing vividly painted tombstones of dead cavalrymen from the *ala* Augusta Sebosiana. One memorial, to Insus son of Vodullus, citizen of the Treveri, is particularly eye-catching. It graphically depicts the deceased quartermaster astride his horse triumphantly holding the severed head of an unfortunate Briton in his right hand, together with the sword that has just performed the decapitation.[19]

To begin a tour of inspection at the western part of Hadrian's Wall, Severus can now reach the north-west and Luguvalium by taking to the water, embarking at the estuary of the Lune and tracking the coastline north of Morecambe Bay.‡ Members of the Cohort I Aelia Classica[20] may be put at his disposal, a naval detachment based at the fort of Glannoventa (Ravenglass). This is the most southern of a series of coastal forts that stretches for 25 miles (40km) up to the Wall's westernmost point at Maia (Bowness-on-Solway). Iron ore is extracted at Glannoventa, and the fort there also connects with one to the north-east at Galava (Ambleside), at the head of Windermere, via one of the steepest and most spectacular roads in the country. Here, the breathtakingly situated new

---

* A maritime route from Deva, stopping along the way to visit inland bases near the estuaries of the rivers Mersey, Ribble and Lune, would also have been a possibility.

† Tantalizingly, beyond an initial letter 'L' the Latin name for Lancaster is unknown.

‡ It is uncertain exactly where ships would have found safe harbour for the night along the Lancashire coast—the coastline has changed greatly since the second century, and evidence for Roman harbours has disappeared.

fort at Mediobogdum (Hardknott) commands superb views north to the Scafell range and west along Eskdale to the sea.* It is manned by the Fourth Cohort of Dalmatians—soldiers originally raised in Severus's home province.[21]

Maenius Agrippa, in his new post as commander of the *classis Britannica*, may well accompany Severus on this leg of the journey along the coastline to Alauna (Maryport). Here, the *cohors I Hispanorum millaria equitata* (First Cohort of Spaniards, 1,000-strong) recently commanded by Maenius Agrippa himself, protects this part of the province from attack by sea from Caledonia. The camp's legate is currently Caius Caballius Priscus. Like Agrippa, Priscus is Italian, born in Verona. He has been at Alauna since AD 128 and will remain here for another year. While making a tour of the camp, Julius Severus will not fail to miss the neat rows of altars made of local St Bees sandstone, which are dedicated annually by the fort's tribune. Maenius Agrippa himself dedicated several of these altars while he was commander here.[22]

Impressing a new governor or legionary legate (especially those in favour with the emperor, as Julius Severus clearly is) can make a young man's career.[23] While to some, serving at Alauna might feel like being at the end of the earth, it is certainly no barrier to career progression. Marcus Censorius Cornelianus, born in Gaul (in Nîmes) but serving at Alauna, will win promotion, eventually serving in Judaea when Severus's fortunes take him there.[24] Among others now serving in the north whose career is in the ascendant is the young equestrian officer M. Statius Priscus, prefect of the Fourth Cohort of Lingones, which was originally raised in Gaul and is now stationed on the Wall.† As with Severus, Priscus comes from Dalmatia. The governor will also take him to Judaea, where he will be promoted to tribune in the Legion III Gallica—and his dazzling rise will continue thereafter.[25]

There will be many young officers determined to make a good impression on Severus as he makes his tour of inspection. But they

---

* Identification of Hardknott with Mediobogdum is uncertain.

† His presence is probable, if not definitive.

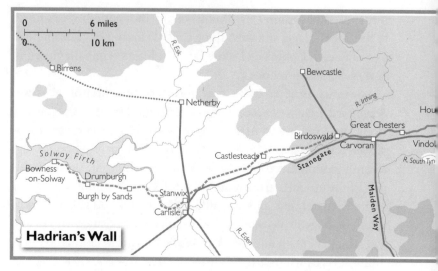

must remember always to pitch their level of keenness carefully, of course, and not go over the top. No one would wish to replicate the disappointing fate of one young man who appeared—doused in rather too much scent—before the Emperor Vespasian to thank him formally for his appointment to the praefecture. Vespasian told him sharply, 'I would have preferred it if you had smelt of garlic,' and promptly recalled his letters of appointment.[26]

AT THE EDGE OF EMPIRE

From Alauna to Luguvalium, a distance of some 30.5 miles (49km), Julius Severus will be able to travel by the good road that runs via the fort at Derventio (Papcastle, near Cockermouth).[27] There is also a maritime route, along the coast to the Solway Firth as far as Maia (Bowness-on-Solway). This is the westernmost part of Hadrian's Wall (Vallum Aelium), and—at some 1,480 miles away from Rome—the most north-westerly frontier point in the whole Roman Empire.*

From Maia, the Wall continues for 80 Roman miles (73 miles/

---

* Apart from a few outposts north of the Wall whose status is uncertain.

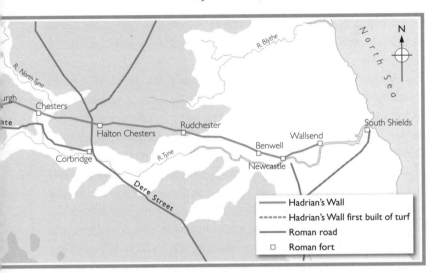

117km), slicing across the narrow neck of northern Britain from the Irish Sea to the North Sea. This most audacious building project began at the time of Hadrian's visit to Britannia in AD 122, when he 'put many things to rights, and was the first to build a wall, 80 miles long, to separate the Romans from the barbarians'.[28] It bears all the hallmarks of the emperor's passions and preoccupations, embodying as it does his interests in monumental architecture, the consolidation of his empire and military discipline.

At the beginning of Hadrian's reign, 'the Britons could not be kept under Roman control'.[29] If there was trouble in the province at that time, it was almost certainly in the north, and the emperor's arrival in Britannia possibly coincided with the end of a period of campaigning. M. Maenius Agrippa was chosen by Hadrian to join an *expeditio* in Britannia in command of the I Hispanorum Cohort, and a top-ranking centurion (*primus pilus*) T. Pontius Sabinus led a very considerable force of 3,000 men on such a campaign, drawn from three legions stationed in the provinces of Upper Germany and Spain.[30] Many men lost their lives in this, and the many other, wars fought in the north—men such as Titus Annius, a centurion serving with the First Cohort of Tungrians based at Vindolanda.[31] Others showed great heroism and lived to tell the tale, such as

Gaius Iulius Karus, prefect of the II Asturum Cohort, who was heavily decorated for his service in 'the British war' before being transferred to Egypt.[32]

It is entirely possible, therefore, that Hadrian's decision to build a wall was a response to those recent troubles; but it was also part of his wider instinct to demarcate the bounds of the empire and declare that he was an emperor interested in consolidation rather than expansion. Early in his reign he had—very controversially—given up his predecessor Trajan's conquests in Parthia, and at about the time of his visit to the Rhine and Britannia in AD 122, as the historians said, 'he began to look at the many regions where the barbarians are held back not by rivers but by artificial barriers, and Hadrian shut them off by means of high stakes planted deep in the ground and fastened together in the manner of a palisade'.[33]

The empire has, of course, had various forms of frontier and border controls in the past—such as the watch towers on the Danube, as depicted on Trajan's Column. In Britannia, before the Wall, there was a series of northern lookout posts, which connected with a solid network of forts positioned along a road (Stanegate) running from Luguvalium to Coria (Corbridge) through the gap in the Pennines cut by the rivers Irthing and Tyne. But Hadrian has been the first to construct barriers on a grand scale: in Germany this has meant a palisade of timbers running 330 miles (530km) along its eastern frontier.[34] In the wilder, much higher and harsher terrain of the Carpathian Mountains of Dacia, with which Julius Severus is so familiar, stone or earth barriers built in conjunction with towers and forts have been erected in places; and in North Africa there is a mud-brick wall with a ditch beyond it (the *fossatum Africae*), punctuated by gates with a single tower in between and forts spaced out at wider intervals.[*]

By starting from the west at the Solway coast, Julius Severus, as a first-time visitor to the Wall, will secure a gentle introduction to it. This stretch is flat and holds no hint of the drama that awaits

---

[*] The date of the African wall is not certain but most probably dates from Hadrian's reign.

further east. From Maia, he can follow a road that sticks to high ground near the southern shore of the Solway Firth, keeping close behind the security of the Wall. It is then a mere 12.5 miles (20km) to Luguvalium, a place that will only grow in size and importance in the years ahead.* Over recent years its timber fort has become something of a works depot, with a *fabrica* (workshop) in what was once the camp's *praetorium*. With smoky, smelly iron-smithing and copper alloy-working being carried out at several places on site, it is not a place at which anyone will choose to tarry.[35] A better bet is the fort at Uxelodunum (Stanwix), dominating the road just half a mile to the north. This houses the most prestigious unit on the Wall, the *ala* Petriana Milliaria, a 1,000-strong pure cavalry regiment, originally raised in Gaul, whose commanding officer holds the highest rank of any auxiliary unit on the British frontier.†

THE WESTERN WALL

Although legionaries have built the Wall, helped by members of the provincial fleet, it is manned by auxiliary troops, who are mainly drawn from north-western provinces such as Batavia, northern Gaul and the Rhineland. These are beer-drinking, trouser-wearing men for whom the conditions on this coastal and western section —where a gloomy sea and sky meet on so many days of the year in one great grey, murky mass—will be familiar enough. The scenery might even remind them of home, especially as the land is flatter here than further east along the frontier. But to men from units raised further away, such as the 500-strong cohort *Hamiorum Sagittariorum* (Hamian Archers) from Syria, who are based at Magnis (Carvoran), or anyone coming from Spain and south-western

---

* By the third century AD, Luguvalium was a flourishing town, the probable *civitas* capital of the Carvetii, which was a branch, or sept, of the Brigantes tribe based in the Eden Valley. But in the 130s it still lacked a clear urban identity. The timber fort was demolished in the 140s and subsequently rebuilt.

† The *ala* Petriana is presumed to have been here under Hadrian but is not attested until much later. Little is known about Stanwix in the Hadrianic period. The stone fort is generally dated to the 160s.

France, the damp environment of the Wall may well be a strange and perhaps isolating experience. They might well look for consolation. Many soldiers in Britannia put their trust in the goddess Fortuna, and sometimes specifically Fortuna Redux—Fortune the Homebringer. These are men such as Gaius Cornelius Peregrinus, an officer from the province of Mauretania Caesariensis in North Africa. While serving as an officer at Alauna he dedicates an altar to the local spirit (*genius loci*) and to Fortune the Homebringer, Eternal Rome and Good Fate, perhaps hoping that fate, fortune and the power of Rome will take him back one day to his sunny life as a town councillor in his faraway home town of Saldae.[36]

There are six different sizes and types of auxiliary regiments in existence, and all may be found on the Wall: two pure cavalry units or *alae* (wings), two infantry units (*cohortes peditatae*), with two being mixed infantry and cavalry (*cohortes equitatae*), of which each of the types can be 500- or 1,000-strong. In total, if you were to include the forts along the Cumbrian coast, well over ten thousand auxiliary soldiers are stationed up here. In addition, there are the officers' wives and families, slaves and freedmen, as well as visiting officials and troops from the south, the soldiers' concubines and children, and other men and women servicing the military in various ways who live in the *vici*, or settlements, outside the forts.

This western section of the Wall from Maia east for 30 miles (48km), as far as the River Irthing and just beyond the fort at Banna (Birdoswald), is made of layers of turf, a huge bank of it 20 Roman feet wide (6 metres) and roughly 4.2 metres (14 feet) high.[37] In some places this wall has a stone base of large cobbles; in others, it is entirely composed of turf, from the ground up. Although less than a decade old, some of the Wall's turf section is just now starting to be rebuilt in stone.

Leaving the fort at Uxelodunum, Julius Severus can make his way along the Stanegate, which runs south of the Wall from Luguvalium to Coria. Before the Wall was built, a series of observation towers situated along what would be its course communicated with the forts on the Stanegate. Now, along the entire stretch of the Wall, at every Roman mile, are gates, each defended by small guardposts, or milecastles, and between every milecastle are two regularly spaced turrets, or lookout posts. On this western section, the milecastles are made of turf and timber, although the turrets are made of stone, as they are all along the Wall.

Running along the whole of the northern side of the Wall, except in places where the steep, rocky terrain makes it unnecessary, is a deep ditch, which measures between 8 and 12 metres wide (26–40 feet) and around 3 metres (10 feet) deep. Between the ditch and the Wall is an open flat area, or 'berm', which can vary between almost 2 metres and 6 metres in width (7–20 feet), usually being narrower nearer to the towers. In places this berm had been studded with holes, which were filled with densely packed branches with sharpened points—a particularly nasty form of obstacle. Anyone stumbling into them would be impaled. Julius Caesar, who employed them at the siege of Alesia in Gaul, during the rebellion of Vercingetorix in 52 BC,[38] recorded that in soldiers' slang—so rich in irony and gallows' humour—the barbed branches were known as *cippi*, a word meaning both boundary marker and tombstone.

THE DACIANS ARE COMING

The first Wall fort that Julius Severus now comes to is Banna. Positioned within a meander of the River Irthing, it sits high on top of an escarpment with magnificent views to the south over the river valley and Cold Fell. The original timber fort is about to be replaced by a large stone one, which will also sit astride the Wall. Containing the usual layout of streets, barracks, headquarters and storehouses, it will also boast a *basilica exercitatoria*, or indoor drill hall, so that the men can continue to keep fit and to train even in atrocious weather.

It was originally intended that the forts would be built to the south of the Wall. Something happened during the Wall's construction, however, to cause a major change of plan, and all the forts now sit astride the Wall, so that soldiers can mobilize more effectively and move north or south as required. This is an innovation found on no other frontier. Perhaps the act of building the Wall had stirred up trouble and, as a result, demonstrated the limitations of the earlier plan. After all, the Wall could have become a potential trap for its own soldiers, hampering movement and giving little room to manoeuvre, north or south. It must be remembered that the Wall is not easy to defend. Stretched out as it is over such a distance, any band of determined enough marauders might overpower the men on duty at the turrets and milecastles. The latter can house up to thirty-two men, but some have a maximum capacity of as few as eight.[39]

On the south side of the Wall the soldiers have now built a *Vallum*, a flat-bottomed ditch 6 metres deep by 3 metres wide (20 × 10 feet), flanked by banks on each side.* Crossings through the *Vallum* are only provided at forts by means of causeways leading directly into the fort gates, with no provision to cross elsewhere, even at milecastles. In adopting this approach, the number of potential crossing points has been reduced from eighty to about sixteen. In this way, the Wall has also become a means of control for those living south of the border, forcing people to cross it only at those points where there is a heavily defended fort. The original width of the stone Wall has also been reduced from the original 10 Roman feet to 8 feet (around 3 metres to 2.4 metres), presumably to speed up its building.

Running direct from the north gate of Banna is a road leading to an outpost fort six miles away. Perched on a bluff above the river, the fort at Fanum Cocidi (Bewcastle)† is manned by the *cohors I Aelia Dacorum milliaria* (First Cohort of Dacians, 1,000-strong), a unit that helped to build the *Vallum* and whose job now is to patrol the uneasy no-man's-land north of the Wall. The cohort was raised in Dacia soon after Trajan's dramatic conquests there in AD 101–2

---

* The banks are set back 9 metres (almost 30 feet) and are 6 metres (20 feet) wide.

† Fanum Cocidi means Shrine of Cocidus, a Celtic warrior god. It is not known if the fort had another 'official' name.

and 105–6, and it was possibly dispatched to Britannia as soon as it was formed.

These original Dacian recruits will be coming up for retirement in the next year or so, having served their twenty-five years. Perhaps the new governor may even have the pleasure of presenting them with their discharge certificates. Julius Severus is, of course, extremely familiar with their native land, after his unusually long six-year governorship of Dacia Superior. As he served there as recently as five years ago and has just come from the neighbouring province of Moesia Inferior, he can give the soldiers well-informed and up-to-date news from their part of the world. The unit appears to maintain strong traditions derived from their homeland: they call their sons 'Decebalus' after the Dacian king and hero who fought Trajan at the time of the conquest, and they continue to employ, if only for ceremonial use, the distinctive curved knife known as a *falx*, which they proudly depict on inscriptions.[40] Although far apart in geographical distance, there are parallels between the two provinces. Dacia, like Britannia, lies on the edges of empire and is surrounded to its north and east by barbarian forces. Both have large garrisons (and in Dacia there is a cohort of Britons), and over the years many high-flying career officers will see service in both provinces.[41]

Returning south to the Wall at Banna, Severus and his party must now turn their faces east, towards the distant crags of the Great Whin Sill, and head past Harrow's Scar milecastle to cross the River Irthing over Willowford Bridge.* The next forts that Severus will come to lie south of the Wall on the Stanegate: Magnis (Carvoran) and Vindolanda (Chesterholm). At the latter, Severus can inspect not just the garrison—the First Cohort of Tungrians—but also watch trainee Britons being put through their paces. In a derisory letter from Vindolanda from an earlier time, they had been described disparagingly as *Brittunculi* ('little Brits') who wear

---

* Milecastles and turrets along Hadrian's Wall are numbered according to a modern convention from east to west, starting from 0 at Wallsend and finishing at 80 at Bowness-on-Solway. Harrow's Scar is No. 49.

no armour and do not mount to throw javelins.[42]

There is handsome accommodation at Vindolanda, fit for an emperor let alone a governor. It comes in the form of a courtyard building of palatial proportions, built of timber but richly decorated with painted plaster.[43] A visit from the new governor will have been long planned, and the commanding officer will be expected to entertain him handsomely, ordering special provisions up from London, such as sets of dining bowls, and ingredients such as mustard, anise, caraway and thyme.[44]

Officers are expected to provide hospitality for official guests at the drop of a hat. Even when they themselves are absent, they must ensure that their visitors are well received and offered a decent lunch, such as chicken and wine.[45] While the Tungrian officers might have acquired a taste for Roman staples such as pork, wine and olive oil, as well as more exotic ingredients, this is not to say that they do not quietly prefer dishes from their homeland when dining with their immediate family or friends from the same part of the world. Their Batavian predecessors at Vindolanda had their own treasured recipes for food made 'in the Batavian fashion', which contained garlic paste and spice.[46]

A LAND RENT ASUNDER

As Julius Severus and his party leave Vindolanda and head north, back to the Wall, they will note how the landscape becomes more expansive, ever wilder and more magnificent. The Wall strides brazenly over the land, crowning the crags and plunging into the gaps between them. In the cold northern light, this great white scar streaks over the grey-green landscape, 'gleaming with more brilliance than bronze', as the orator Aelius Aristides will describe other boundaries at the limits of empire.[47] For the Wall is painted (perhaps also rendered) white and, like the amphitheatre at Isca and many other buildings, the grooves are painted red in imitation of ashlar joining.[*]

At one milecastle (No. 37), the massive handiwork of the Legion II Augusta is again in evidence; and beyond it lies breathtaking Vercovicium (Housesteads). Riding astride the Whin Sill escarpment, this is the most dramatically situated of all the forts on the Wall. What emotion must the sight of it—and of the view of the Wall itself—inspire in men such as Julius Severus? It is at once reassuring, a sign that Rome has managed to draw a nice tidy line even here, in this uncouth place; but also alarming, its very existence a tacit—or perhaps glaring—admission of how fragile the ideal of *Romanitas* really is, that only a wall separates civilization from restless barbarism beyond, from tribes with unspeakable names who are only too happy to seize the riches of Rome while refusing to succumb to the discipline that created them.

The underlying, ever-present tension is manifested in the presence of the large military zones to north and south of the Wall—both areas are potential sources of trouble, and there are severe restrictions on people mixing across the line. Looking north over the Wall, towards the barbarian lands, the countryside may now seem ominously empty; but it is full of the ghosts of British settlements, abandoned less than ten years ago. That people's lives have been severely disrupted in this region, not to say uprooted and torn apart, would be painfully apparent were you to stray north over the ditch into what is now no-man's land.

The Wall has hacked a brutal and in many ways unimaginative course—the most direct route across country, without this always being the best even from a purely military view. The people who have lived here for centuries have had to watch their ancestral land being severed in two, with those living north of the Wall suddenly

---

[*] Evidence for whitewashing has been found at Heddon-on-the-Wall, where hard white mortar is still preserved on some of the facing stones; and at Peel Gap between turrets 39a and 39b. The view that the whole wall was painted white is highly speculative. See Bidwell (1996), pp. 19–32. For a brief discussion about whitewashing, see Crow (1991), pp. 51–63.

finding their access to lands, or family, or markets to the south severely restricted. The kind of humiliation that these displaced people must have suffered as a consequence was expressed—albeit through an entirely Roman filter—in a speech that Tacitus gave to a Germanic tribe in AD 70, but which might just as well have come out of the mouth of a northern Briton in the 120s. An envoy from the Tencteri tribe addresses fellow countrymen who have settled in Colonia Claudia Ara Agrippinensium (Cologne)* and from whom they have been separated by a frontier on the Rhine: 'Having shut off the rivers, the land, even the very sky so to speak, the Romans have prevented us from mixing and meeting—and to add insult to injury for men born to be warriors, we are allowed contact only if unarmed—practically naked—and under escort—and only on payment of a toll fee.'[48] The Tencteri demanded the right to settle on either side of the river bank 'as once our ancestors did'. The inhabitants of the *colonia* eventually agreed that they would allow the Tencteri to cross the Rhine into their city without escort or having to pay toll or tax, but only during daylight hours and so long as they remained unarmed. The inhabitants around Hadrian's Wall have most certainly not been offered even these rights; the restricted crossing points at forts mean that they can only ever cross the border under the watchful eye of soldiers.[49]

While some provincials might have been partially seduced by Roman blandishments, or at least been prepared to make the best of it and seize what opportunities they could within the new order, the severance and seizure of ancestral land must have proved intolerable to some, who decided to make affiliations further north. Perhaps it is these disaffected, but clearly once quite prosperous and powerful, people who lie behind the emergence now of previously unheard-of tribes in Caledonia. And perhaps their armed struggle over the loss of land influenced the change in the Wall's design soon after construction first started.†

---

* The modern city of Cologne derives its name from the Latin *colonia*.

† A different type of society seems to have emerged in Scotland after the imposition of the Wall, with new tribal names like the Maeatae and eventually the Picts being

The rebuilding of the turf section in stone and construction of new forts on and around the frontier suggests that the situation is still tense and unpredictable, with an expectation that trouble can flare up at any time. Indeed, the very presence of Julius Severus—crack soldier and troubleshooter that he is—suggests the sort of problems in Britannia's far north that need to be addressed. Hostility can be encountered from many quarters—from the unconquered tribes of Caledonia, from the disaffected and uprooted peoples who have moved further north, or from those within the frontier zone itself.*

Violence committed in Britannia was not confined to wars or to the everyday brutality of occupation, of course.[50] As with anywhere else, it could occur on a domestic scale. Buried under the clay floor of a shop (or inn) just outside the south gate of Vercovicium were the bodies of a woman and a man, the latter with the tip of the knife that killed him still wedged between his ribs. Whether the crime was committed by a civilian or a soldier, no one will ever know—all evidence of the crime was carefully concealed by a clean layer of clay.†

Any fear that officers and men on the Wall have may well be masked by bravado and a disparaging attitude towards the native *Brittunculi*.[51] Arrian, governor of Cappadocia, refers in his *Periplus* (an otherwise rather pedestrian catalogue of harbours and places) to the Sanni people, who 'have recently become addicted to plunder and do not pay tribute regularly, but now, by the gods' assistance, we will either oblige them to be more punctual or exterminate them.'[52] Romans have a ruthless attitude towards people who do not comply with their demands. These demands include taxes, which provincials normally pay in cash—though up near the Wall they may still pay wholly in kind.

---

documented. Such developments seem to have left the people of the coastal plain north-east of the Wall exposed.

* Whether the trouble was in the far north, in Caledonia, or in the region immediately around the Wall is not known.

† It is not known who manned Housesteads during the Hadrianic period. Later, the First Cohort of Tungrians, formerly at Vindolanda, was stationed there.

Across the North Sea the unsophisticated Frisii gave hides specifically for 'army use' in the first century AD, and in the south of Britannia cereal crops were given in payment in the years after the conquest.[53]

The collection of taxes and tribute is universally loathed, and daily throughout the empire letters are written and petitions drawn up complaining about tax collectors and soldiers extorting too much from the local population.[54] In Britannia, those unpopular individuals whose job it is to collect taxes or to organize the distribution of the payments in kind to the depots or collection points (before being dispensed to the military) must make many journeys through the northern frontier. Tax farming is less common in Hadrian's day, however, and in the southern parts of Britannia, where there are established *civitas* capitals, the duty of organizing and collecting tax falls largely on the local *decuriones*, or town councillors. In the northern military zone, by contrast, soldiers in the north may be responsible for collecting the taxes; they are certainly employed to carry out censuses, which are used to ensure that everyone eligible pays the *tributum capitis* (poll tax) and *tributum soli* (land tax).[55]

When it comes to tax collection, the potential for abuse, wilful misinterpretation and consequent local disturbance is great. In the case of the Frisii, when the chief centurion (*primus pilus*) responsible for extracting hides wilfully decided they should be from aurochs—huge wild cattle, difficult to hunt—rather than from domestic stock, the tribe rebelled and strung up the soldiers who came to collect the tribute.[56] Needless to say, the Roman response was firm. The Frisii ultimately came off the worse, losing their lands, and their wives and children into slavery, as a consequence.

A SOLDIER'S LOT

The fact is that Britannia has tens of thousands of soldiers planted on her soil, who have to be fed, equipped and paid a salary in cash—and Britons are expected to foot the bill. In a place with a large military presence, such as in the north, the burden is felt particularly deeply and on a day-to-day basis. Not only are the soldiers and their military installations all too visible in the landscape—built on land that has been recently confiscated—but the taxes required to pay for it all are now being extracted from people whose reduction in landholdings has made them less well off. In addition, there is the unwelcome burden of having to billet soldiers passing through towns and villages. From the number of complaints arising and the volume of legislation passed on this subject, it is evidently a constant and common grievance throughout the empire, despite several attempts to define the system and clarify the use of what will become known as the *cursus publicus*. Officially, soldiers can demand a free billet but not food for themselves or their animals; but both of the latter are commonly exacted, nonetheless.[57]

In Apuleius's *Metamorphoses*, a legionary soldier confiscates the ass from a poor old market gardener in Greece for 'army use' and beats up the owner for good measure because he (not speaking Latin) cannot answer the soldier's question. Centurions, in particular, are notoriously heavy handed all over the empire, but also heavy footed too: the satirist Juvenal winces as a clumsy soldier steps on his foot with his hobnailed boot in the streets of Rome, though that is to be let off lightly; it is better not to admit that 'your smashed-in teeth, swollen face black and blue with bruises and the one eye left to you which the doctor is doubtful he can save' came from being beaten up by a soldier, else 'you will make enemies of the cohort' and risk being beaten up even worse. In Britannia, perhaps around the time of Hadrian's visit, at least one man from overseas (*transmarinus*) was outraged at being flogged savagely enough by centurions to draw blood—a treatment, it is implied, that is on a level with that meted out to natives.[58]

It is not always easy being a soldier, of course, and the job, while varied and relatively well paid, is full of risk even in times of peace. If the experiences of the Cohort I Hispanorum Veterana in Moesia Inferior are anything to go by, all manner of eventuality can await you: you can be seconded to the fleet; transferred to a neighbouring province; drowned; killed by bandits; sent to Gaul to get clothing or to the mountains to round up cattle; or dispatched elsewhere to obtain grain, horses, or to visit the mines. Other tasks include guarding draft animals, scouting with the centurion, helping at the grain ships or taking part in a military mission across the River Danube.[59] Being detained by bandits is one of the few acceptable excuses for returning to camp late from leave. A soldier will be charged as AWOL unless delayed by storms, bad weather at sea or by bandits on land.[60]

Military personnel in Britannia carry out similar duties to their counterparts in Moesia or elsewhere and are exposed to the same sort of risks, and the same variety of duties. At one time, the First Cohort of Tungrians at Vindolanda reports that of its 752 men, two-thirds are absent, with 332 at nearby Coria, 46 acting as guards of the governor, 1 centurion away in Londinium, 6 'outside the province', 9 having set out to Gaul and 11 conducting business in Eboracum. Of the 296 men present, 15 are sick, 6 are wounded and 10 are suffering from inflammation of the eyes.[61]

One thing that soldiers in the ranks will not be spending their time doing is getting married, for they are legally prevented from doing so. As soldiers are still deployed regularly in far-off provinces, the army does not want to be saddled with the problem of moving hundreds, if not thousands, of women and children from one part of the empire to another.

The rules do not mean, of course, that soldiers are obliged to remain celibate, and in the settlements surrounding the forts there are plenty of women—and children. Back in the time of the Third Macedonian War, in 171 BC, troops on duty in Spain were said to have fathered some 4,000 offspring with local women.[62] Neither the children of such unions nor their mothers have any legal status, however, until a soldier is honourably discharged on retirement; then he is eligible to marry and to legitimize his union. Until that time, his children will be deemed illegitimate, even if he himself is already a Roman citizen. Children can only inherit if they are named specifically as heirs in their soldier-father's will. Hadrian has now ruled, though, that the children of soldier-citizens who have died intestate can inherit if there are no surviving legitimate children or relations who might take precedence.

The marriage ban brings other social and legal problems, too.* Soldiers' relationships with local women might well be a source of resentment among the native men, who in the main have rather less cash in their pockets and no promise of Roman citizenship in the distant future. Many women who strike up partnerships with Roman soldiers around the Wall are British but not from the immediate vicinity, or were formerly slaves. One of the most poignant inscriptions on the Wall belongs to a tombstone in draughty Arbeia (South Shields), which commemorates the death of Regina, a Catuvellaunian woman from the south of Britannia, whose *civitas* capital is Verulamium. She was enslaved and acquired by Barates, a Syrian originally from Palmyra. He freed her, married her, and on her death in Arbeia he paid for someone to carve a handsome tombstone. On it, Regina is depicted seated in a wicker chair like any self-respecting Roman matron, with a distaff and spindle in her lap, an open jewellery box at her right hand and a basket of wool on the floor beside her. Beneath the formal Latin inscription is carved, in her husband's native Palmyrene, a most poignant cry from the heart: 'Regina, the freedwoman of Barates—alas!'[63]

However touching the story of Regina and Barates as depicted on the tombstone may seem, at its root is a British woman from the peaceful south sold into slavery. The truth is that not everyone who is enslaved becomes so as a result of war or of being kidnapped by pirates or bandits. Some children have slaves as parents and are born into slavery; others are sold by parents who cannot afford to keep them, or are even exposed at birth and picked up, from the rubbish heaps, by opportunists who will raise them as slaves.[64] Girls are particularly dispensable—as one Egyptian papyrus letter from a man to his wife chillingly records: 'If you bear a child and it is male, leave it be; if it is female, throw it out.'[65] People can also be enslaved

---

* The ban on soldiers marrying remained in place until the early third century.

for debt or, in desperation, even sell *themselves* into slavery.

Unlike soldiers in the ranks, commanding officers are permitted to take their wives and children on tour with them, as well as their household staff.* The wives of officers on the Wall can feel rather isolated, with their husbands fully occupied in their work and their sport. As they can socialize only with people of the same sort of status as themselves, then their female company is limited to the wives of other officers at neighbouring camps—unless they bring out members of their own family. Unsurprisingly, the wives seize every opportunity to write letters to each other and, best of all, to meet up when weather and their own commitments permit them—and are prepared to travel considerable distances to do so. They long to share special occasions with each other, such as birthdays, and dictate their invitations, adding more personal greetings in their own hand.†

While men can ride about the countryside with relative ease and visit their friends at neighbouring forts comparatively easily, officer's wives are no doubt dependent on travelling by carriage with an escort, and so might only be able to meet on special occasions and long-planned trips.

HORSEMANSHIP AT CILURNUM

When the weather is bad in winter, travel along muddy or frozen roads is difficult, for man, woman and beast. Often there is nothing else to do but to sit it out and wait until the weather improves. No one will risk damage to their carts or animals or put their own lives in danger by setting out in poor weather on bad roads unless it is an emergency.[66] It is small wonder that Titus Irdas, who is in

---

* It is not clear whether centurions, who were provided with more spacious accommodation than the ranks, were also accorded this privilege.

† 'On 11 September, sister, for the celebration of my birthday, I ask you warmly to come to us, you will make the day more enjoyable by your presence. Greet your Cerialis. My Aelius and our little son greet you. Farewell, sister, dearest soul, as I hope to prosper and hail.' The commanding officer's wife, Claudia Severa, added the last sentence, with its sweet sign-off, in her own slightly uncertain hand. Vindolanda Tablet 291.

charge of procurement at the busy military supply centre at Cataractonium (Catterick), will dedicate an altar in that town 'to the
god who devised roads and paths'.[67]

As Julius Severus is travelling in summer with his own dedicated
transport officer, all roads should be accessible for him, including
those that follow the wild course east of the Wall from Vercovicium
towards the River Tyne, which is where he must now head. Even so,
during the course of his journey along the 8 or so miles from here
to the fort at Cilurnum (Chesters) he may get a sense that the area
is vulnerable and consequently order a fort to be built at Brocolita
(Carrawburgh),[68] which will be situated just to the west of the most
northern point of the Wall.

After the wild drama of the landscape around Vercovicium,
Cilurnum lies in tranquil contrast on the west side of a lush valley of the North Tyne. The fort is situated at a major river crossing, where the Wall is carried across the river by a bridge of nine
4-metre-wide (13 feet) arches. The fort itself is a mere five years old.
It is home to the 500-strong *ala Augusta ob virtutem appellata* ('the
cavalry unit named Augusta on account of its courage'), who live
with their horses in sixteen stable-barracks, each housing thirty
men, which corresponds to the number in a cavalry *turma* (troop).

The cavalrymen at Cilurnum will no doubt be keen, if not a little nervous, to display their riding skills when the governor comes
to visit. To pass muster they must first ensure that their horses
look resplendent in decorated harnesses, fancy trappings and
bright saddle cloths, while they themselves, sitting resolutely in
their horned saddles and awaiting the order to begin manoeuvres,
will cut unearthly figures in their gilded parade helmets with face
masks drawn down, crowned with brightly coloured plumes.

When addressing them after their demonstration, Julius Severus
will doubtless echo the kind of observations made by Hadrian after
inspecting the *ala* I Pannoniorum in Lambaesis (in North Africa)
a couple of years earlier: 'You filled the parade ground with your
wheelings, your spear-throwing was not ungraceful, though performed with short, stiff shafts. Several of you hurled lances skilfully;

you jumped onto horses in a lively way; and yesterday you did this speedily. Had anything been lacking, I would note it; had anything stood out, I would mention it. The entire manoeuvre was equally pleasing.'[69] Hadrian remarked approvingly that 'omnia per ordinem egistis'—everything was in order—and the ala Augusta will surely be just as keen to show Severus that everything is tip-top at Cilurnum so that he can make a favourable report to an emperor who is so keenly interested in military matters. Hadrian's reforms of the army are commemorated on coins celebrating 'the discipline of Augustus', and indeed so highly rated is the ideal of discipline that it is now deified as Discipulina.* The ala Augusta are clearly keen to demonstrate their allegiance to the ideal and have dedicated an altar to the Discipline of the Emperor Hadrian Augustus. It stands in the shrine of their headquarters building, sternly reinforcing the idea that military discipline as practised by the Romans is divinely ordained.[70]

Hadrian knows that his men need to train continually to be ready to defend the empire, and although keen to keep the peace rather than foment war, Hadrian is passionate about keeping soldiers in prime condition. Many of his reforms are said to have been made during his tour of the north-western provinces, which included his visit to Britannia, where the recent unrest doubtless informed his ideas, as would have his inspections of British troops. He likes to lead by example, too, demonstrating that he is physically strong and fit and willing to share in the soldiers' hardships. To this end he cheerfully eats army field rations, such as bacon, cheese and vinegary wine, and is said to be able to march 20 miles (32km) a day, fully armed. He is as determined to establish discipline in the camp as in the field. Accordingly, he has taken great interest in the regulation of soldiers' duties and in camp expenses, looking into everything from conditions of leave—to prevent officers using the promise of leave to curry favour with troops—to the improvement of arms and equipment. Legionary legates such as Minicius Natalis,

---

* Possibly this was Hadrian's idea.

now in Eboracum, will be well aware of the emperor's reputation for examining receipts from provinces scrupulously and of his desire to acquire a sound knowledge of military stores in every province.

Minicius Natalis, who clearly likes to cut a dash, may feel less in tune with Hadrian's disapproval of the flashy-dress and bejewelled-wine-cooler style of officer life. The emperor refuses to wear gold ornaments on his sword belt, jewels on his clasp or ivory on his sword hilt, and is said to have cleared the camps of 'banqueting rooms, porticoes, grottoes and bowers'.[71] It is tempting to speculate whether the rather fancy *nymphaeum* attached to the long swimming pool at Isca runs the risk of now being classified as a *crypta* (grotto) and therefore banned, not to mention the porticoed courtyard next to the fortress's amphitheatre.*

Hadrian knows, of course, that an army is not a machine operated by abstracts but a body of men governed by officers. Consequently, he is keen to ensure that the tribunes have enough maturity and authority, that only centurions who are fit and have an upstanding reputation are appointed to the post, that no one enters the army who is too young, and that no one stays in service when they are too infirm. As with every good leader who encourages morale, Hadrian is said to make a point of visiting sick soldiers in their quarters.

GHOSTS IN THE LANDSCAPE

After Cilurnum, and the displays of horsemanship, the governor must cross the Tyne and proceed east, visiting Coria next, a supply fort about 2.5 miles (4km) south of the Wall, lying at the junction of the Stanegate with Dere Street. Dere Street runs north of Coria all the way to the outpost fort at Bremenium (High Rochester) and into Caledonia. Were Severus to turn south at this point, his route would take him along Dere Street to the military supply centre at Cataractonium (Catterick), and then through the centre of Isurium

---

* Although there is no record of their nature, Hadrian is said to have corrected many abuses in Britain while on his tour. *Scriptores Historiae Augustae* (Hadrian), 1, 11.

Brigantum (Aldborough), the capital of the Brigantes tribe (whose territory covers the greater part of northern England). It would continue to Eboracum—and a welcome from Minicius Natalis at the legionary fortress there—and then on to Lindum (Lincoln) and Verulamium (St Albans) before reaching Londinium.

But Julius Severus must first finish his inspection of the Wall, which stretches a further 20 or so miles (32km) further east. As Severus and his party will see, as surely as they did further west, old tracks and ancestral land have been sliced through along the frontier. In the fertile open land of this eastern section, parts of the Wall have been constructed on fields fresh from ploughing, and the area to the north bears the scars of enclosures, which were being dug right up until the building of the Wall. In the not too distant landscape on this eastern stretch are the remains of once-great native landholdings, ripped apart only recently. Even at places considerably further north, centuries-old settlements have been left or replaced by much smaller stock enclosures. Some of these properties had been continuously occupied for more than 300 years.

Far from being squalid little smallholdings, randomly dotted in the landscape, many of these ancestral enclosures were substantial, and had contained in their innermost core large roundhouses, sometimes grouped together or in pairs, where two or more high-status families (presumably related) would have lived and farmed side by side.[72] The biggest of these two-storey houses were as large as any found in southern Britain, big enough to accommodate livestock if necessary on a low-ceilinged ground floor, with the family quartered on the upper level. These places also had subsidiary enclosures where metal—the preserve of the powerful—could be worked, and droveways for cattle and horses, with ditches either side to prevent livestock wandering off. Around these dwellings of chiefs, and presumably dependent on them in some way, lay smaller clusters of roundhouses, protected by much less substantial ditches.[73] The deep foundations of the largest roundhouses and the drainage gullies around them, which collected water from their conical thatched roofs, can still be seen clearly, scarring the ground.

In common with the Cornovii before the conquest, these people evidently prized cattle but showed little interest in material goods. In contrast with tribes further south, these northern people seem to have kept themselves to themselves, at least where the Romans were concerned, right up until the construction of the Wall. A few old bangles,[74] made from melted-down Roman glass, and the odd Roman pot mark the limited extent of their interaction with the alien Roman culture.[75]

Things are different now. Unlike in the west, in Cumbria, where people continue to live in traditional enclosures south of the Wall,* some richer chiefs who live south of the Wall in this eastern sector are showing signs that they are succumbing at last to the blandishments of Roman life, to the shops, fine dining, baths and togas. Some villas and settlements, similar to those of small towns in the south, have gradually begun to appear.†

Nowadays, some provincials seem to have adopted an idiosyncratic 'pick and mix' attitude to Roman culture. Down at Faverdale, which lies between Dere Street and another major north–south route, Cade's Road, some 25 miles (40km) south of the Wall, one family group continues to live in a roundhouse but has adapted Roman methods of stock-rearing, producing bigger specimens of cattle, sheep and pigs. Although they clearly have the means to buy imported pottery and have assembled an impressive number of Samian-ware drinking vessels, they continue to use handmade pottery of ancient, Iron Age form. While maintaining time-honoured rituals, such as the careful burial of broken quernstones, they have acquired new ones, including a miniature bath house, startlingly painted in red, white, green, yellow, orange, black and pink. It contains two heated rooms and a waterproof (*opus signum*) floor; but it may strike a visitor used to traditional baths as a little odd, as there is no pool or basin. The remnants of seafood snacks, such as cockles, mussels and oysters, lying about the place, however, suggest

---

* They would continue to do so into the fourth century.
† Although some of these places may equally have been the preserve of retired soldiers and merchants profiting from business on the Wall.

that the inhabitants are eagerly embracing the enticements of baths and dining rolled into one. If so, these shellfish sauna parties must be intimate gatherings, for the room can only accommodate a maximum of six people.[76]

HUNTING AND FISHING, READING AND WRITING

Although Julius Severus is on a tour of duty and clearly has a great deal of work to do, he will surely not miss the opportunity to take advantage of the marvellous hunting country in this area and to join some of the senior officers in their favourite—and in many cases pretty much only—pastime. Even when officers cannot leave their work commitments for the day, they write to each other about hunting and fishing—and send each other requests for kit. 'If you love me, brother, I ask that you send me hunting-nets,' implores Flavius Cerialis from Vindolanda to his friend Brocchus.[77]

Friends also exchange news about their hunting hounds. Two Celtic breeds seem to be popular, the *segusius* and the *vertragus*.[78] The former are shaggy and ugly—the purer the breed, the uglier they are, according to Arrian (who will also find time to write a treatise on hunting while in Cappadocia). In addition to their unfortunate looks, they also make a terrible noise, a point not lost on Arrian: 'Among the Celts, there is a famous comparison of these dogs with roadside beggars because of their mournful and miserable voice and because they follow their prey not with a keen sound but with importunate and pitiful howls.'

Arrian himself owned a *vertragus* bitch called Horme (Ορμη), meaning something like 'Dash'. It is a good name, for this breed is renowned for its speed and is rather better looking than the unfortunate segosian hound. 'There is nothing finer to look at than the shape and appearance of the best bred of these dogs... First of all they are long from head to tail, and there is no other sign of speed and good breeding in any dog which is so important for speed as length.'[79] If the officers on the Wall care for their hounds as much as Arrian does for his, they will be well looked after—sensibly fed, praised and fondled after a good chase, and given a soft, warm bed at night where (Arrian advises) 'it is best that they sleep with a man so as to become more affectionate and appreciate companionship, and to love the person who sleeps next to them no less than the one who nurtured them'.[80]

Keen though Arrian and these officers are on hunting, there is no one in the empire more passionate about the chase than Hadrian, who holds both his horses and his hounds in deep affection. He famously erected a tomb with a *stele* and inscription for his favourite hunter, Borysthenes, who died at Apte in Gallia Narbonensis while on the first leg of the journey that brought Hadrian to Britannia.[81] As a young man, Hadrian was so fond of hunting that he was criticized for it; but he continued to hunt passionately— and, some would say, theatrically—throughout his life. If eating bacon in the camps with the men helps him gain political kudos by suggesting he has the common touch, stagey hunts celebrated by carefully selected poets elevate him to the level of hero, putting his spectacular bravery and strength on a par with Hercules and Alexander.[82] They say he founded a town called Hadrianotherae at the place where he killed a bear.[83]

Lesser mortals can continue to rejoice in the thrill of the hunt and also commemorate their achievements in monuments, even if, in scale at least, they are rather more modest than those of the emperor. Some 27 miles (43km) south of Coria on Dere Street, near Vinovia (Binchester) auxiliary fort, Gaius Tetius Venturius Micianus, prefect of the Sebosian Cavalry Regiment, who hunts in the wild beauty of Weardale, has been unable to contain his pride and excitement at bagging an elusive boar. It was an animal he was so determined to catch that he made a pact with the hunting god, Silvanus, to whom he dedicates an altar 'in fulfilment of his vow... for having caught a remarkably fine wild boar which many of his predecessors had been unable to catch'.[84] Britannia may not be able to provide lions, but up in the north country, in addition to wild boar, there are polecats, grey wolves, beavers, and the odd brown bear lurking in the remote fells; and lynx have been spotted as far south as Yorkshire.[85]

It is to be hoped that the soldiers do enjoy their hunting, for beyond the daily military duties there is precious little else to do, except to make occasional visits to friends at other forts and to look forward to periods of leave or a secondment to one of the legionary bases or to Londinium. If you like to read or study, then the winters can be particularly hard, with heat and light both in short supply. Anyone who employs a secretary in winter will need to ensure his hands are well protected by sleeves so that the cold does not prevent him from taking dictation.[86]

Oil lamps are far less common in Britannia than in other parts of the empire, and outside the most prosperous houses in the cities and the military camps they are a rarity. As olive oil has to be brought hundreds of miles into Britannia it is a luxury, rather than an everyday staple, and is used sparingly, even by the military. Oil lamps are so desirable because they provide a steady, clear flame, provided that the wick is not too long, and even a small lamp can burn for about three or four hours before it needs a refill.[87] In Britannia, however, open lamps, in the form of shallow iron dishes, are more common, fuelled by either liquid tallow (the rendered fat of cattle or sheep), lard from pigs, dripping from cows—or occasionally even fish oil. These lamps can be hung on a wall or carried around.

Candles made out of tallow are also an option, but far from ideal. Mutton tallow is firm but very smelly, while pig tallow gives off a lot of smoke. Quite apart from their unsteady, smoky flames, tallow candles are also greasy to hold and leave fatty marks wherever they drip. They also need constant attention, as their wicks burn only partially, so they need to be trimmed regularly to keep the flame bright. Far better, if you can afford it, are candles made from beeswax.

Once you are up here on the Wall you just have to get on with it and try to maintain the traditions of army and home as best you can. In this wild place, you must hope for the companionship of a fellow officer with all the qualities of a *bonus vir*, a cultured man of steady character.[88] Dressed in formal dinner attire, with scarves as accessories, officers invite each other to taste the fruits of their sport at dinner: game such as roe deer and venison may appear alongside the thrushes, duck and swans they have taken pleasure in hunting, all washed down with Massic wine from Campania.

Out in the barracks, the men are provided with plainer food, including a weekly ration of wheat for themselves and barley for any horses. For the most part they are well fed, and well clothed in long-sleeved tunics and trousers (also available in hard-wearing, waterproof leather) and thick woollen cloaks. They wear under-clothes and woollen socks (which, in their letters, they request friends and family to send), and when the weather is particularly bitter they can wrap great thick wads of wool around their legs. Having cash to spend, they are able to supplement their rations with treats such as oysters and go drinking, gambling and whoring in the small settlements outside the camp and the larger towns when on leave or secondment. While sour wine is standard army issue, many of the auxiliary troops from the north-west provinces have more of a taste for beer.

JOURNEY'S END

As winter approaches, unless there is serious and pressing trouble at the frontier, Julius Severus may choose to return south after he has finished his inspection of the Wall. The great bridge across the Tyne marked the Wall's original terminus. As it seems that work on the Wall began here, this bridge must have been one of the very first structures to be built as part of Hadrian's great project.

The bridge's main purpose is not so much practical as symbolic and magnificent. It is flanked by altars at either end, to the two watery gods Neptunus and Oceanus, both dedicated by the Legion VI Victrix.[89] Its name—Pons Aelius (Hadrian's Bridge)—is of such consequence that the fort built later* on a promontory above it will go by the same name.[90] Wherever the emperor goes on his travels, he gives impetus—and often his name—to monumental projects, so it will be said that one can 'see memorials of his journeys in most cities of Europe and Asia'.[91] Pons Aelius bears the same name as the bridge he built in Rome. The two monuments, such worlds apart, are united by Hadrian's name and vision.†

The bridge no longer marks the terminus of the Wall, which is to be found a little further on at Segedunum (Wallsend). Should Maenius Agrippa be accompanying Severus at this point, he will be able to give him an eyewitness account of Hadrian's visit eight years before, as he was present in person. Both men can pause to reflect on the words of the monumental inscription at Segedunum, which records that Hadrian, having scattered the barbarians and restored the province, added a frontier between the shores of both oceans.[92]

Now Britannia's new governor has completed his first tour of the remote frontier between those two oceans. It is time for him to embark on one of the ships of the *classis Britannica* anchored in the Tyne, underneath the watchful eye of the garrison at the fort of Arbeia, who defend the lower reaches of the river.

Of those left behind on the Wall as winter approaches, the officers and men from the north-western provinces (especially the Batavians) might be hardened to the rain and the grey, brooding skies; at least they can cherish their recipes from home. The Dacians here might well find in the wintry hills and forests something to remind them of their homeland, the memory of which they try so hard to preserve. Those from sunnier parts of the world, such as the Syrian merchants and Mauretanian town councillors, cannot help but spare a thought now and then for their native cities. Some will die here, their only remaining journey being the one

---

* The fort was constructed in the later second century AD.

† It is tempting to speculate that there was also some sort of monument high on the promontory above the northern bridgehead (on the site of the later fort which retained the name of the bridge) in the form of a mausoleum, perhaps commemorating the end of the wars in the manner of Augustus's monument at La Turbie, above the Bay of Monaco. But there is no archaeological evidence to support this.

they will take to the Underworld. But others will live to return to their homes or, like Julius Severus, will make further remarkable journeys throughout the length and breadth of the empire.

Beyond AD 130:
People, Politics
and Places

*

PEOPLE

As 'the first of Hadrian's best generals', Julius Severus was summoned from Britannia in the spring of AD 133 to take charge of
operations in Judaea following the serious revolt there led by Simon
Bar Kokhba. His mission was to annihilate the Jewish rebels,[1] and
he was so successful that some 580,000 men on the Jewish side were
said to have been killed.[2] For his role in the campaign, Severus was
awarded the highest military honours, the *ornamenta triumphalia*.
He was appointed proconsul (governor) of the newly formed province Syria Palaestina, which incorporated Judaea. At this point he
vanishes from the record—presumably he died in Syria.[3] Nothing is
known about his wife or children, although he appears to have had
a son or nephew called Gnaeus Julius Verus, who was appointed
governor of Britannia in the 150s (*c*.155–158).

The commander of the *classis Britannica*, Marcus Maenius
Agrippa, appears to have thrived in Britannia, for he was afterwards
appointed procurator of the province. Minicius Natalis, however,
returned to Rome on completion of his commission as legionary
legate in York. There, he was appointed *praefectus alimentorum*
(prefect of the food supply) and then *curator viae Flaminiae*

(curator of the Via Flaminia). He was made consul in AD 139, after Hadrian's death, and held a further post in Rome with responsibility for temples and public works. He then acceded to Julius Severus's old job as governor of Moesia Inferior, where he had first served as a tribune. His career was crowned with the proconsulship of Africa, a post that his father had also held.

POLITICS

After Hadrian's death in AD 138, Antoninus Pius succeeded as emperor. Within a year the northern frontier of Britannia was overrun and the province's governor, Quintus Lollius Urbicus, was forced to drive back the barbarians and to build a wall of turf between the Forth and the Clyde, 37 miles (60km) long. In the 160s, under Marcus Aurelius, this 'Antonine Wall' was abandoned, and Hadrian's Wall once again formed the northern frontier. There was a further war in Britannia, about which little is known, and under Commodus in the 180s tribes again wreaked havoc across the Wall, though the Romans eventually celebrated victory in AD 184. When Commodus was murdered at the end of AD 192, Pertinax, one-time governor of Britannia, became emperor for eighty-six days before he, too, was assassinated.

Years of civil war in the empire followed, until the North African Septimius Severus narrowly defeated, near Lyon, the army of his compatriot Clodius Albinus, another governor of Britannia and pretender to imperial power, who had the support of the British and Spanish legions. Albinus killed himself, Lyon was pillaged and the fall-out was felt all over the empire. During the course of his reign, Septimius Severus divided Britannia into two provinces, the south part becoming Britannia Superior ('Upper Britain', i.e. nearer Rome) and the north Britannia Inferior ('Lower Britain'). Britannia Inferior was governed from York. In AD 208 Severus himself arrived in Britannia to invade Scotland, accompanied by his wife and two sons, Caracalla and Geta. The war was a failure, and the emperor died in York in 211. His sons succeeded as joint emperors and abandoned the war. The following year Caracalla killed his brother and gave all free men Roman citizenship. Caracalla, too, was killed—by the Praetorian prefect Macrinus, in 217, who claimed imperial power. But Caracalla's cousin Bassianus (a.k.a. Elagabulus), a man of bizarre tastes, managed to snatch that power away from him within the year. He came to a bad end in March 222, when his decapitated body ended up in the Tiber alongside that of his mother. His blander young cousin Severus Alexander succeeded, only to be murdered in his tent, together with his mother, in AD 235 by mutinous soldiers on the Rhine.

Thereafter there followed a dizzying succession of emperors, who mostly died by violent means. Mid-century, plague and Goths hit the empire hard, soon followed by Franks and Alemanni, who crossed the Rhine and pillaged Gaul and Spain, and by Saxons, who appeared on the shores of the North Sea to threaten Britannia. During these deeply troubled times, British cities began to be fortified, and forts were built on the south and east coasts to guard against these barbarian pirates. Christians were persecuted. In the east, the Emperor Valerian was captured, humiliated and put to death by the Persians in AD 259/60.

Aristocratic Gallienus began to re-establish order before being assassinated by his own officers in AD 268. His tough 'Illyrian' soldier successors continued the interminable struggle against external enemies and internal instability. It was the last of the Illyrian emperors, Diocletian, who managed to make the greatest headway. Under him (in AD 284) the army, administration and monetary system were reformed, and the empire was split into two, with his co-emperor (or co-augustus) Maximian ruling the West. Two 'Caesars', Constantius Chlorus and Galerius, helped them govern, thus forming the Tetrarchy, or rule of four.

Britannia continued to cause trouble. In AD 286 Belgic-born Carausius made himself head of an independent state in Britain, declaring himself emperor. He was, however, murdered in AD 293 and succeeded by his curly-haired, snub-nosed chancellor of the exchequer, Allectus, who was himself killed by Constantius Chlorus when he recovered the British provinces for Rome in AD 296. After twenty years, the two emperors abdicated in AD 305, Diocletian retiring to his palace at Split, near his birthplace at Salona.

Under the Tetrarchy, Britannia had been reorganized again, and by AD 312–314 it was divided into four provinces within a diocese of Britannia ruled by a *vicarius*, under whom were four separate governors who were no longer in charge of both the administration and the military. Soldiers were under the command of a *dux Britanniarum* (Duke of Britain), while a *comes* (count) controlled the coastal forts (known as the Saxon Shore forts). Another *comes* controlled the cavalry. In AD 305, Constantius Chlorus returned to Britannia for a new campaign in Scotland. He died in York in 306. There, the troops declared his son Constantine emperor. He faced much competition for the position—at one point there was a Heptarchy, or rule of seven emperors—but after years of war, Constantine emerged triumphant in AD 324 and became sole ruler.

During the course of these unsettling years Constantine managed to carry out reforms, and in AD 313 he issued the Edict of Milan, legitimizing Christianity. Britannia was sufficiently organized to send bishops from the sees of London and York (probably also Lincoln) to the Council of Arles in AD 314. Constantine founded Constantinople, the 'New Rome', and died in AD 337. The empire had now shifted significantly eastwards, culturally as well as politically.

In the West—and although the times remained troubled, pirates infested the seas and the frontiers were unsafe—Britannia was, in many ways, more settled in her Romanized skin, with magnificent country houses in the south and west and provincial capitals such as York and Cirencester booming. But with the empire's power shifted so far east, this most north-westerly province was now even more geographically and culturally remote.

For the poets, Britannia would forever be clothed in the skin of a 'Caledonian beast, her cheeks tattooed, her azure cloak sweeping around her feet, imitating the billowing ocean.'[4]

PLACES OF NOTE

ALAUNA (MARYPORT). The names of the units that were subsequently stationed here, in the third and fourth centuries, are unknown. The earth-works of the fort are well preserved and there is a fine museum adjoining it. The north-east gate of the fort now forms the chancel arch of Cross-canonby Church.

The bulk of the museum's collection is known as the Netherhall Col-lection. It was first begun in 1570 by John Senhouse, recorded by William Camden in 1599, and built upon by subsequent generations. The highlight of the museum is the astonishing group of Roman military altars, the lar-gest in Britain, from the site of the fort lying adjacent to the museum. In 2013 excavations at the fort uncovered the most north-westerly Classical temple known in the Roman world.

*

AQUAE SULIS (BATH). The temple was modified in the late second cen-tury when two small side chapels were added on either side of the steps. The spring was enclosed by a building whose entrance was on the south side of the temple courtyard. The so-called 'four seasons building' was built on the north side of the courtyard. The baths also underwent many changes over time, becoming progressively larger and reaching their max-imum extent in the fourth century. Thereafter the complex declined.

Aquae Sulis was surrounded by a defensive wall in the third century. The area contained within the wall was built up, although it is not cer-tain whether these were private dwellings or buildings connected with the development of the site as a centre of religious tourism, with local people living outside the walls.

The Roman baths are astonishingly well preserved, and the sight of the thermal water still gushing through the original Roman channels, and the steam rising from the green waters of the sacred spring, is one of the most thrilling of any Roman remains anywhere. The gilded bronze head of the cult statue of Sulis Minerva and the head of the 'Gorgon' from the temple pediment are two of the most hypnotic treasures of Roman Britain.

*

ARBEIA (SOUTH SHIELDS). The Hadrianic fort was replaced, probably under Marcus Aurelius in the AD 160s. Shortly after AD 200, the south wall was taken down and the fort extended. Many of the buildings were replaced by thirteen granaries, converting the fort into a supply base, probably to serve Septimius Severus's attempts at conquest north of the Wall. Nine more granaries were subsequently built. One hundred years later, following a devastating fire, the granaries were adapted as barracks and a new headquarters and commanding officer's house were built.

The fort was first excavated in the 1870s, and the finds from this time form the nucleus of the small but sensational collection at the fort's museum, which includes some of the most important finds from Roman Britain. Highlights include the funerary monument to Regina, the British ex-slave and then wife of Barates the Syrian; the elaborate funerary monument to handsome Victor, a North African slave evidently much cherished by a Spanish soldier stationed here; a complete ringmail suit; a large collection of Roman jet; and the recently discovered second-century head of a deity, possibly the northern goddess Brigantia. On the site are a number of reconstructed buildings, including the fourth-century commanding officer's house, a barrack block and the west gate modelled on that at Housesteads.

*

BANNA (Birdoswald). The I Aelia Dacorum Miliaria Cohort originally raised in Dacia (modern Romania) had arrived at Birdoswald by AD 219 and remained there through the third and fourth centuries, although the fort might have been briefly abandoned in the late third century. An extensive settlement grew up outside the fort. The important discovery of a series of timber halls on the site of the granaries indicates that descendants of the soldiers continued to live in the fort long after the end of Roman rule in Britain and into the sixth century.

Lying within a meander of the River Irthing, Birdoswald affords spectacular views of the surrounding countryside. The complete circuit of the fort walls, Roman granaries with the position of the Dark Age hall marked out, a sixteenth-century bastle house and foundations of a medieval tower house may all be seen. The museum has a selection of finds from the site. To the east and west of Birdoswald, Hadrian's Wall survives up to 2.5 metres (8 feet) high, providing one of the most impressive stretches along its entire length. Turret 49b and Milecastle 49 (Harrow's Scar) lie nearby.

*

BREMETENACUM VETERANUM (Ribchester). At some point after AD 175, Sarmatians from the Ukraine and southern Russia were stationed at Ribchester. Superb horsemen, they were among 5,500 men drafted to Britannia following Marcus Aurelius's victory over them in what is now Hungary. The baths had fallen into disuse by AD 225, and the granaries appear to have been burned down, but it is not clear whether this was by accident or a deliberate act when the auxiliaries were posted elsewhere.

The site is charming and picturesque, on the banks of the River Ribble. There is a small museum with some excellent finds, including the tombstone of an Asturian cavalryman trampling down a Celtic warrior. The remains of the baths and two of the granaries may be viewed. The Ribchester Hoard, including the famous parade helmet found in 1796 by the son of a village clogmaker, is on display at the British Museum.

*

CALLEVA ATREBATUM (SILCHESTER). In about AD 270, a substantial wall was built around the town, covering an area of 2.4 square kilometres. Also in the third century, the amphitheatre was refurbished (by this time it had assumed a typical elliptical shape). Calleva was abandoned between AD 550 and 650. Why a town of such size and status was left in this way and never subsequently developed or built on—there are indications that the inhabitants were forced to leave—is one of the mysteries of Roman Britain.

At Silchester, the amphitheatre and parts of the town walls may still be seen. The large number of finds from the town are on display at the nearby Reading Museum. The most celebrated of them is the bronze eagle, discovered in the forum basilica in 1866 between layers of burned material, and which was romantically interpreted as the imperial standard of a Roman legion lost during a desperate struggle; it is now thought to have formed part of a statue of Jupiter or of an emperor. The find inspired Rosemary Sutcliff's 1954 children's novel, *The Eagle of the Ninth*, on which the 2011 film *The Eagle* was based.

*

CILURNUM (CHESTERS). Lying in a tranquil valley, with a flourishing civilian settlement, Chesters remained occupied until the end of Roman rule in Britain in the early fifth century.

The site has the finest example of a Roman bath building in Britain. There is also the remarkable survival of the strongroom, with its vaulted roof intact, and the superb remains of the bridge abutment across the

North Tyne. An Edwardian museum contains one of the best collections of inscriptions and sculpture on the Wall. The collection was put together by John Clayton, who was responsible for excavating and saving central sections of the Wall, including Chesters, which was situated in the parkland of his family's estate.

*

CORIA (CORBRIDGE). Lying south of Hadrian's Wall, this fort was occupied into the 160s. It then became a base for legionary soldiers, around which a civilian settlement developed. The legionary soldiers both supported and helped garrison Hadrian's Wall and a chain of outpost forts up Dere Street. They also supervised and administered Corbridge as a supply base and market for the frontier. By the early third century an extensive town had grown up around the base, which was abandoned rapidly when Roman administration in Britain collapsed in the early fifth century.

The exposed site of 1.8 hectares represents the central nucleus of the town, although it is only a fraction of the whole original site, which covered up to 20 hectares. The granaries are the best preserved in Britain. A fountain, main street and massive courtyard building ('site XI') are among the most obvious remains. The museum houses one of the biggest collections of architectural fragments from the north-western provinces, as well as a large collection of pottery and everyday objects. Of great significance is the Corbridge Hoard, the discovery of which enabled the workings of *lorica segmentata*—Roman plate armour—to be understood for the first time.

*

DEVA (CHESTER). The legionary fortress and amphitheatre were neglected for much of the second century as the Legion XX Valeria Victrix was deployed up on Hadrian's Wall. It was only in the late second/early third century that major construction work resumed, when the legion returned to its base. The original amphitheatre was replaced with an ambitious new one, which is the largest and most elaborate of all British amphitheatres. In the post-Roman period many timber buildings were built in the amphitheatre, which might have become a defended settlement connected in some way with the royal church established next to it by the Mercian King Aethelred in the seventh century.

Two-fifths of the late-second-century amphitheatre are on display in the heart of modern Chester. The arena wall survives to a maximum height of 2.2 metres (7 feet) and the arena is floored with yellow gravel to reflect the original yellow sand. Deposits laid down outside the early amphitheatre and sealed by the construction of the second amphitheatre provide evidence for activities outside the amphitheatre, such as hot-snack and souvenir stalls. All the excavated remains are held by the Grosvenor Museum, Chester, including the altar to Nemesis.

*

DUROVERNUM CANTIACORUM (CANTERBURY). In the early third century, the Romano-Celtic theatre was rebuilt to a new plan, making it more Classical in form and enlarging it to accommodate 3,000 people. The town was fortified much later than other towns in Britannia—in the later third century—with coarsed flint and mortar walls, 2.25 metres (7 feet 6 inches) thick, enclosing an area of 120 acres. Many private houses in town were provided with suites of baths, and civic life continued to flourish longer than elsewhere as affluent citizens and local landowners maintained their links with the town rather than retiring to villas in the country, as happened in other places. The town went into a gradual decline from the mid-fourth to the mid-fifth century, after which time the city was repopulated, with small timber-framed houses being built among the ruins.

Finds from Roman Canterbury are displayed at the Roman Museum, built around the remains of a large Roman town house that was excavated after German bombing during the Second World War. Mosaics and the hypocaust system are displayed, as well as an extremely rare soldier's helmet dating from the time of Julius Caesar's invasions of Britain: it was probably made in Gaul and reused as a burial urn. Outside the city walls, St Martin's Church, where Saint Augustine set up his mission when he arrived from Rome in AD 597, contains much Roman fabric and may have been first built in antiquity. Elsewhere in town, the remains of a second-century bath complex lie in the basement of a bookshop.

*

HADRIAN'S WALL (VALLUM AELII). Hadrian's successor, Antoninus Pius, abandoned the Wall, slighting it by removing milecastle gates and throwing crossings across the *Vallum* ditch. He moved the frontier up to the Forth–Clyde isthmus, where he built a new turf wall. This was abandoned after twenty years, and the soldiers returned to Hadrian's Wall and got it up and running once more. After a war in the 180s, when enemy tribes crossed the Wall, many changes took place and soldiers were re-deployed at key points east and west. In the late second or early third century there was a major repair to the Wall, and many mile-castles had their north gates narrowed so that only pedestrians could use them. The Wall was manned into the early fifth century.

Hadrian's Wall, the most famous of all the frontiers of the Roman Empire, is a UNESCO World Heritage Site and has been studied for more than 400 years. Sections of the Wall, the associated forts on the Wall (and to the south and along the Cumbrian coast), its mile-castles, turrets, signal towers, *Vallum*, civilian settlements and bridges may all be visited. A number of museums containing important collections lie on and around the length of the Wall.

*

ISCA AUGUSTA (CAERLEON). The legionary fortress baths appear to have been maintained until about AD 230–240. By AD 290–300, at the time of the Emperor Carausius or his successor Allectus, the fortress had been stripped of most reusable material. Parts of the buildings were still standing in the twelfth century, when Gerald of Wales, out recruiting for the Third Crusade in 1188, admired 'a lofty tower and beside it remarkable hot baths'.

The excavated remains are extensive: they include the defences, the amphitheatre, the only legionary barracks buildings to be seen in Britain, and the baths. The last are displayed under a covered building. Numerous finds can be viewed at the National Roman Legion Museum in the town.

*

LANCASTER. The auxiliary fort at Lancaster underwent numerous changes, with at least six phases of development. In about AD 340 a stone fort was constructed on a different alignment, which remained in use until the early fifth century.

Little of Roman Lancaster remains: a Roman bath house, part of a large courtyard house and possible *mansio* connected to the fort, can be visited in Vicarage Fields. A fragment of the fort's massive fourth-century wall, known as the Wery Wall, may also be seen. On display at Lancaster City Museum is the Rider tombstone of Insus, showing him triumphantly holding the head of a Briton whose decapitated body lies at his feet.

*

LETOCETUM (WALL, Staffordshire). Letocetum, an important staging post on Watling Street, provided overnight accommodation at its *mansio*. A settlement developed and eventually there was a small Romano-British town. The town ran into difficulties towards the end of the third century, and baths and *mansio* were destroyed by fire and abandoned. Substantial defences were built to the east of these buildings and astride Watling Street around this time, and by the fourth century the whole population appears to have moved within the defences.

The *mansio*'s foundations and those of the bath house (both of which underwent several phases of development and construction, the best understood of which date from about AD 130) can still be seen, together with many excavated finds on display in the museum.

*

LONDINIUM (LONDON). London was enclosed by some 2 miles (3km) of stone wall in the late second century, and the fort (at Cripplegate) was incorporated into these new defences. At Newgate, where the road west to Calleva left the city, the gate was equipped with twin portals flanked by square towers projecting in front of the line of the curtain wall. Ermine Street, the main road north to York, left the city at Bishopsgate, and the main road for Colchester and East Anglia ran from Aldgate. Towards the end of the second century a temple to Mithras was built on the site of Bucklersbury House, north of Cannon Street, which continued in use with several changes to its interior into the middle of the fourth century, after which it was rebuilt and dedicated to Bacchus.

The Museum of London contains much of interest, including a leather bikini and sculptures from the temple of Mithras, the site of which lies at the corner of Queen Street and Queen Victoria Street. Beneath the Guildhall, at Guildhall Yard, the remains of the amphitheatre are on show. The remains of the late-second-century Billingsgate house and baths in Lower Thames Street, once on the waterfront, are generally not open to the public. More accessible are the remains of the Roman wall and gates, although the medieval wall was built on them.

*

LUGDUNUM (LYON). As capital of Tres Galliae, Lugdunum continued to enjoy great prosperity for several more decades after AD 130, but by the advent of the third century the city had run into difficulties. In AD 197 Lyon declared for Clodius Albinus, governor of Britannia and pretender to the imperial throne. He fought Septimius Severus just outside

Lyon—and was defeated. The depth of the repercussions the city suffered for supporting the losing side is unclear, but the urban cohort, the only military unit stationed in the interior of Gaul, was disbanded. Under Diocletian's administrative reforms, Lugdunum became the capital of a reduced province. Trèves, Arles and Vienne now assumed greater importance, and during the third century the city contracted.

On the hill known as Fourvière, the 10,000-seat theatre and the smaller 3,000-seat Odeon next to it may be visited. The neighbouring Gallo-Roman Museum contains a breathtaking collection, including the Lyon tablet recording Claudius's speech to the Senate in AD 48, in which he proposed to admit citizens from Gaul as senators, a speech for which we also have Tacitus's version. The second-century Coligny calendar, written in Gaulish, is another of the many treasures in this museum. There is also an amphitheatre on Croix-Rouge, which is where the sanctuary of the Three Gauls was sited and where the Lyon tablet was discovered in the sixteenth century.

*

LUGUVALIUM CARVETIORUM (Carlisle). The fort, which essentially lies underneath Carlisle Castle, was occupied until the early fifth century. At some point in the third century, possibly as a consequence of Caracalla's settlement of the northern frontier in the early third century, Carlisle became the *civitas* capital of the Carvetii. The town was fortified, possibly encompassing some 70 acres, and the walls were still standing in the seventh century, when Saint Cuthbert walked around them and was shown a Roman fountain.

The Tullie House Museum contains a large collection of Roman artefacts, including a significant number of wooden and leather objects and a small number of writing tablets from the town, together with numerous artefacts from sites along the western half of Hadrian's Wall.

*

NARBONENSIS (Narbonne). Narbonne suffered from a terrible fire in about AD 150, which destroyed many of its public buildings. These were restored with the help of Emperor Antoninus Pius. The city began to decline in the third century as trade slowed, and Arles became more important as a commercial centre. Under Diocletian's administrative reforms, Gallia Narbonensis was divided up and Narbonne became the capital of the south-west part of the province named Narbonensis Prima.

It remained an important and relatively prosperous city, however, into the fifth century.

Nothing substantial remains of the city's celebrated public monuments so admired by Martial in the first century and Sidonius Apollinarius in the fifth, apart from extensive *horrea*, or warehouses, which survived as cellars. There are fine collections of artefacts, though, in the Palais des Archevêques, including mosaics and wall-paintings, while the l'église Lamourguier holds an extensive lapidary.

*

OSTIA. Later in the second century and into the early part of the third, little monumental new building took place here, with the exception of a large temple resembling the Pantheon in Rome, constructed near the forum during the reign of Alexander Severus (AD 222–235). During the long period of turmoil following the end of the Severan dynasty, building activity at Ostia almost ceased, the size of the population shrank, and local government collapsed. In the second half of the third century and the first part of the fourth, Ostia and Portus were struck by earthquakes and tsunamis.

Most of the excavated buildings at Ostia date from the first half of the second century, during the reigns of Trajan, Hadrian and Antoninus Pius, with a large number dating from Hadrian's time, so the visitor here will be able to get a strong flavour of the Hadrianic period.

*

PONS AELIUS (NEWCASTLE UPON TYNE). Newcastle Castle occupies the site of the Roman fort. Fragments of the headquarters building, commanding officer's house and granary are visible under a railway arch beside the castle keep.

The city's Great North Museum (Hancock) now houses the collection of the Society of Antiquaries of Newcastle upon Tyne, whose Roman material is of international significance. The museum contains altars, building inscriptions, relief sculpture, tombstones and many other artefacts, including jewellery, pottery, weapons and organic material. The sensational statue of the Birth of Mithras from Housesteads is on display in the museum.

*

ROMA (ROME). After a terrible fire in AD 191, many buildings were reconstructed. The Severans also erected major new monuments, including the baths of Caracalla. During the years of turmoil in the third century, construction work slowed down and practically stopped. Aurelian (AD 271–275) erected walls around the city. Diocletian resumed work, reconstructing a large part of central Rome destroyed in a great fire in AD 283. He also built the largest baths ever constructed in the empire. Maxentius, the son of Diocletian's co-ruler Maximian, chose Rome as his base after the Praetorian Guard proclaimed him emperor, and he began to tend to the neglected city. Constantine the Great took on his work, but soon became engrossed in his new capital, Constantinople. As the old monuments were patched up or fell into disuse, Rome was finished as a political force but emerged as a religious one. With Christians no longer persecuted, Christian monuments began to rise out of the neglected pagan city.

The two outstanding Hadrianic monuments to survive in Rome itself are the Pantheon and his Mausoleum, now the Castel Sant'Angelo. Outside the city there is his stupendous palace at Tivoli.

*

RUTUPIAE (Richborough) and REGULBIUM (Reculver).

Rutupiae thrived as a port until the early third century, when it began to decline, possibly because of the increasing importance of Dover. In the mid-third century, large ditches and an earthen rampart were built around the monumental arch, whose days were numbered. In the 270s, work began on the construction of a massive fort in response to increasing attacks by Saxon and Frankish raiders. The arch was taken down for building material and its marble cladding broken up and burnt to provide lime for concrete. The fort formed part of the Saxon Shore fortifications defending the coast. But despite these radical changes, Rutupiae retained its symbolic importance as the gateway to Britannia.

At the other end of the Wantsum Channel, a new fort was also built at Regulbium in response to the Saxon threat, although it seems to have been abandoned by AD 375. It later became an important Anglo-Saxon monastery, the remains of which still dominate the coastline today. The Roman foreshore now lies two miles inland from the sea.

At Richborough, the most striking standing remains are the walls of the Saxon Shore fort, but there is also much else of interest, including the excavated Claudian invasion ditches, a rare Roman baptismal font, the remains of the *mansio* and other buildings in the town, and the site of the gigantic arch. The museum displays a small but significant collection of finds from the site, including decorative fragments from the monumental arch.

*

SEGEDUNUM (WALLSEND). As early as the eleventh century the settlement was called 'Wallesende'. Lying at the heart of industrial Tyneside and buried under housing until the 1970s, the whole Roman fort has now been excavated, making Segedunum one of very few places where a fort plan is laid out more or less whole. It is one of the best understood and best excavated sites along the Wall. The barracks, south of the headquarters building, revealed how horses were stabled alongside their cavalrymen.

There is a viewing tower over the site, a reconstructed bath house modelled on that at Chesters, and a museum displaying finds from the site.

*

VENTA SILURUM (CAERWENT). Despite its forum basilica and *mansio*, Venta remained something of a straggling backwater along the Caerleon–Gloucester road until the later second century. The street grid was then modified and the town surrounded by a ditch, bank and wooden palisade. Towards the end of the third century a stone wall was built in front of the bank, and in about AD 350 stone towers were added to the north and south walls. The town started to decline in the fourth century, but the Roman remains were impressive enough in the 1540s for John Leland to remark that it was 'sometime a fair and large city'.

Now a small village, the defences are still astonishingly well preserved, their circuit just over a mile. The foundations of shops, houses and a Romano-Celtic temple are also on view, as well as the forum basilica—interestingly, the only town in Britain where this can be seen. The road through the village is more or less on the line of the Roman road, although the latter was much wider than the present one. Some stone inscriptions are displayed in the church. Other significant finds from the town are in the National Museum of Wales, Cardiff.

*

VERCOVICIUM (HOUSESTEADS). About halfway along the Wall's length, Housesteads was manned from the later second century until after AD 395 by the First Cohort of Tungrians, raised in eastern Belgium. Early in the third century they were strengthened by a war band of Frisians, recruited from outside the empire.

Perched high on a windswept ridge, with sweeping views over the surrounding countryside, Housesteads is one of the most iconic sites, not just on the Wall but throughout the whole empire. The latrine, west gate, commanding officer's house and granaries are exceptionally well preserved. There is a small exhibition, including finds from the site. The extraordinary sculptures from the Mithraeum are at the Great North Museum (Hancock) in Newcastle upon Tyne and also at Chesters Museum.

*

VINDOLANDA (CHESTERHOLM). Vindolanda lies on the Stanegate, south of Hadrian's Wall. The fort underwent at least nine phases of construction. After the end of Roman rule, Vindolanda remained in use for over 400 years until it was finally abandoned in the ninth century.

Ongoing excavations constantly add to knowledge of the site. Together with the excavated parts of the fort there are also reconstructed buildings and a museum containing a marvellous collection, including the Vindolanda letters and a remarkable display of leather shoes and other organic material. The nearby Roman Army Museum is located next to Walltown Crags, one of the highest-standing sections of Hadrian's Wall.

*

VIROCONIUM CORNOVIORUM (WROXETER). The substantial baths complex was finally completed around AD 150 and the town's defences were built towards the end of the second century. They were refurbished in the fourth century. The baths basilica was maintained into the fifth century and then dismantled; over the ruins, timber buildings were constructed, some of which were substantial. The town was probably abandoned in the sixth century.

The most substantial remains of what was once the fourth-largest town in Britannia are the baths, including the remains of the huge wall of the baths basilica. There is also a reconstructed town house and small museum with an excellent collection of finds from the site. Other significant finds may be seen at Shrewsbury Museum.

Checklist of Latin and English Place Names

―――

(For names of Roman provinces, see map on pages 10–11)

LATIN PLACE NAME	LATER/MODERN NAME
Abonae	Sea Mills
Alauna	Maryport
Andematunnum	Langres, in Champagne, France
Antipolis	Antibes, France
Arbeia	South Shields
Augusta Suessonium	Soissons, France
Augustodunum	Autun, France
Baeterra	Béziers, France
Banna	Birdoswald
Barcino	Barcelona, Spain
Blestium	Monmouth
Bonna	Bonn, Germany
Branodunum	Leintwardine
Bremenium	High Rochester
Bremetenacum Veteranorum	Ribchester
Brocolita	Carrawburgh
Burrium	Usk
Caledonia	Scotland
(generally north of the Forth–Clyde isthmus)	
Calleva Atrebatum	Silchester
Camerinum	Camerino, Italy
Camulodunum	Colchester
Cataractonium	Catterick
Carcasso	Carcassonne, France
Carthago Nova	Cartagena, Spain
Centumcellae	Civitavecchia, Italy

Cilurnum Chesters
Coccium Wigan
Colonia Agrippina Cologne, Germany
(in full, *Colonia Claudia Ara Agrippinensium*)
Condate Northwich
Condercum Benwell
Coria Corbridge
Corinium Dobunnorum Cirencester
Cunetio Mildenhall
Derventio Papcastle
(also the name of several rivers,
including the Derwent and Dart,
and the Roman fort and town
at Littlechester, Derbyshire)
Deva Chester
Dubris Dover
Durnovaria Dorchester
Durobrivae Rochester
Durovernum Cantiacorum Canterbury
Eboracum York
Forum Iulii Fréjus, France
Gades Cadiz, Spain
Galava Ambleside
Gesoriacum Boulogne, France
Glannoventa Ravenglass
Glevum Gloucester
Gobannium Abergavenny
Isca Augusta Caerleon
Isca Dumnoniorum Exeter
Isurium Brigantum Aldborough
Lemonum Poitiers, France
Letocetum Wall
Lindum Lincoln
Londinium London
Lugdunum Lyon, France
Luguvalium Carlisle
Magnis Carvoran

Magnis	Kenchester
Maia	Bowness-on-Solway
Mamucium	Manchester
Massilia	Marseille, France
Mediolanum	Whitchurch
Narbonensis	Narbonne, France
Noviomagus	Crayford
Noviomagus Regnorum	Chichester
Oceanus Britannicus	English Channel
Pons Aelius	Newcastle upon Tyne
Pontes/Pontibus	Staines
Pontus Euxinus	Black Sea
Portus Lemanis	Lympne
Puteoli	Pozzuoli, Italy
Ratae Corieltauvorum	Leicester
Regulbium	Reculver
Rutupiae	Richborough
Salinae	Middlewich
Samarobriva	Amiens, France
Segedunum	Wallsend
Spina [*Spinis*]	settlement near Speen or Woodspeen
Tibur	Tivoli, Italy
Tolosa	Toulouse, France
Uxelodunum	Stanwix
Vagniacis	Springhead
Vallum Aelii	Hadrian's Wall
Venta Belgarum	Winchester
Venta Silurum	Caerwent
Vercovicium	Housesteads
Verlucio	Sandy Lane
Verulamium	St Albans
Vienna	Vienne, France
Vindolanda	Chesterholm
Vinovia	Binchester
Viroconium Cornoviorum	Wroxeter

Bibliography

——

ACCADEMIA ERCOLANESE DI ARCHEOLOGIA, *Le Antichità di Erocolano*, Vol. III (Naples, 1762)

ADAMS, C. and R. Laurence (eds), *Travel and Geography in the Roman Empire* (London and New York, 2001)

ADAMS, C.E.P., 'Feeding the Wolf: Logistics and the Roman Army', *Journal of Roman Archaeology*, Vol. 14 (2001): pp. 465–72

ADAMS, J.N., 'British Latin: The Text, Interpretation and Language of the Bath Curse Tablets', *Britannia*, Vol. 23 (1992): pp. 1–26

——, *The Regional Diversification of Latin 200 BC–AD 600* (Cambridge, 2007)

AICHER, P.J., *Rome Alive: A Source-Guide to the Ancient City*, Vols 1 and II (Wauconda, IL, 2004)

ALLASON-JONES, L., 'Health Care in the Roman North', *Britannia*, Vol. 30 (1999): pp. 133–46

——(ed.), *Artefacts in Roman Britain: Their Purpose and Use* (Cambridge, 2011)

ANDRÉ, J.-M. and M.-F. Baslez, *Voyager dans l'antiquité* (Paris, 1993)

ANDREWS, P., 'Springhead, Kent: Old Temples and New Discoveries' in D. Rudling (ed.), *Ritual Landscapes of Roman South-East Britain* (Oxford and Great Dunham, 2008): pp. 45–62

AUSTEN, P.S. and D. Breeze, 'A New Inscription from Chesters on Hadrian's Wall', *Archaeologia Aeliana*, Vol. VII (1979): pp. 114–26

AYMARD, Jacques, *Essai sur les chasses romaines* (Paris, 1951)

BARRATT, A.A., 'Knowledge of the Literary Classics in Roman Britain', *Britannia*, Vol. 9 (1978): pp. 307–13

——, 'Claudius' British Victory Arch in Rome', *Britannia*, Vol. 22 (1991): pp. 1–19

BARTUS, D. and J.M. Grimm, 'A Knife Handle from Caerwent (Venta Silurum) Depicting Gladiators', *Britannia*, Vol. 41 (2010): pp. 321–4

BASS, G.F., 'Underwater Excations at Yassi Ada: A Byzantine Shipwreck', *American Archaeology* (1962): pp. 537–64

BATEMAN, N., *Roman London's Amphitheatre*, Museum of London Archaeology (London, 2011)

BATEMAN, N., C. Cowan and R. Wroe-Brown, *London's Roman Amphitheatre: Guildhall Yard, City of London*, Museum of London Archaeology Services Monograph 35 (London, 2008)

BEARD, M., 'A British Dedication from the City of Rome', *Britannia*, Vol. XI (1980): pp. 313–40

BEARD, M., J. North and S. Price, *Religions of Rome*, Vols I and II (Cambridge, 1998)

BEDOYERE, G. de la, *Gods with Thunderbolts: Religion in Roman Britain* (Stroud, 2002)

BEHR, C.A., *Aelius Aristides and the Sacred Tales* (Amsterdam, 1968)

———, *Aelius Aristides: The Complete Works Translated into English*, Vol. 2, *Orations XVII–LIII* (Leiden, 1981)

BENNETT, J., *Sea Mills, the Roman Town of Abonae: Excavations at Nazareth House 1972*, City of Bristol Museum and Art Gallery Monograph 3 (Bristol, 1985)

BIDWELL, P., *Hadrian's Wall Bridges* (London, 1989)

———, 'The Exterior Decoration of Roman Buildings in Britain' in P. Johnson with I. Haynes (eds), *Architecture in Roman Britain*, Council for British Archaeology Research Report 94 (York, 1996): pp. 19–32

BIDWELL, P. *et al.*, 'The Roman Fort at Newcastle upon Tyne', special issue of *Archaeologia Aeliana*, 5th Series, Vol. XXXI (2002)

BIRD, D.G., 'The Environs of Londinium: Roads, Roadside Settlements and the Countryside' in I. Haynes, H. Sheldon and L. Hannigan (eds), *London Underground: The Archaeology of a City* (2000): pp. 9–34

BIRLEY, A., *The People of Roman Britain* (London, 1979)

———, *The Fasti of Roman Britain* (Oxford, 1981)

———, *Hadrian: The Restless Emperor* (London, 1997)

———, *Garrison Life at Vindolanda: A Band of Brothers* (Stroud, 2002)

———, *The Roman Government of Britain* (Oxford, 2005)

———, 'Two Governors of Dacia Superior and Britain', *Graecia, Roma, Barbaricum* (Iasi, 2013): pp. 241–60

BIRLEY, E., *Roman Britain and the Roman Army* (1961)

BISHOP, M.C., 'The Camomile Street Soldier Reconsidered', *Transactions of the London and Middlesex Society*, Vol. 34 (1983): pp. 31–48

BLACK, E.W., *Cursus Publicus: The Infrastructure of Government in Roman Britain*, British Archaeological Reports British Series 241 (Oxford, 1995)

BLAGG, T.F.C., 'Architectural Munificence in Britain: The Evidence of the Inscriptions', *Britannia*, Vol. 21 (1990): pp. 13–32

——, 'The External Decoration of Romano-British Buildings' in P. Johnson with I. Hayes (eds), *Architecture in Roman Britain*, Council for British Archaeology Research Report 94 (York, 1996): pp. 9–18

BLAGG, T.F.C. and A.C. King (eds), *Military and Civilian in Roman Britain: Cultural Relationships in a Frontier Province*, British Archaeological Reports British Series 136 (Oxford, 1984)

BLAGG, T.F.C. and M. Millett (eds), *The Early Roman Empire in the West* (Oxford, 1990)

Boatwright, M.T., *Hadrian and the Cities of the Roman Empire* (Princeton, NJ, 2000)

——, *Hadrian and the City of Rome* (Princeton, NJ, 1987)

BOGAERS, J.E., 'King Cogidubnus in Chichester: Another Reading of RIB 91', *Britannia*, Vol. 10 (1979): pp. 243–54

BOON, G., *Isca: The Roman Legionary Fortress at Caerleon* (Cardiff, 1972)

——, *Silchester: The Roman Town of Calleva* (Newton Abbot, 1974)

——, 'Potters, Oculists and Eye-Troubles', *Britannia*, Vol. 14 (1983): pp. 1–12

——, 'Review: Silchester Amphitheatre', *Britannia*, Vol. 21 (1990): pp. 397–400

BOOTH, K., 'The Roman Pharos at Dover Castle', *English Heritage Historical Review*, Vol. 2 (2007), pp. 8–21

BOULAKIA J.D.C., 'Lead in the Roman World', *American Journal of Archaeology*, Vol. 76, No. 2 (1972): pp. 139–44

BOWMAN, A.K., 'Literacy in the Roman Empire: Mass and Mode' in J.H. Humphry (ed.), *Literacy in the Roman World*, Journal of Roman Archaeology Supplementary Series 3 (Ann Arbor, MI, 1990): pp. 119–31

Bowman, A.K., , *Life and Letters on the Roman Frontier: Vindolanda and Its People*, 3rd edition (London, 2003)

Bowman, A.K. and J.D. Thomas, *Vindolanda: The Latin Writing Tablets* (London, 1983)

———, 'Two Letters from Vindolanda', *Britannia*, Vol. 21 (1990): pp. 33–52

———, *The Vindolanda Writing Tablets (Tabulae Vindolandenses II)* (London, 1994)

———, *The Vindolanda Writing Tablets (Tabulae Vindolandenses III)* (London, 2003)

Bradley, M., '"It all comes out in the wash": Looking Harder at the Roman *Fullonica*', *Journal of Roman Archaeology*, Vol. 15 (2002): pp. 1–44

Breeze, D., 'The Organisation of the Career Structure of the *Immunes* and *Principales* of the Roman Army', *Bonner Jahrbücher*, Vol. 174 (1974): pp. 245–92

———, 'The Impact of the Roman Army on the Native Peoples of North Britain' in D. Breeze and B. Dobson, *Roman Officers and Frontiers*, Mavors Roman Army Researches 10 (Stuttgart, 1993)

———, *Hadrian's Wall*, English Heritage Red Guide (London, 2006)

——— (ed.), *J. Collingwood Bruce's Handbook to the Roman Wall*, 11th edition (Newcastle upon Tyne, 2006)

———, *The Frontiers of Imperial Rome* (Barnsley, 2011)

———, *The First Souvenirs: Enamelled Vessels from Hadrian's Wall* (Kendal, 2012)

Breeze, D. and B. Dobson, *Hadrian's Wall*, 4th edition (London, 2000)

Breeze, D., B. Dobson and V. Maxfield, 'Maenius Agrippa: A Chronological Conundrum', *Acta Classica*, Vol. LV (2012): pp. 17–30

Brewer, R.J., *Caerwent: Roman Town* (Cardiff, 2006)

———, *Corpus Signorum Imperii Romani: Great Britain*, Vol. 1, Fasicule 5, *Wales* (Oxford, 1986)

Brigham, T. with N. Crowley, 'Reconstructing the Basilica' in G. Milne (ed.), *From Roman Basilica to Medieval Market, Archaeology in Action in the City of London* (London, 1992)

Brunt, P.A., 'Princeps and Equites', *Journal of Roman Studies*, Vol. 73 (1983): pp. 42–75

Bull, S., *Triumphant Rider: The Lancaster Roman Cavalry Tombstone* (Lancaster, 2007)

BURNHAM, B.C. and J.L. Davies (eds), *Roman Frontiers in Wales and the Marches*, Royal Commission on the Ancient and Historical Monuments of Wales (Aberystwyth, 2010)

BURNHAM, B.C. and J.S. Wacher, *The Small Towns of Roman Britain* (London, 1990)

CAMPBELL, B., 'The Marriage of Soldiers Under the Empire', *Journal of Roman Studies*, Vol. 68 (1978): pp. 153–66

CARCOPINO, J., *Daily Life in Ancient Rome*, new edition (London, 1991)

CARRERAS MONFORT, C., *Una reconstrucción del comercio en cerámicas: la red de transportes en Britannia* (Barcelona, 1994)

CARRERAS MONFORT, C. and R. Morais (ed.), *The Western Roman Atlantic Facade: A Study of the Economy and Trade in the Mar Exterior from the Republic to the Principate*, British Archaeological Reports International Series 2162 (Oxford, 2010)

CARRINGTON, P., 'Feeding the Wolf in Cheshire: Models and (a Few) Facts' in S. Stallibrass and R. Thomas (eds), *Feeding the Roman Army: The Archaeology of Production and Supply in NW Europe* (Oxford, 2008): pp. 18–31

CASSON, L., 'Harbour and River-Boats of Ancient Rome', *Journal of Roman Studies*, Vol. 55 (1965): pp. 31–9

——, *Travel in the Ancient World* (Baltimore, MD, and London, 1994)

——, *Ships and Seamanship in the Ancient World* (Baltimore and London, 1995; first published 1971)

CHEVALLIER, R., *Voyages et déplacements dans l'empire romain* (Paris, 1988)

——, *Roman Roads* (London, 1989)

——, *Les voies romaines*, new edition (Paris, 1997)

CLARK, K., 'The Dog Assemblage' in Fulford and Clarke (eds), *Silchester, City in Transition*, op. cit.: pp. 271–8

——, 'The Dog Assemblage' in Fulford, Clarke and Eckardt (eds), *Life and Labour in Late Roman Silchester*, op. cit.: p. 195

CLEENE, M. de and M.C. Lejeune, *Compendium of Symbolic and Ritual Plants in Europe*, Vols 1 (*Trees and Shrubs*) and 2 (*Herbs*) (Ghent, 2004)

CLEERE, H., 'The *Classis Britannica*' in D.E. Johnson (ed.), *The Saxon Shore* (London 1977)

COARELLI, F., *Rome and Environs: An Archaeological Guide*, translated by J.J. Clauss and D.P. Harmon (Berkeley, CA, 2007)

COOLEY, A.E. (ed.), *Becoming Roman, Writing Latin: Literacy and Epigraphy in the Roman West, Journal of Roman Archaeology* Supplement 48 (Portsmouth, RI, 2002)

CORNEY, M., 'The Romano-British Nucleated Settlements of Wiltshire' in P. Ellis (ed.), *Roman Wiltshire and After: Papers in Honour of Ken Annable* (Devizes, 2001)

COWAN, C., *Urban Development in North-West Southwark: Excavations 1974–90*, Museum of London Archaeology Services Monograph 16 (London, 2003)

COWAN, C., F. Seeley, A. Wardle, A. Westman and L. Wheeler, *Roman Southwark Settlement and Economy: Excavations in Southwark 1973–91*, Museum of London Archaeology Services Monograph 42 (London, 2009)

CROOM, A., *Roman Clothing and Fashion* (Amberley, 2010)

———, *Running the Roman Home* (Stroud, 2011)

CROW, J., 'A Review of Current Research on the Turrets and Curtain of Hadrian's Wall', *Britannia*, Vol. 22 (1991): pp. 51–63

———, *Housesteads: A Fort and Garrison on Hadrian's Wall* (Stroud, 2004)

———, *Housesteads: Roman Fort*, English Heritage Red Guide (London, 2012)

CRUMMY, N., 'A Campanian Vessel Foot from Silchester', *Britannia*, Vol. 42 (2011): pp. 157–65

——, 'Characterising the Small Finds Assemblage from Silchester's Insula IX (1997–2009)' in M. Fulford (ed.), *Silchester and the Study of Romano-British Urbanism* (Portsmouth, RI, 2012)

CRUMMY, N. and H. Eckardt, 'Regional Identities and Technologies of Self: Nail-Cleaners in Roman Britain', *Archaeological Journal*, Vol. 160 (2003): pp. 44–69

CRUMMY, P., *City of Victory: The Story of Colchester—Britain's First Roman Town* (Colchester, 1997)

———, 'The Roman Circus at Colchester', *Britannia*, Vol. 39 (2008): pp. 15–32

CUNLIFFE, B., *Roman Bath*, Reports of the Research Committee of the Society of Antiquaries 24 (London, 1969)

———, *The Regni* (London, 1973)

———, *Roman Bath Discovered*, 4th edition (Stroud, 2000)

——, *Facing the Ocean: The Atlantic and Its Peoples* (Oxford, 2001)

—— (ed.), *The Temple of Sulis Minerva at Bath*, Vol. II, *The Finds from the Sacred Spring* (Oxford, 1988)

CUNLIFFE, B. and P. Davenport (eds), *The Temple of Sulis Minerva at Bath*, Vol. 1, *The Site* (Oxford, 1985)

DARK, K. and P. Dark, *The Landscape of Roman Britain* (Stroud, 1997)

DARK, P., 'The Pollen and Trichurid Ova from Pit 5251' in Fulford and Clarke (eds), *Silchester, City in Transition*, op. cit.: pp. 294–300

DAVIES, H., 'Designing Roman Roads', *Britannia*, Vol. 29 (1998): pp. 1–16

DAVIES, R.W., 'The Roman Military Diet', *Britannia*, Vol. 2 (1971): pp. 122–42; also in his *Service in the Roman Army*, eds. D. Breeze and V.A. Maxfield (1989): pp. 187–206

DILKE, O.A.W., *Greek and Roman Maps* (London 1985)

——, 'Itineraries and Geographical Maps in the Early and Late Roman Empires' in J.B. Harley and D. Woodward (eds), *The History of Cartography*, Vol. I, *Cartography in Prehistoric, Ancient, and Medieval Europe and the Mediterranean* (Chicago, IL, 1987)

DIONISOTTI, A.C., '"From Ausonius' Schooldays?" A Schoolbook and Its Relatives', *Journal of Roman Studies*, Vol. 72 (1982): pp. 83–125

DIXON, K.R. and P. Southern, *The Roman Cavalry* (London, 1992)

DOLONEY, K., 'A Place at the Table: The Role of Vertebrate Zooarchaeology: Within a Roman Research Agenda for Britain' in S. James and M. Millett (eds), *Britons and Romans: Advancing an Archaeological Agenda* (York, 2001)

DRAPER, S., *Landscape, Settlement and Society in Roman and Early Medieval Wiltshire*, British Archaeological Reports British Series 419 (London, 2006)

DRINKWATER, J., 'The Rise and Fall of the Gallic Julii: Aspects of the Development of the Aristocracy of the Three Gauls under the Early Empire', *Latomus*, Vol. XXXVII, No. 7 (1978): pp. 817–50

——, *Roman Gaul* (London, 1983)

DRUMMOND-MURRAY, J., P. Thompson with C. Cowan, *Settlement in Roman Southwark: Archaeological Excavations (1991–8) for the London Underground Limited Jubilee Line Extension Project*, Museum of London Archaeology Services Monograph 12 (London, 2002)

DUNCAN-JONES, R., *The Economy of the Roman Empire: Quantitative Studies* (Cambridge, 1974)

DURHAM, E., 'Symbols of Power: The Silchester Bronze Eagle and Eagles in Roman Britain', *Archaeological Journal*, Vol. 70 (2013): pp. 78–105

ECKARDT, H., *Illuminating Roman Britain* (Montagnac, 2002)

EDWARDS, B.J.N., *The Romans at Ribchester* (Lancaster, 2000)

ELLIS, P., *The Roman Baths and Macellum at Wroxeter: Excavations by Graham Webster 1955–85*, English Heritage Archaeological Report 9 (Swindon, 2000)

ELLIS EVANS, D., 'Language Contact in Pre-Roman and Roman Britain', *Aufstieg und Niedergang der Römischen Welt* (*ANRW*) Series 2.29.2 (1983)

ELLMERS, D., 'Shipping on the Rhine During the Roman Period: The Pictorial Evidence' in J. du Plat Taylor and H. Cleere (eds), *Roman Shipping and Trade: Britain and the Rhine Provinces*, Council for British Archaeology Research Report 24 (London, 1978)

EPPLETT, C., 'The Capture of Animals by the Roman Military', in *Greece and Rome*, Vol. 48 (2001): pp. 210–22

ERDKAMP, P. (ed.), *The Cambridge Companion to Ancient Rome* (Cambridge, 2013)

ERIM, K., 'A New Relief Showing Claudius and Britannia from Aphrodisias', *Britannia*, Vol. 13 (1982): pp. 277–81

FAGAN, G.G., *Bathing in Public in the Roman World* (Ann Arbor, MI, 1999)

FISHWICK, D., 'Dated Inscriptions and the *Feriale Duranum*', *Syria*, Vol. 65 (1988): pp. 349–61

———, 'The Provincial Centre at Camulodunum: Towards an Historical Context', *Britannia*, Vol. 28 (1997): pp. 31–50

FONTANELLA, F. (ed.) *Elio Aristide a Roma: traduzione e commento* (Pisa, 2007) (text based on R. Klein's edition *P. Aelii Aristides Orationem ΕΙΣ ΡΩΜΗΝ*, Darmstadt, 1982)

FRANCE, J., *Quadragesima Galliarum: L'organisation douanière des provinces alpestres, gauloises et germaniques de l'empire romain* (Rome, 2001)

FRASER, T.E., *Hadrian as a Builder and Benefactor in the Western Provinces* (London, 2006)

FRERE, S., 'Civic Pride: A Factor in Roman Town Planning', in F. Grew and B.A. Hobley (eds), *Roman Urban Topography in Britain and the*

Western Empire, Council for British Archaeology Research Report 59
(London, 1985)

FRERE, S. and M. Fulford, 'The Collegium Peregrinorum at Silchester',
Britannia, Vol. 33 (2002): pp. 167–75

FULFORD, M., *The Silchester Amphitheatre Excavations of 1979–85*,
Britannia Monograph Series 10 (London, 1989)

——, 'Britain and the Roman Empire: The Evidence for Regional and
Long Distance Trade' in R.F.J. Jones (ed.), *Roman Britain: Recent
Trends* (Sheffield, 1991)

——, 'Links with the Past: Pervasive "Ritual" Behaviour in Roman
Britain', *Britannia*, Vol. 32 (2001): pp. 199–218

——, *A Guide to Silchester: The Roman Town of Calleva Atrebatum*
(Stroud, 2002)

FULFORD, M. and A. Clarke (eds), *Silchester, City in Transition—The
Mid-Roman Occupation of Insula IX c. AD 125–250/300: A Report on
Excavations Undertaken Since 1997*, *Britannia* Monograph Series 25
(London, 2011)

FULFORD, M., A. Clarke and H. Eckardt, *Life and Labour in Late Roman
Silchester: Excavations in Insula IX Since 1997*, *Britannia* Monograph
Series No. 22 (London, 2006)

GARNSEY, P., *Famine and Food Supply in the Graeco-Roman World:
Responses to Risk and Crisis* (Cambridge, 1988)

GOETZ, G. (ed.), *Colloquia Monacensia 10*, Corpus Glossariorum
Latinorum III 651 (Leipzig, 1892)

GOLVIN, J.-C. and J.-P. Adam, *L'Europe et la Gaule romaine: voies
commerciales, moyens de transport*, exhibition catalogue (Paris, 2003)

GREEN, M., *Animals in Celtic Life and Myth* (London and New York,
1992)

GRENIER, A., *Manuel d'archéologie gallo-romaine, l'archéologie du sol*,
Part 2, Vol. 2, *Les Routes* (Paris, 1934)

——, 'La Gaule Romaine' in T. Frank (ed.), *An Economic Survey of
Ancient Rome 3: Britain, Spain, Sicily, Gaul* (Baltimore, MD, 1937)

GROCOCK, C. and S. Grainger, *Apicius: A Critical Edition* (Totnes, 2006)

GRÜNEWALD, T., *Bandits in the Roman Empire*, translated by
J. Drinkwater (London and New York, 2004)

GUEST, P., M. Luke and C. Pudney, 'Archaeological Evaluation of the
Extramural Monumental Complex ("The Southern Canabae") at

Caerleon, 2011: An Interim Report', Cardiff Sudies in Archaeology
Specialist Report 33 (Cardiff, 2012)

HALFMANN, H., *Itinera Principum: Geschichte und Typologie der
Kaiserreisen im römischen Reich* (Stuttgart, 1986)

HARRIS, W.V., 'Towards a Study of the Roman Slave Trade', *Memoirs of
the American Academy in Rome*, Vol. 36 (1980): pp. 117–40

———, *Ancient Literacy* (Cambridge, MA, 1989)

HASSALL, M., 'Britain and the Rhone Provinces: Epigraphic Evidence
for Roman Trade' in Plat Taylor and Cleere (eds), *Roman Shipping
and Trade*, op. cit.

———, 'Altars, Curses and Other Epigraphic Evidence' in W. Rodwell
(ed.), *Temples, Churches and Religion: Recent Research in Roman
Britain, with a Gazetteer of Romano-Celtic Temples in Continental
Europe*, British Archaeological Reports British Series 77 (Oxford
1980): pp. 79–89

———, 'London as Provincial Capital' in J. Bird, M. Hassall and H. Sheldon
(eds), *Interpreting Roman London: Papers in Memory of Hugh
Chapman* (Oxford, 1996): pp. 19–27

———, 'The 2nd-Century AD Garrison of Londinium' in John Shepherd
(ed.), *The Discovery of the Roman Fort at Cripplegate, City of London:
Excavations by W.F. Grimes 1947–68* (London, 2012)

HASSALL, M.W.C. and R.O.S. Tomlin, 'Roman Britain in 2002',
Britannia, Vol. 34 (2003): pp. 362–3

HENIG, M., *The Art of Roman Britain* (London, 1995)

———, *Religion in Roman Britain*, 2nd edition (London, 1995)

HETHERINGTON, D., T. Lord and R. Jacobi, 'New Evidence for the
Occurrence of Eurasian Lynx (*Lynx lynx*) in Medieval Britain',
Journal of Quaternary Science, Vol. 21 (2006): pp. 3–8

HILL, J. and P. Rowsome, *Roman London and the Walbrook Stream
Crossing: Excavations at 1 Poultry and Vicinity, City of London*, Parts
I and II, Museum of London Archaeology Services Monograph 37
(London, 2011)

HOBSON, B., *Latrinae et Foricae: Toilets in the Roman World* (London,
2009)

HODGSON, N. (ed.), *Hadrian's Wall 1999–2009: A Summary of
Excavation and Research Prepared for the Thirteenth Pilgrimage of
Hadrian's Wall, 8–14 August 2009* (Kendal, 2009)

————, *Chesters Roman Fort*, English Heritage Red Guide (London, 2011)

————, *Roman Corbridge*, English Heritage Red Guide (London, 2015)

————, 'Divide and Conquer: Hadrian's Wall and the Native Population', *Current Archaeology* (April 2013)

HOPKINS, H. 'Taxes and Trade in the Roman Empire (200 BC–400 AD)', *Journal of Roman Studies*, Vol. 70 (1980): pp. 101–25

HOPKINS, K. and M. Beard, *The Colosseum* (London, 2005)

HORNUM, M.B., *Nemesis, the Roman State and the Games* (Leiden, 1993)

HOSTETTER, E. and T. Noble Howe (eds), *The Romano-British Villa at Castle Copse, Great Bedwyn* (Bloomington, IN, 1997)

HULL, M.R., 'The Roman Potters' Kilns of Colchester', *Society of Antiquaries (London) Research Report 21* (1963): pp. 47–74

HYLAND, A., *Equus: the Horse in the Roman World* (New Haven, CT, 1990)

ILES, P. and D. Shotter, *Lancaster's Roman Cemeteries* (Lancaster, 2010)

JACKSON, K., *Language and History in Early Britain* (Edinburgh, 1953)

JACKSON, R., 'The Chester Gladiator Rediscovered', *Britannia*, Vol. 14 (1983): pp. 87–95

JARRETT, M.G., 'Non-Legionary Troops in Roman Britain: Part One, the Units', *Britannia*, Vol. 25 (1994): pp. 35–77

JENKINS, F., 'Role of the Dog in Romano-Gaulish Religion', *Latomus* (1957): pp. 60–76

JENNISON, G., *Animals for Show and Pleasure in Ancient Rome* (Manchester, 1937)

JONES, A.H.M., 'The Roman Civil Service (Clerical and Sub-Clerical Grades)', *Journal of Roman Studies*, Vol. 39 (1949): pp. 38–55

JONES, B. and I. Keillar, 'Marinus, Ptolemy and the Turning of Scotland', *Britannia*, Vol. 27 (1996): pp. 43–50

JONES, P., *Roman and Medieval Staines: The Development of the Town* (Kingston, Surrey, 2010)

KEAY, S., *Roman Spain* (London 1988)

KEAY, S., M. Millett, L. Paroli and K. Strutt, *Portus: An Archaeological Survey of the Port of Imperial Rome*, Archaeological Monographs of the British School at Rome 15 (London, 2005)

KEAY, S. (ed.), *Portus and Its Hinterland*, Archaeological Monographs of the British School at Rome 18 (London, 2011)

KEAY, S. (ed.), *Rome, Portus and the Mediterranean*, Archaeological Monographs of the British School at Rome 21 (London, 2012)

KING, A., 'Animals in the Roman Army' in A. Goldsworthy and I. Haynes (eds), *Roman Britain: Recent Trends* (Sheffield, 1999)

KLEBERG, T., *Hôtels, restaurants et cabarets dans l'antiquité romaine: études historiques et philologiques* (Uppsala, 1957)

LA REGINA, A. (ed.), *Lexicon Topographicum urbis Romae: Suburbium*, Vols 1–5 (Rome, 2001–8)

LANNA, S., *Mesomede Inno a Φύσις: Introduzione, testo critico, traduzione e commento*, Seminari Romani di Cultura Greca 15 (Rome, 2013)

LEARY, J. and D. Field, *Story of Silbury Hill* (London, 2010)

LEARY, J., D. Field and G. Campbell (eds), *Silbury Hill* (London, 2013)

LIDDLE, A., *Arrian: Periplus Ponti Euxini*, with introduction, translation and commentary (Bristol, 2003)

LING, R., 'A Stranger in Town: Finding the Way in an Ancient City', *Greece and Rome*, Vol. 37 (1990): pp. 204–14

MARGARY, I., *Roman Roads in Britain*, 3rd edition (London, 1973)

MARSDEN, P., 'A Boat of the Roman Period Discovered on the Site of New Guy's House, Bermondsey, 1958', *Transactions of the London and Middlesex Archaeological Society*, Vol. 21 (1965): pp. 118–31

——, 'The County Hall Ship', *Transactions of the London and Middlesex Archaeological Society*, 21 (1965): pp. 109–17

——, *A Roman Ship from Blackfriars, London*, Guildhall Museum (London 1967)

——, *International Journal of Nautical Archaeology*, Vol. 5 (1976): pp. 23–55

——, *Ships of the Port of London: First to Eleventh Centuries*, English Heritage Archaeological Report 3 (1994)

MASON, D.J.P., 'The Roman Site at Heronbridge, Near Chester, Cheshire: Aspects of Civilian Settlement in the Vicinity of Legionary Fortresses in Britain and Beyond', *Archaeological Journal*, Vol. CXLV (1988): pp. 123–57

——, *Roman Chester: City of the Eagles* (Stroud, 2001)

——, *Roman Britain and the Roman Navy* (Stroud, 2003)

MATTINGLY, D., 'Being Roman: Expressing Identity in a Provincial Setting', *Journal of Roman Archaeology*, Vol. 17 (2004): pp. 5–25

MEIGGS, R., *Roman Ostia*, 2nd edition (Oxford, 1973)

MERRIFIELD, R., *London: City of the Romans* (London, 1983)

MILLAR, F., *The Roman Empire and Its Neighbours*, 2nd edition (London, 1981)

——, *The Emperor in the Roman World*, 2nd edition (London, 1992)

MILNE, G., *The Port of Roman London* (London, 1985)

——, 'Maritime Traffic Between the Rhine and Roman Britain: A Preliminary Note' in S. McGrail (ed.), *Maritime Celts, Frisians and Saxons*, Council for British Archaeology Research Report 71 (1990): pp. 82–4

MOMMSEN, Th., *Römisches Staatsrecht*, Vol. II, 3rd edition (Lepzig, 1887)

——, *Le Droit public romain*, Vol. III, translated from the German by P. Girard (Paris, 1893)

MORLEY, N., 'Populations: Size and Social Structure', in P. Erdkamp (ed.), *The Cambridge Companion to Ancient Rome* (Cambridge, 2013)

NEAL, D.S. and S.R. Cosh, *The Roman Mosaics of Britain*, Vol. III, *South-East Britain Including London* (London, 2009)

NIXON, C.E.V. and B. Saylor Rodgers, *In Praise of Later Roman Emperors: The Panegryrici Latini—Introduction, Translation and Historical Commentary, With the Latin Text of R.A.B. Mynors* (Berkeley, CA, 1994)

NOY, D., *Foreigners at Rome: Citizens and Strangers* (London, 2000)

O'BRIEN, L. and B. Roberts, 'Excavations on Roman Ermine Street at the New Restaurant Facility, GlaxoSmithKline, Ware', *Hertfordshire Archaeology and History*, Vol. 14 (2004–5): pp. 3–39

OPPER, T., *Hadrian: Empire and Conflict*, British Museum exhibition catalogue (London, 2008)

PEACOCK, D.P.S., 'The Rhine and the Problem of Gaulish Wine in Roman Britain', in Plat Taylor and Cleere (eds), *Roman Shipping and Trade*, op. cit.: pp. 49ff.

PERRING, D., *Roman London* (London, 1991)

——, *The Roman House in Britain* (Oxford, 2002)

PERRING, D. and T. Brigham, 'Londinium and Its Hinterland: The Roman Period', in K. Frederick, P. Garwood, P. Hinton, M. Kendall and E. Macadam (eds), *The Archaeology of Greater London: An Assessment of Archaeological Evidence for Human Presence in the Area Now Covered by Greater London* (London, 2000)

Pflaum, H.G., *Les Procurateurs équestres sous le Haut-Empire Romain* (Paris, 1950)

Phang, S.E., *The Marriage of Roman Soldiers (13 BC–AD 235): Law and the Family in the Imperial Army* (Leiden, 2001)

Philp, B., *The Excavation of the Roman Forts of the Classis Britannica at Dover 1970–1977* (Dover, 1981)

Picard, G.C., 'Ostie et la Gaule de l'Ouest', *Mélanges de l'Ecole Française de Rome Antiquité*, Vol. 93, No. 2 (1981): pp. 883–915

Piso, I., *Fasti Provinciae Daciae I: Die senatorischen Amsträger* (Bonn, 2003)

———, *Fasti Provinciae Daciae II: Die ritterlischen Amsträger* (Bonn, 2013)

Pitt, K., *Roman and Medieval Development South of Newgate: Excavations at 3–9 Newgate Street and 16–17 Old Bailey, City of London*, Museum of London Archaeology Services Monograph 14 (London, 2006)

Plat Taylor, J. du and H. Cleere (eds), *Roman Shipping and Trade: Britain and the Rhine Provinces*, Council for British Archaeology Research Report 24 (London, 1978)

Pomey, P. (ed.), *La Navigation dans l'antiquité* (Aix-en-Provence, 1999)

Proctor, J., *Faverdale, Darlington: Excavations at a Major Settlement in the Northern Frontier Zone of Roman Britain*, Pre-Construct Archaeology Monograph 15 (Darlington, 2012)

Reardon, B.P. (ed.), *Collected Ancient Greek Novels* (Berkeley and Los Angeles, CA, 1989)

Remesal Rodriguez , J., 'Baetican Olive Oil and the Roman Economy', in S. Keay (ed.), *The Archaeology of Early Roman Baetica*, *Journal of Roman Archaeology* Supplementary Series 29 (Portsmouth, RI, 1998): pp. 183–99

Ricci, C., *Orbis in Urbe. Fenomeni migratori nella Roma imperiale* (Rome, 2005)

Rickman, G., *The Corn Supply of Ancient Rome* (Oxford, 1980)

Rivet, A.L.F. and C. Smith, *The Place-Names of Roman Britain* (London, 1979)

Robinson, M., 'The Macroscopic Plant and Invertebrate Remains' in Fulford and Clarke, *Silchester, City in Transition*, op. cit.: pp. 281–93

ROGERS, I.R. and D.J. Garner, *Wilderspool and Holditch: Roman Boom-Towns on the 'Road North'*, British Archaeological Reports British Series 449 (Oxford, 2007)

The Roman Inscriptions of Britain (RIB), Vol. I eds. R.G. Collingwood and R.P. Wright (Oxford, 1965); Vol. II (8 fascicules), eds. SS. Frere and R.S.O. Tomlin (Oxford, 1990–5); Vol. III, eds. R.S.O. Tomlin, R.P. Wright and M.H. Hassall (Oxford, 2009)

ROTH, J., *The Logistics of the Roman Army at War (264 BC–AD 235)* (Leiden, 1999)

ROUGÉ, J., 'La Navigation hivernale sous l'empire romain', *Revue des Études Anciennes*, Vol. 54 (1952): pp. 316–52

———, *Recherches sur l'organisation du commerce maritime en Méditerraneé sous l'empire romain* (Paris, 1966)

SAILLANT, P.-Y. and C. Sanchez, *La Voie de Rome entre Mediterranée et Atlantique*, exhibition catalogue (n.p., 2008)

SAINT-DENIS, E. de, 'Mare Clausum', *Revue des Études Latines* (1947): pp. 196–214

SARTORIO, G.P., *Mezzi di trasporto e traffico*, Vita e costumi dei Romani Antichi 6 (Rome, 1994)

SCHEIDEL, W., I. Morris and R. Saller (eds), *The Cambridge Economic History of the Greco-Roman World* (Cambridge, 2007)

SCOBIE, A., 'Slums, Sanitation and Mortality in the Roman World', *Klio*, Vol. 68 (1986): pp. 399–433

———, 'Spectator Security and Comfort at Gladiatorial Games', *Nikephoros*, Vol. 1 (1988): pp. 191–243

SESTILI, A. (ed.), *Arrian Cynegetica: Il Cinegetico trattato sulla caccia—introduzione, traduzione e note* (Turin, 2011)

SHERWIN-WHITE, A., *The Letters of Pliny: A Historical and Social Commentary* (Oxford, 1966)

SHOTTER, D., *Romans and Britons in North-West England*, 3rd edition (Lancaster, 2004)

SKEAT, T.C. (ed.), *Greek Papyri in the British Museum*, Vol. VII, *The Zenon Archive* (London, 1974)

SMITH, C., 'Vulgar Latin in Roman Britain: Epigraphic and Other Evidence', *Aufstieg und Niedergang der Römischen Welt* (*ANRW*), 2.29.2 (1983): pp. 893–948

SOLLEY, T.W.J., 'Roman Remains from the Severn Bridge Approach at Aust', *Transactions of the Bristol and Gloucestershire Archaeological Society*, Vol. 85 (1966): pp. 36–44

SORDI, M., 'L'epigrafe di un pantomimo', *Epigraphica*, Vol. 15 (1953): p. 104

SPEIDEL, M.P., *Emperor Hadrian's Speeches to the African Army: A New Text* (Regensburg, 2007)

STALLIBRASS, S. and R. Thomas (eds), *Feeding the Roman Army: The Archaeology of Production and Supply in NW Europe* (Oxford, 2008)

STEINBY, E.M. (ed.), *Lexicon Topographicum urbis Romae*, Vols 1–6 (Rome, 1993–2000)

SYME, R., 'Journeys of Hadrian', *Zeitschrift für Papyrologie und Epigraphik*, Vol. 73 (1988): pp. 159–70

———, *The Provincial at Rome* (Exeter, 1999)

TALBERT, R.J.A., *The Senate of Imperial Rome* (Princeton, NJ, 1984)

TCHERNIA, A. and J.-P. Brun, *Le Vin romain antique* (Grenoble, 1999)

TIMBY, J., 'The Pottery', in Fulford and Clarke, *Silchester, City in Transition*, op. cit.: pp. 143–203

TERPSTRA, T., *Trading Communities in the Roman World: a micro-economic and institutional perspective* (Leiden, 2013)

TODD, M., 'Roman Britain, British Leaders (55 BC–AD 84)', *Oxford Dictionary of National Biography* (Oxford, 2004)

TOMLIN, R.S.O., 'Inscriptions on Metal Vessels' pp. 55–59 and 'The Curse Tablets' pp. 59–270 in B. Cunliffe (ed.), *The Temple of Sulis Minerva at Bath*, Vol. 2, *The Finds From the Sacred Spring* (Oxford, 1988)

———, 'Roman Manuscripts from Carlisle: The Ink-Written Tablets', *Britannia*, Vol. 29 (1998): pp. 31–84

———, '"The Girl in Question": A New Text from Roman London', *Britannia*, Vol. 34 (2003): pp. 41–51

TOYNBEE, J.M.C., *Art in Roman Britain* (Oxford, 1962)

TYLECOTE, R.F., 'Roman Lead Working in Britain', *British Journal for the History of Science*, Vol. 2, No. 1 (1964): pp. 25–43

VÁRHELYI, Z., *The Religion of Senators in the Roman Empire: Power and the Beyond* (Cambridge, 2010)

VARONE, A., *Erotica Pompeiana: Love Inscriptions on the Walls of Pompeii* (Rome, 2002)

Victoria County History of Hampshire and the Isle of Wight, Vol. IV (London, 1912)

WACHER, J., *The Towns of Roman Britain*, 2nd edition (London, 1995)

WHITE, R., *Wroxeter: Roman City*, English Heritage Red Guide (London, 2011)

WHITE, R. and P. Barker, *Wroxeter: The Life and Death of a Roman City* (Stroud, 1998)

WIEDEMANN, T., *Emperors and Gladiators* (London and New York, 1992)

WILD, J.P., *Textile Manufacture in the Northern Provinces* (Cambridge, 1970)

——, 'Bath and the Identification of the Caracalla', *Britannia*, Vol. 17 (1986): pp. 352–3

——, 'The Textile Industries of Roman Britain', *Britannia*, Vol. 33 (2002): pp. 1–42

WILMOTT, T., 'Cohors I Aelia Dacorum: A Dacian Unit on Hadrian's Wall', *Acta Musei Napocensis*, Vol. 38 (Cluj-Napoca, 2001): pp. 103–23

——, *Birdoswald Roman Fort*, English Heritage Red Guide (London, 2005)

——, *The Roman Amphitheatre in Britain* (Stroud, 2008)

——, *Richborough and Reculver*, English Heritage Red Guide (London, 2012)

WILSON, P., *Lullingstone Roman Villa*, English Heritage Red Guide (London, 2009)

WOOLF, G., *Becoming Roman: The Origins of Provincial Civilization in Gaul* (Cambridge, 1998)

——, 'How the Latin West Was Won', in Cooley (ed.), *Becoming Roman*, op. cit.

——, 'Pliny's Province' in T. Bekker-Nielson (ed.), *Rome and the Black Sea Region* (Aarhus, 2006)

WRIGHT, R.P., 'A Hadrianic Building Inscription from Hardknott', *Transactions of the Cumberland and Westmorland Archaeological and Antiquarian Society*, Vol. 65 (1965): pp. 169–75

YEGUL, F., *Baths and Bathing in Classical Antiquity* (Cambridge, MA, 1992)

YOUTIE, H.C. and J.G. Winter, *Papyri and Ostraca from Karanis*, Michigan Papyri Vol. VIII (Ann Arbor, MI, 1951)

YULE, B., *A Prestigious Roman Building Complex on the Southwark Waterfront: Excavations at Winchester Palace, London, 1983–90*,

Museum of London Archaeology Services Monograph 23 (London, 2005)

ZANT, J., *The Carlisle Millennium Project Excavations in Carlisle 1998–2001*, Vols I and II (Lancaster, 2009)

ZIENKIEWICZ, J.D., *The Legionary Fortress Baths at Caerleon*, Vol. I, *The Buildings* (Cardiff, 1986)

——, *The Legionary Fortress Baths at Caerleon*, Vol. II, *Finds* (Cardiff, 1986)

USEFUL WEBSITES

LATIN LIBRARY:
for a variety of useful classical links and texts,
www.thelatinlibrary.com

OSTIA, HARBOUR OF ANCIENT ROME:
www.ostia-antica.org

ROMAN LAW LIBRARY:
with a good internet resources page, including links to
papyrology resources,
www.droitromain.upmf-grenoble.fr

VINDOLANDA TABLETS ONLINE:
www.vindolanda.csad.ox.ac.uk

Notes to the Text

———

Unless otherwise indicated in the Notes that follow, citations of texts by Greek and Roman authors refer to editions in the Loeb Classical Library (1912–), published by Heinemann and later by Harvard University Press. My English translations are based upon them. For Dio Cassius, the standard edition is by U.P. Boissevain (5 vols, 1895–1931) and the Loeb English translation (1927), edited by E. Cary, is numbered one book higher than Boissevain. The Loeb numbering is used here. For Tacitus, and for Pliny the Younger, the Oxford Texts have been used.

Short-form citations such as 'Opper (2008)' refer to items appearing in the Bibliography.

ABBREVIATIONS

The following abbreviations are used in the Notes:

CIL   *Corpus Inscriptionum Latinarum* (1862–)

ILS   *Inscriptiones Latinae Selectae* (1892–1916)

RIB   *The Roman Inscriptions of Britain*, Volume I, *Inscriptions on Stone*, compiled by R.G. Collingwood and R.P. Wright, edition with addenda and corrigenda by R.S.O Tomlin (Stroud, 1995); Volume II, *Instrumentum Domesticum*, Fascicles 1–8, edited by S.S. Frere *et al.* (Stroud, 1990–5)

SHA   *Scriptores Historiae Augustae*

I. ROME, HEART OF EMPIRE

1. 'Their boundary is the ocean both where the sun god rises and where he sinks, while they control the entire Mediterranean and all its islands as well as Britain in the ocean,' writes Appian of Alexandria (*Preface to History of Romans*), 9. Appian was living in Rome after AD 120.

2. Halfmann (1986), p. 193; pp. 204–7.

3. Sordi (1953), p. 104.

4. For his life and career, and that of his father, see Birley (2005), pp. 249–50.

5. CIL II 4509 = 6145; ILS 1029.

6. The area around Tivoli was popular with the Spanish elite: Opper (2008), p. 135 and footnote 7. Hadrian's Villa Tiburtina was designed as a public space as much as a private one, and the emperor conducted imperial business there: Opper (2008), p. 159.

7. This number of *insulae*, which is taken from fourth-century descriptions of Rome, is considered to be extremely high, and many argue for a more conservative figure. For a discussion on the size of Rome, see Morley (2013), pp. 29–45.

8. Pseudo Sextus Aurelius Victor (*Epitome de Caesaribus*) 13.

9. The grain dole was regarded as a privilege, rather than as a handout for the destitute. Those eligible were assigned a specific day of the month and collection point. At the time of Augustus, some 200,000 of Rome's population received a monthly handout. From the time of Trajan, 5,000 boys became eligible as a special mark of favour. See Rickman (1980), pp. 184 and 179–97 for the way corn was distributed and the likely size of queues during the month. See also ILS 6069 = CIL VI 10224 *C(aius) Sergius C(ai) fil(ius) Alcimus/ vixit ann(is) III mensib(us) III/ diebus tribus/ frumentum accepit/ die x ostio XXXIX*, 'In memory of Gaius Servius Alcimus, son of Gaius, who lived 3 years, 3 months and 3 days. He received grain on the 10th day from entrance arcade 39', which is cited in Aicher (2004) Vol. 1, pp. 222–5 and Vol. II, p. 130.

10. There are numerous references to attempts to ban traffic in the city and various exemptions, such as for public building works. SHA (*Hadrian*) XX states that Hadrian banned heavy wagons entering Rome and banned riding on horseback in the cities.

11. Suetonius (*Augustus*) 7. It was once owned by Suetonius, who presented it to Hadrian. It showed Augustus as a boy, and Hadrian kept it in

honour among the household gods in his bedroom.

12. Suetonius (*Nero*) 38.

13. Boatwright (1987), p. 101 and footnote 5.

14. Even non-combatant auxiliaries at the faraway fort of High Rochester, north of Hadrian's Wall in the mid-second century, set up an altar to *Dea Roma n(atali) eius*, 'Goddess Roma on her birthday'. RIB 1270, see Hassall (1980), p. 82.

15. Opper (2008), p. 119.

16. SHA (*Hadrian*) XI, 2.

17. Opper (2008), p. 104 and footnote 15.

18. The Porticus Aemilia was 90 metres (295 feet) from the river and was of immense size: 487 metres long and 60 metres wide (1,600 × 197 feet), with its interior divided by 294 piers into a series of rooms, arranged seven rows deep. It is depicted with 'remarkable precision' on the Severan Marble Plan (Coarelli, 2007), p. 345.

19. By the end of its life, in the mid-third century, it contained the broken remains of an estimated 24.75 million amphorae, which once contained some 1.7 billion kilos of olive oil. Today it stands more than 40 metres (130 feet) high with a perimeter of 1 kilometre (3,300 feet) or more. More than 80 per cent of the oil came from Baetica in south-western Spain. Baetican imports reached their peak during the second century, when they comprised between 90 and 95 per cent of the total. See Remesal Rodriguez (1998), pp. 183–99.

20. Opper (2008), p. 38.

21. Men such as L. Marius Phoebus, whose name appears on many of the amphorae stamps from Monte Testaccio: see CIL VI 1935 and Noy (2008), p. 208 and footnote 41, who thinks he could have been a Roman trading with Baetica. The Spanish trade associations had Rome-based distributors, men such as the Roman *eques* (knight) C. Sentius Regulianus, a *diffusor olearius*, which probably means that he was responsible for repackaging the oil, distributing it—and dumping all those used-up amphorae on Monte Testaccio. In addition to his interests in Baetican olive oil he also described himself as a wine merchant of Lyon: CIL VI 29722, in Noy (2008), p. 208.

22. Claudius ruled that senators could visit estates in Gallia Narbonensis and Sicilia, however, without seeking this permission. See Talbert (1984), pp. 139–40.

23. In *c.* AD 139 Minicius Natalis was honoured as patron of the municipality by the people of Tibur, indicating that he had a villa there. See Millar (1981), p. 159.

24. Martial (*Epigrams*) XIII, 54 mentions ham *de Menapis* (the Menapii being a tribe in Belgic Gaul between the rivers Meuse and Scheldt) and ham from Cerretans, or Cerdana, in Spain.

25. Martial (*Epigrams*) XIV, 99: *Barbara de pictis veni bascauda Britannis; sed me iam mavolt dicere Roma suam*, 'A barbarian basket, I came from the painted Britons; but now Rome prefers to say I belong to her'.

26. Propertius (*Elegies*) II, 1.78: *esseda caelatis siste Britannia iugis*, 'stop your British chariot with its fancy harness'. *Caelatus* means figures engraved/ in bas relief.

27. Caesar (*Gallic War*) IV, 33.

28. Hyland (1990), p. 226.

29. There is very little evidence for a British presence in Rome, either in associations or as individuals. Only one fragmentary inscription has been found, dating from the third century or later, when Britannia had been divided into two provinces, 'Upper' and 'Lower' Britain (*Britannia Citerior et Inferior*). On a slab of coarse marble, found within the precinct of the church of S. Pancrazio in the area of the Villa Doria Pamphili, it records a dedication made by the *provinciae Brittann(iae)* (provincial councils of Britain). See Beard (1980), pp. 313–14.

30. Of all the surviving inscriptions of foreigners in Rome from the whole of the Roman era, only three are British, and they record deaths during military service. See CIL VI 3279 *Nig. Marinianus natione Britanicianus*; CIL VI 3301 *M. Ulpius Iustus natione Britto*; CIL VI 32861 [name lost] *natione Brit…* in Noy (2000), p. 295.

31. See, for example, Suetonius (*Caligula*) 44; Dio Cassius (*Roman History*) LX, 19; Augustus (*Res Gestae*) 32.

32. The reference to elephants taking part in the expedition is in Dio Cassius (*Roman History*) LX, 21.

33. Suetonius (*Claudius*) 17.

34. Dio Cassius (*Roman History*) LX, 21.

35. Erim (1982), pp. 277–81.

36. See, for example, *British Museum Catalogue of Coins in the Roman Empire*, Claudius 32, a gold *aureus* minted at Rome now in the collection of the British Museum, London; and the silver *didrachm* minted in

Caesarea (*British Museum Catalogue of Coins in the Roman Empire,* Claudius 237).

37. A 16th-century drawing of fragments associated with the Claudian arch shows a frieze depicting fighting between Romans and Celtic-looking barbarians and some large panels depicting a procession of Roman soldiers, possibly Praetorians. See Barratt (1991), pp. 1–19. A fragment of inscription is in the courtyard of the Palazzo dei Conservatori and other fragments of sculpture are held in the Museo Nuovo Capitolino: see Coarelli (2007), p. 255.

38. Tacitus (*Annals*) XII, 31–8.

39. Tacitus (*Annals*) XII, 36.

40. Tacitus (*Annals*) XII, 31–9, tells the story of the British uprising.

41. Dio Cassius (*Roman History*) LXI, 33. This anecdote reflected not just the sort of ambivalence about imperialism voiced by Tacitus, but perhaps criticism of Rome throwing quite so much money and resources at such an unpromising place as Britannia.

42. Dacia Superior was a praetorian province formed following Hadrian's swift reorganisation of the area as a result of unrest in the region in the last years of Trajan's reign and the start of his own. Moesia Inferior reverted to its original boundaries south of the Danube, and the territories it had encompassed north of the river became Dacia Inferior, with Trajan's original province of Dacia renamed Dacia Superior. In Dacia, Julius Severus oversaw further changes in the administration of the province when, in AD 124, it was split again, and *Dacia Porolissensis* (roughly corresponding to north-western Transylvania) was created. Perhaps it was Severus's experience of reorganizing a troublesome province as much as his reputation as one of Hadrian's best generals which led to his appointment as governor of Britannia. See Piso (2013), pp. 27–8.

43. Piso (1993), p. 44.

44. Birley, A. (1981), pp. 6–7.

45. Tacitus (*Histories*) II, 1: *et praecipui fama quartadecumani, rebellione Britanniae compressa. Addiderat gloriam Nero eligendo ut potissimos.*

46. For a discussion of Maenius Agrippa's career and uncertainties over dates in light of recent excavation at Maryport, see Breeze, Dobson, Maxfield (2012), pp. 17–30

47. Just how erratic and sketchy information about Britannia in the wider

world could be is demonstrated by Ptolemy's monumental eight-volume *Geography*, written in about AD 140–150. In compiling his section on Britain, he used sources from different periods, having access only to information about the south of Britain up to AD 70, for example, although he was a little more up-to-date with the north—despite omitting to mention Hadrian's Wall. He left out key places such as Gloucester and Caerleon, but included insignificant ones and mislocated others. Most spectacularly, Ptolemy tilted Scotland through a right angle—an error, it seems, from his mistaken corrections to information from the earlier geographer Marinus of Tyre, who produced a map of the world around the start of the second century AD. For simply collating old material, see Pliny the Younger (*Letters*) V, 8.12: *Vetera et scripta aliis? Parata inquisitio, sed onerosa collatio…*, 'Old stuff written by others? Your research is done—you just have the bore of collating it…' For Ptolemy's mistake, see Jones and Keillar (1996), pp. 43–50, and Davies (1998), pp. 1–16, for a discussion of orientation with respect to road design in Britain.

48. As Tacitus (*Agricola*) 10–12 remarked, writing decades before, 'the position and inhabitants of Britain have been recorded by many writers'.

49. Herodian (*History*) III, 14.7.

50. Vindolanda Tablet 164.

51. Cicero (*Ad Atticum*) IV, 16.7 (written in early July 54 BC).

52. Pliny (*Letters*) X, 11.2.

53. Horace (*Satires*) I, 6.101–6.

54. Josephus (*Jewish War*) V, 49; Velleius Paterculus (*History of Rome*) II, 114, for Tiberius's baggage while campaigning in Pannonia. Both cited in Roth (1999), pp. 89–90.

55. As a clothing list from the fortress at Vindolanda (just south of Hadrian's Wall, dating from the early years of the second century) shows, the commanding officer there, Flavius Cerialis, who came from Batavia (roughly the modern Netherlands), needed a bit of a helping hand in this respect from his fellow officers. The list (Vindolanda Tablet 196) mentions that some are sent from 'Tranquillus'. Birley (2002), pp. 138–9, suggests that this uncommon name may refer to Suetonius Tranquillus, for whom the younger Pliny obtained a commission in Britain, but which he did not in the event take up.

56. Suetonius (*Augustus*) 36; for the she-mules and concubines, see SHA

(*Severus Alexander*) XLII, 4; and see SHA (*The Deified Claudius*) XIV, 2ff., with its fascinating letter from Valerian to Zosimio, procurator of Syria.

57. See Talbert (1984), p. 208, and (*Digest*) 33.7.12.40–1, quoting Ulpian (*On Sabinus*) XX, describing a proconsul about to set out for his province putting tables, furniture, clothes and medicines into store.

58. Tiberius in AD 25 determined that it should be 1 June; Claudius, in AD 43, mid-April.

59. For provincial quaestors returning to Rome at the end of the proconsular year in July and before the kalends of September, cf. Pliny the Younger (*Letters*) IV, 12.4; IV, 15.6nn; V, 21 in Sherwin-White (1966). For a good discussion, see Talbert (1984), Appendix 3 and Chapter 4.2.

60. Agricola arrived in Britain in AD 77/8 to take up his governorship 'in the middle of summer', *media iam aestate*; see Tacitus (*Agricola*) 9.6 and 18.1.

61. An example of one letter of appointment survives from the time of Marcus Aurelius, because its recipient, Q. Domitius Marsianus, promoted to *procurator patrimonii* of Narbonensis, had it set up as an inscription in his home town of Marsianus, Bulla Regia, in Africa. See Millar (1992), pp. 288 and 311, for a freedman dispatched to Britain with *codicilli* nominating Agricola as governor of Syria; Tacitus (*Agricola*) 40.

62. Dio Cassius (*Roman History*) LIII, 15–16; Dio Cassius (*Epitome*) LX, 17, for the mid-April date.

63. See Pliny the Younger (*Letters*) for visits to his estates in September and October: X, 8; X, 9; III, 4; 1.7.4; VII, 30; VIII, 1

64. Pliny the Younger (*Letters*) V.21. The young quaestor Julius Avitus died at sea on his way home from a province during the summer. See note on the letter in Sherwin-White (1966), op. cit.

65. Dio Cassius (*Roman History*) LIII, 13.

66. *Vota pro itu et reditu*, 'prayers for leaving and returning': see, for example, Suetonius (*Tiberius*) 38; Suetonius (*Caligula*) 14.

67. Examples are many; see for instance Juvenal (*Satires*) 3.

II. ROME TO PORTUS OSTIENSIS

1. For a discussion of the date of the speech, see Behr (1981). For a commentary on the text and the boundaries of empire under Hadrian and Antoninus Pius, see notes on the passage in Fontanella's commentary (2007).

2. These are attested from at least the mid-second century AD. Terpstra (2013), p. 140.

3. Pliny the Younger (*Letters*) II, 17.

4. See La Regina (ed.), Vol. IV (2006), pp. 223–30, and Steinby (ed.) Vol. 5 (1999), p. 144 for Via Portuensis and p. 143 for Via Ostiensis.

5. Ovid (*Fasti*) VI, 773–86.

6. Casson (1995), p. 212 and ref. 49 citing G. Jacopi, 'Scavi in prossimità del porto fluviale di S. Paolo', *Monumenti Antichi*, Vol. 39 (1943), pp. 45–96 and plates 3–12.

7. For traffic from Rome to Ostia, the road heading through the Porta Raudusculana seems to have become more important than that from the Porta Trigemina in the Forum Boaiarum, which led through Emporium. See J.R. Patterson in Steinby, Vol. 5 (1999). For a detailed description of the Via Ostiensis route outside Rome, see La Regina, Vol. IV (2006), pp. 135–48, and of the route along Via Portuensis, pp. 223–42 of the same.

8. Juvenal (*Satires*) VI: *flava ruinosi lupa… sepulchri*; Martial (*Epigrams*) III, 93, 15: *cum te lucerna balneator extincta admittat inter bustuarias moechas*, 'when the bath attendant has extinguished his lantern, he lets you in among the grave-haunting whores'.

9. Petronius (*Satyricon*) 71: *Praeponam enim unum ex libertis sepulcro meo custodiae causa, ne in monumentum meum populus cacatum currat.*

10. CIL VI 2357: *Hospes ad hunc tumulum ni meias ossa precantur/tecta hominis [set] si gratus homo es misce bibe da mi.*

11. CIL IV 3782, 3832, 4586, 5438, in Croom (2011), p. 117.

12. Croom (2011), p. 77; for private houses, see that of Pascius Hermes, Pompei CIL IV 7716; for the arch near the forum at Thigibba in Africa, see Croom (2011).

13. Pliny the Elder described the River Tiber as 'the most gentle merchant (*mercator placidissimus*) of all that is produced on earth and perhaps with more villas built on its banks and overlooking it than all the other rivers on earth'. Pliny (*Natural History*) III, 5.54: *rerum in toto orbe*

nascentium mercator placidissimus, pluribus prope solus quam ceteri in omnibus terris amnes adcolitur adspiciturque villis.

14. Ammianus Marcellinus 17.4.14: *tertio lapide ab urbe.*
15. Symmachus had a suburban villa here in the late fourth century: Symmachus (*Epistles*) 1.6; 2.52.
16. CIL VI 3539; Birley (1990), p. 10.
17. Pliny the Younger (*Letters*), II, 17.2 and 17.3.
18. Pliny the Younger (*Letters*) II, 17.26.
19. Tacitus (*Annals*) XV, 43.4.
20. Aelius Aristides (*Orations: On Rome*) XXVI, 11.
21. In AD 133 the emperor was honoured by the city for having preserved and enhanced it with all indulgence and generosity: *colonia Ostia conservata et aucta omni indulgentia et liberalitate eius.*
22. Keay (ed.) *et al.* (2005), p. 35.
23. Suetonius (*Claudius*) 17.2; Dio Cassius (*Epitome*) LX, 21.
24. Pliny the Elder (*Natural History*) XIX, 3–4: *herbam esse quae Gadis ab Herculis columnis septimo die Ostiam adferat et citeriorem Hispaniam quarto, provam Narbonensem tertio...*
25. A singular reference to a merchant ship from Gaul at Ostia comes from an eyewitness account by the elder Pliny (*Natural History*), IX, 14–15. He described how a cargo of hides from Gaul sank at Portus while the harbour was under construction during the reign of Claudius. The hides attracted the attentions of a whale wanting to feed on them, but it became trapped and beached. The whale in turn attracted much attention, not least from the Emperor Claudius, who decided to make an entertainment of it by putting nets and ropes across the harbour and then baiting the poor creature with darts and javelins, which he and members of the Praetorian Guard threw from boats. One of the boats was submerged by water which the whale spurted out.
26. The mosaics are thought to date from the Severan period, when the theatre complex was restored by Commodus and Septimius Severus. Coarelli (2007), p. 457.
27. *Stuppatores res[tiones]*, 'tow-rope and cordmakers'; *corpus pellion(um)*, 'tanners corporation'; *codicari(i) de suo*, 'barge owners'; *navicul(arii) et negotiantes Karalitani*, 'ship owners and merchants of Cagliari'.
28. Sadly, he came to a sticky end when taken in by a charlatan oracular snake in the 160s. Lucian of Samosata (*Alexander*) 27.

29. In Achilles Tatius's mid-second-century Greek novel *Leucippe and Clitophon* the protagonists run down to the harbour to look for a ship 'and by chance even the wind seemed to invite us', as they find one on the point of throwing off its stern cables and manage to jump on board. Achilles Tatius (*Leucippe and Clitophon*) 31.

30. Juvenal conjured up the dodgiest possible clientele in a large *popina* in Ostia. Juvenal (*Satires*) 8, 171–76: … *mitte Ostia, Caesar,/ mitte, sed in magna legatum quare popina:/ invenies aliquot cum percussore iacentem. permixtum nautis et furibus ac fugitivis,/ inter carnifices et fabros sandapilarum/ et resupinati cessantia tympani Galli./ aequa ibi libertas, communia pocula, lectus/ non alius cuiquam, nec mensa remotior ulli.*

31. See, for example, Horace (*Satires*), I, 1.29: *perfidus (hic)copo*; Apuleius (*Metamorphoses*) 1.8ff. and St Augustine (*City of God*) 18.18 on landladies and poisoned cheese.

32. Seneca (*Epistles*) 104.6: *illum odorem culinarum fumantium quae motae quicquid pestiferi vaporis cum pulvere effundunt…*, 'that reeking odour of working kitchens which cover everything in pestilential steam and smoke'. For Nero imposing restrictions, see Dio Cassius (*Epitome*) LXII, 14.2; and for Vespasian, Dio Cassius (*Epitome*) LXV, 10.3.

33. CIL IV 3948, from Pompeii, in Kleberg (1957), 112.

34. A notice put up by Hedone at Pompeii CIL IV 1679 in Kleberg (1957), 107: *Edone dicit: assibus hic bibitur, dipundium si dederis, meliora bibes, quattus si dederis, vina Falerna bib(es).*

35. CIL IV 8442: *futui coponam*, found scrawled on an election poster next to a Pompeian bar (Reg. ii, 2, 3); *futui ospita*, found on a drinking vessel in Bonn, CIL XIII 10018, 95 Kleberg (1957) 90.

36. *Digest* 3.2.4.2–3, quoting Ulpian (*On the Edict*) 6: *ut puta si caupo fuit vel stabularius et mancipia talia habuit ministrantia et occasione ministerii quaestum facientia…*, 'he is liable to punishment for procurement whether this is his principal occupation, or whether he carries on another trade (for instance, if he is an inn- or tavern-keeper and has slaves of this kind serving and taking the opportunity to ply their trade)'. He also goes on to say that a *balneator*, or bath-keeper, who keeps a servant for guarding clothes and hires them out for other services would be guilty too.

37. Apicius (*The Art of Cooking*) 1.2: *conditum melizomum viatorium: conditum melizomum perpetuum, quod subministratur per viam*

peregrinanti, 'long-life honey wine used by tourists on journeys', Grocock and Grainger (2006), p. 134.

38. Petronius (*Satyricon*) CIII–CIV.

39. See Simon Keay, 'The Port System of Imperial Rome', pp. 33–70, particularly pp. 48–52, in (ed.) Keay (London, 2012).

40. Papyrus Michigan VIII, 490, for the letter from the young Egyptian naval recruit: 'I am now writing to you from Portus for I have not yet gone up to Rome and been assigned.' Papyrus Michigan VIII, 491, for the follow-up letter informing his mother that he has arrived in Rome on the same day. Both letters reproduced and translated in Youtie and Winter (1951).

41. Trajan brought out a commemorative *sestertius* showing on its reverse the buildings along sides I, III, IV and VI of the basin where a huge statue of Trajan and temple were located, although these are not shown on the coin. Keay *et al.* (2005), pp. 308–9.

42. Each side of the hexagon measured 357.77 metres (1,173 feet), with over a mile of bank around the main basin and a water surface of more than 32 hectares. This is less than half the size of Claudius's harbour.

43. Juvenal (*Satires*) 12.78–9: *non sic igitur mirabere portus quos natura dedit.*

44. A *modius* was a unit of measurement for dry goods corresponding to 566.4 cubic inches or 9.28 litres, similar in capacity to a British imperial peck (554.84 cubic inches or 9.092 litres). The figure of 20 million *modii* comes from a fourth-century epitome. For North Africa supplying twice as much as Egypt, see Josephus (*Jewish War*) II, 383, 386, writing in the mid-first century. The figures have been questioned. For a discussion, see Garnsey (1988), pp. 231–2, and Rickman (1980), pp. 118–21.

45. Tacitus (*Annals*) 43.

46. Suetonius (*Claudius*) 18.2. That ships did travel off season, often in extremely dangerous conditions, is dramatically shown in the Acts of the Apostles, when the Alexandrian grain ship bound for Rome to which St Paul is transferred as a prisoner, at Myra in Lycia, is shipwrecked while sailing in the 'closed' season, with 276 passengers on board: Acts of the Apostles 27.

47. Seneca (*Letters*) 77.1. It is not certain when the grain ships ceased to use Puteoli. It is possible that during the Hadrianic period some continued to dock here.

48. Pomey (ed.) (1999), p. 113.

49. For colours of sails, see Casson (1995), pp. 234–5 and references 45–9. He cites e.g. Pliny the Elder (*Natural History*) XIX, 22: 'Cleopatra had a purple sail when she came with Mark Antony to Actium and with the same sail she fled.' A purple sail was subsequently the distinguishing mark of the emperor's ship.

50. Aelius Aristides (*On Rome*), Oration XXVI, 13.

51. The Alexandrian grain ship that brought St Paul to Rome went under the sign of *Castor and Pollux* (Acts of the Apostles) 28.11.

52. Casson (1995), p. 358.

53. Pliny the Elder (*Natural History*) XXXV, 41: 'in painting ships of war the wax colours are melted and laid on with a brush while hot. Painting of this nature, applied to vessels, will never spoil from the action of the sun, winds, or salt water'.

54. See, for example, Catullus (*Poems*) 4: *phaselus ille, quem videtis, hospites/ ait fuisse navium celerrimus.* That phaselus which you see, guests, says she was the fastest of ships.

55. For St Paul's journey by grain ship, see Acts of the Apostles 27. For a discussion of ships' tonnage and passenger numbers, see Casson (1995), Chapter 9 Appendix, pp. 183–200.

56. Statius (*Silvae*) III, 2: *Propempticon for Maecius Celer.* A propempticon is an escort or send-off.

57. Achilles Tatius (*Leucippe and Clitophon*) 15. Melite and Clitophon have their own private cabin on the ship.

58. Literary sources only provide vague information about life below deck. In Petronius's *Satyricon*, the maid takes Giton below deck to disguise him with her mistress's false hair and eyebrows, while in a poem of Paulinus of Nola, Martinianus falls into a deep sleep in *prorae sinu*, 'in the bosom of the prow', on a hard bed (*duro cubili*), presumably meaning the floor. Paulinus of Nola (*Poems*) 24, v.167: *qui tunc remoto fessus in prorae sinu et securus innocentia,/ Ionas ut olim ventre navis abditus, somnos anhelabat graves. Sed excitatus luctuosis undique pereuntium clamoribus/ pedibusque turbae membra quassus omnia,/ duro cubili prosilit.*

59. Casson (1995), p. 176 and footnote 40, citing Paulinus of Nola (*Epistles*) 49.1; Lucian (*Zeus Tragoedus*) 48; Suetonius (*Tiberius*) 51 for bilge duty as punishment.

60. There is one that is astonishingly well preserved in the Musée d'Archéologie at Antibes.

61. Papyrus London 1979 for leather cushions in Skeat (ed.) (1974), pp. 74–5, cited in André and Baslez (1993), p. 424; see Aelius Aristides (*The Sacred Tales*) II, 65–8, and IV, 32–6, for vivid descriptions of the discomforts of sailing. Papyrus London 1979, which was written from Alexandria, mentions people having to leave their leather pillows and cushions behind because the captain cannot get them cleared through customs and they have to be sent on later. The letter, however, dates from 2 January 252 BC. The January date is interesting as the travellers have evidently sailed the Mediterranean in winter.

62. Petronius (*Satyricon*) CIX. In the *Satyricon*, Lichas, the owner of a ship that is about to go down, implores Encolpius to restore a sacred cloak and *sistrum* (ceremonial rattle), which the latter has stolen from a votive statue of Isis on board the ship. See also Achilles Tatius (*Leucippe and Clitophon*) 32.

63. A poetic version of the form such a ceremony might take is preserved in the *Anthology*: 'Phoebus Apollo, who lives on the sheer height of Leucas visible from afar to sailors, and washed by the Ionian Sea, accept from the sailors a feast of barley cake kneaded by hand and a libation mixed in a small cup, accept too, the poor light of this lamp lit from a mean little oil-flask. In return for these offerings, be kind to us and send to our sails a favourable breeze carrying us with it to the shore of Actium.' The *Greek Anthology* (Philippus) VI, 251 to Apollo: see also *The Greek Anthology* (Macedonius the Consul) VI, 69 and 70.

64. For a reconstruction drawing and description of such a kitchen based on the galley found in the excavation of a seventh-century Byzantine wreck, the *Yassi Adi I*, in Turkey, see Pomey (ed.) (1999), pp. 106 and 189–91, and also the excavation report of Bass (1962).

65. Pomey (ed.) (1999), p. 107, cites excavations where evidence for animals onboard has been found.

66. Achilles Tatius (*Leucippe and Clitophon*) 32.

67. As depicted on the third-century Torlonia relief, Museo delle Navi, Fiumicino. The arch at Richborough may also have been topped with elephants.

68. Juvenal (*Satires*) XII, 77.

69. Lucian (*Zeus Tragoedus*) 48–9.

70. The small shelter suspended over open water behind the stern post, which is depicted on some illustrations of ships, may be a latrine. Later,

medieval ships had latrines in a similar position. Casson (1995), p. 181 and footnote 61.

71. Pliny the Elder (*Natural History*) XXVIII, 52.

72. Acts of the Apostles 27.3.

73. Philo (*On the Embassy to Gaius*) XXXIII, 251–3.

74. 'At breakfast time, a young man who had settled his belongings next to ours very kindly asked us to eat with him… we put what we had together in the middle and shared both food and conversation.' A scene described by Achilles Tatius in *Leucippe and Clitophon* II, 33. Translation by John J. Winkler, in Reardon (ed.) (1989).

75. Ovid (*Tristia*) I, ii: *nec letum timeo; genus est miserabile leti;/ demite naufragium, mors mihi munus erit./ est aliquid, fatove suo ferrove cadentem/ in solida moriens ponere corpus humo/ et mandare suis aliqua et sperare sepulcrum/ et non aequoreis piscibus esse cibum.*

76. Achilles Tatius (*Leucippe and Clitophon*), III, 1–5, with translation based on that by John J. Winkler, in Reardon (ed.) (1989).

III. PORTUS OSTIENSIS TO OCEANUS BRITANNICUS

1. According to Tacitus, the assassins of Faustus Cornelius Sulla Felix—a small group of men, keen to complete their mission as fast as possible— took six days to travel to Marseille from Rome in AD 62. Tacitus (*Annals*) XIV, 57: *Sulla sexto die pervectis Massiliam percussoribus ante metum et rumorem interficitur, cum epulandi causa discumberet. Relatum caput eius inlusit Nero tamquam praematura canitie deforme,* 'Sulla was killed by the assassins who reached Marseille on the sixth day—before fear and rumour—and when he was reclining at dinner. His head was brought back [to Rome] where Nero was amused to see his unsightly prematurely grey hair.'

2. For a description, see Pliny the Younger (*Letters*) VI, 31.

3. Meiggs (1973), p. 59, but he gives no reference for this statement.

4. Pliny the Younger (*Letters*) 7.16 wrote that he hoped to persuade Calestrius Tiro, travelling to Baetica in AD 107 as the new proconsul of the province, to make a diversion to see his wife's grandfather at Ticinum on the Po River near Mediolanum (Milan) and to manumit some slaves on his behalf, which he was entitled to do through his authority as a proconsul.

5. Pliny the Elder (*Natural History*) II, 46: 'similarly in the province of Narbonne the most famous of the winds is Circius (WNW) which is inferior to none other at all in force and which usually carries a vessel right across the Ligurian Sea to Ostia'.

6. Pliny the Elder (*Natural History*) XIX, 1.

7. Sulpicius Severus (*Dialogues*) 1.1: 'landing on the 30th day at Marseilles, I came on from there and arrived here on the tenth day—so prosperous a voyage was granted to my dutiful desire of seeing you'.

8. Pliny the Elder (*Natural History*) III, 31, and see Syme (1999), p. 73, on Pliny the Younger's account of being asked: *Italicus es an provicialis?*, 'Are you Italian or from the Province?'

9. Pliny the Younger (*Letters*) 5.19.

10. Colonia Claudia Aequum, to give the city its full name. For Severus's ancestry, see Piso (1993), p. 45; see also Birley (1981), pp. 130 and 348.

11. Strabo (*Geography*) IV, 5.1–5, for routes from Gaul; Diodorus Siculus (*History*) V, 21–2, for a description of Britain and the tin trade, including the length of time it took for tin traders to cross Gaul.

12. Tacitus (*Agricola*) 4.3: *arcebat eum ab inlecebris peccantium praeter ipsius bonam integramque naturam, quod statim parvulus sedem ac magistram studiorum Massiliam habuit, locum Graeca comitate et provinciali parsimonia mixtum ac bene compositum.*

13. *The Greek Anthology* (Diodorus) VI, 245.

14. Achilles Tatius (*Leucippe and Clitophon*), 1.1.

15. P. Princeton 220. Quoted in in W. Scheidel (ed.), *The Cambridge Companion to the Roman Economy* (2012), p. 232.

16. Plutarch (*Moralia*) 518e, 'on busybodies'.

17. See Quintilian (*Declamation*) 359—a case of an altercation between a customs man and a woman wearing an expensive string of pearls: *praeter instrumenta itineris omnes res quadragesimam publicano debeant*, 'except for travelling items let all items owe 2.5 per cent excise duty'.

18. For letters of introduction, see, for example, Horace (*Letters*) XII; Pliny the Younger (*Letters*) I, 4; and Apuleius (*Metamorphoses*), 1.22.

19. Plautus (*The Soldier*) I.741.

20. Diodorus Siculus (*History*) V, 22.

21. See Carreras and Morais (2010), pp. 261–4, for a summary of the Atlantic trade routes in the first century BC and the effect of the Roman conquest of Gaul.

22. Dion (1968), 503.

23. Marcus Aurelius Lunaris, a *sevir Augustalis*—a priest of the imperial cult—at both Eboracum (York) and Lindum (Lincoln) was one such prominent Yorkshire businessman trading with Bordeaux. On his safe arrival at Burdigala in AD 237, he dedicated an altar to the presiding goddess of the city, the 'Tutela Bourdigalae', and to Salus (good health) in fulfilment of a vow he had made on leaving York. The altar is carved out of sandstone brought especially from Yorkshire (the stone local to Burdigala is limestone), and is dated AD 237. It is on display at the Musée d'Aquitaine, Bordeaux: Inv.: 60.1.354.

24. Peacock (1978), pp. 49–51.

25. The social pressure to put on gladiatorial shows eventually led to the intervention of the emperor and Senate in the late second century AD; in Woolf (1998), pp. 216–17. The inscription concerning the ruling on shows and fixing the price of gladiators for games given by city magistrates and high priests of provincial councils comes from Italica in Spain but refers to the *concilium Galliarum*; see Millar (1977), p. 195.

26. For Lugdunum as the birthplace of Claudius, see Suetonius (*Claudius*), 2; for the possibility that Claudius spent the winter at Lugdunum on his return from Britain in AD 43–44, see Halfmann (1986), pp. 172–3. Hadrian might also have overwintered at Lugdunum on his journey through the north-western provinces in AD 121–2: see Syme (1988), p. 160.

27. Hotel names in Chevallier (1983), p. 190, who also makes the pleasing suggestion that *ad Decem Pagos*, 'at the Ten Cantons', may be translated as an Inter-Continental. He also provides a list of European place names derived from the Latin *Taberna*.

28. *Mercurius hic lucrum promittit, Apollo salutem, Septumanus hospitium cum prandio, qui venerit, melius utetur post. Hospes, ubi maneas, prospice.* CIL XIII 2031 (Lyon).

29. Galen (*De alimentorum facultatibus*) 3.2, 6.66K. Galen was born in Pergamum in *c.* AD 129.

30. For sex at inns, see a curious inscription, CIL IX 2689, apparently erected by L. Calidius Eroticus (roughly equivalent to Lucius 'Hot Sex'), who 'while he was still living', made it for himself and for 'Voluptuous Fannia'. It depicts two men counting up on their fingers and the following dialogue: 'Boss, let's settle up. You had one *sextarius* of wine,

bread at one *ass*, mezze two *asses*.' 'Correct'. 'A girl, eight *asses*.' 'That's also correct'. 'Hay for the mule, two asses'. 'That mule will ruin me'. *Copo, computemus' Habes vini sextarium unum, pane(m) assem unum, pulmentar(ium) asses duos./ 'convenit'/ puell(am), asses octo'/ et hoc convenit/ faenum mulo, asses duos/ iste mulus me ad factum dabit.* It is not clear whether this is a joke between two lovers or at someone's expense or an advert for an inn.

31. For a porter at the gate, see Apuleius (*Metamorphoses*) 15.1; for a porter arranging dinner, see Petronius (*Satyricon*) 90:7.

32. Apuleius (*Metamorphoses*) I, 11: *grabatulus, alioquin breviculus et uno pede mutilus et putris*, 'my camp bed which was rather short and with one broken, rotten leg'.

33. CIL V 6668.

34. Horace (*Satires*) I, 5.7–8: *hic ego propter aquam, quod erat deterrima, ventri indico bellum, cenantis haud animo aequo expectans comites...*, 'here because of the water which was terrible, my stomach waged war with me and I had to watch my companions dine while feeling out of sorts'.

35. Horace (*Satires*) I, 5.71–2.

36. Horace (*Satires*) II, 4.58–62.

37. Appian (*Gallic Wars*) 5 (fragments preserved in Constantine Porphyrogenitus (*The Embassies*) I, 90.

38. Diodorus Siculus (*The Library of History*) V, 26. See Woolf (1998), pp. 179ff.

39. Martial (*Epigrams*) XIII, 107; XIII, 123; XIV, 118; X, 36; and see also Pliny the Elder (*Natural History*) XXIII, 47, for Marseille. See also Woolf (1998), p. 185.

40. CIL XV 4547, 4553, for more Baeterrae inscriptions.

41. Pliny the Elder (*Natural History*) XIV, 62–94.

42. CIL XIII 10018, 7, found on a curiously shaped bottle in Paris; CIL XIII 10018, 131, 157 see Kleberg (1957), p. 110. Both inscriptions are from a series of cups produced in Gaul in the third century AD.

43. Horace (*Satire*) I, 5, 82–5: *Hic ego mendacem stultissimus usque puellam ad mediam noctem exspecto; somnus tamen aufert intentum veneri; tum inmundo somnia visu nocturnam vestem maculant ventremque supinum...*

44. CIL IV 4957: *Miximus in lecto, Fateor, peccavimus, hospes. Si dices: quare? Nulla fuit matella.*

45. Croom (2010), pp. 135–6, and Wild's work *passim* on Gallic and British clothing cited in Bibliography.
46. Birley (2013), p. 10.
47. The group that accompanies Severus to Britannia would have been the sort of trusted friends, family and colleagues whom Marcus Cornelius Fronto enlisted when appointed proconsul of Asia in about AD 153–4: 'I called from home relations and friends, whose loyalty and integrity I could count on, to assist me. I wrote to my intimates at Alexandria to get to Athens as quickly as they could and wait for me there and I put these very learned men in charge of my Greek correspondence… From Mauretania also I summoned to my side Julius Senex… to help me not only through his loyalty and hard work but in his military expertise at hunting down and fighting bandits.' Fronto (*To Antoninus Pius*) 8. Fronto did not take up the post, because of ill health. See Pliny the Younger (*Letters*) X, 25, for anxiety over the late arrival—towards the end of November—of the legate Servilius Pudens in Nicomedia in Bithynia.
48. This estimate is by comparison with the 50 acres of a standard legionary fortress, which could accommodate about 5,500 men. The size of the barracks is unknown, but Mason (2003), p. 106, estimates that at least 4,000 men could be accommodated there, enough for twenty triremes or more than sixty liburnian biremes.
49. Suetonius (*Caligula*) 46ff.; Dio Cassius (*Roman History*) LIX, 25.2.
50. Arrian (*Periplus Ponti Euxini*) V, 2, '*Circumnavigation of the Euxine Sea*', where everything is salvaged when one of the boats in their convoy is shipwrecked.
51. CIL XIII 3543, 3544.
52. Tacitus (*Histories*) I, 58.
53. Tacitus (*Histories*) IV, 12.
54. AE 1956.249, Cologne: Aemilius son of Saen(i)us who served in the Classis Germanica and was buried at Cologne. If this records a man from the Dumnonii of Devon, then it is the earliest record of a Briton serving in the Roman fleet.
55. A mosaic at Bad Kreuznach depicts a ship with a leather sail. Ellmers (1978), pp. 1–14.
56. Caesar (*Gallic War*) III, 13.
57. Mason (2003), p. 52.
58. Tacitus (*Annals*) II, 6.

59. Arrian (*Periplus*), 3–6, has several ships to escort him around his province of Cappadocia in the AD 130s.
60. (*Digest*) 1.16.4.4, quoting Ulpian (*On the Duties of a Proconsul*) I.
61. CIL XIII 3564, of uncertain date. See Mason (2003), p. 105.
62. Caesar (*Gallic War*) V, 1 for adapting ships to sail in tidal conditions during his second expedition, and Tacitus (*Annals*) II, 6 describes boats being adapted to suit specific conditions and for different purposes during Germanicus's war in Germany.
63. (*Digest*) 37.13.1, quoting Ulpian (*On the Edict*) 45: 'in the fleets all rowers and sailors are soldiers'; see also Casson (1995), p. 310.
64. Dio Cassius (*Roman History*) XLVIII, 51.5, for Agrippa training oarsmen on practice benches.
65. Caesar (*Gallic War*) IV, 23.

IV. ARRIVAL IN BRITANNIA

1. It was occasionally referred to as Albion by later writers, though in a consciously antiquarian way. A fourth-century poem by Avienus describing Britain as the *insula Albionum* is ultimately based on a sixth-century BC journey from Marseille, pre-dating Pytheas. See Rivet and Smith (1979), p. 39.
2. Dio Cassius (*Roman History*) LIII, 13.
3. (*Digest*) 1.18.15, quoting Marcianus (*De iudiciis publicis—On Public Proceedings*), I.
4. Tacitus (*Agricola*) 33.
5. Tacitus (*Agricola*) 18.
6. 'The whole remaining population with wives and children were waiting by the roadsides to receive him and each group cried out as he passed and the whole city was filled like a temple with garlands and incense. On his arrival he offered sacrifices of thanksgiving for his homecoming to the household gods.' Josephus (*Jewish War*) VII, 69–72.
7. On arrival in Asia, for example, the incoming proconsul is obliged always to travel there by sea and to land at Ephesus before continuing to any of the other principal cities—at the request of the people of the province themselves. (*Digest*) 1.16.4–5, quoting Ulpian (*On the Duties of a Proconsul*) I.

8. When a philosopher called Agesilaus failed to join a welcoming party for the emperor Septimius Severus (r. 193–211) in Anazarbus in Cilicia (southern Turkey), claiming that he was too busy being a philosopher, the emperor sent him into exile. Millar (1992), p. 31.

9. Suetonius (*Claudius*) 38.

10. Josephus (*Jewish War*) VII, 69.

11. Juvenal (*Satires*) IV, 139–142; Pliny the Elder (*Natural History*) XXXII, 62. Oyster connoisseurship was not just a passing fad of the first century. Some 300 years later, Ausonius loyally accorded the winning prize to his native Bordeaux oysters, which he described lovingly as 'very tender, with plump white flesh, the sweetness of their *jus* mixing with the taste of seawater to give them a light, salty touch.' Ausonius (*Epistles*) III, 24–5.

12. A sandstone altar found near the Painted House at Dover, RIB 65b, records a dedication to the Mother Goddesses of Italy by Olus Cordius Candidus, who held the office of *strator consularis*, transport officer for the provincial governor. See Hassall and Tomlin (1977), pp. 426–7, no. 4.

13. The road entered Canterbury at the Queningate, (built in the Roman wall in the late third century and passing through the area of the present cathedral precinct). This gate was blocked in the medieval period and replaced by Burgate. Wacher (2nd edition, 1995), p. 189.

14. There is a similar example at Lutetia Parisiorum (Paris), for example. Later in the third century AD it was replaced by an expanded and more thoroughly Classical theatre.

15. It is not clear exactly when this happened.

16. The workaholic elder Pliny kept a secretary by his side complete with book and notebook (*ad latus notarius cum libro et pugillaribus*) when travelling so that he would not waste a moment of work. He scolded his nephew Pliny the Younger for choosing to walk and thus wasting precious work time. Pliny (*Letters*) III, 5.

17. Suetonius (*Claudius*) 33.

18. Horace (*Epistles*) 17.7. Aelius Aristides, travelling in autumn AD 144, was taken ill and felt unable to travel overland, 'for my body would not bear the shaking'. So he and his companions sold their remaining pack animals and risked taking a ship, despite inclement weather. Aelius Aristides (*Sacred Tales*) II, 65ff.

19. Pliny the Younger in *Letters* X ascribed the fever he suffered on his way to Bithynia as being caused by the heat and fatigue of travelling overland.

20. Suetonius (*Augustus*) 49.
21. Pliny the Younger scrupulously asked special permission of Trajan for his wife to be issued with such a permit when she needed to travel unexpectedly because of a family emergency. Pliny (*Letters*) X, 120 and 121.
22. The regulations are contained in the fourth–fifth-century Codex Theodosianus.
23. The site developed over the course of the century, and other temples were built, there as well as a Jupiter column and monumental gateway. See Andrews (2008), pp. 45–62.
24. The route would have taken them through what is now Greenwich Park. Watling Street coming down Shooters Hill was, at this point, aligned directly with Westminster, but because of a loop of the river at Deptford it needed to go south, where its exact course is unknown. It then seems to have followed the course of the Old Kent Road and joined with Stane Street at Borough High Street. Margary (1972), p. 55.

V. LONDINIUM

1. The route from the Kent ports joins Stane Street at Borough High Street. Margary (1973), p. 55.
2. Cowan (2003), p. 56 and *passim*; Cowan *et al.* (2009), pp. 18–24.
3. Drummond-Murray, Thompson and Cowan (2002), p. 6.
4. Yule (2005).
5. The shrine is conjectural. A lead curse tablet (*defixio*) was found on the north foreshore of the Thames, near the site of the bridge, asking 'Metunus' [Neptune] to avenge the supplicant before nine days were up—which could suggest that there was a shrine to Neptune on the bridge, as at Newcastle. For details of the London *defixio*, see Hassall and Tomlin (1987), pp. 360–3.
6. For revolving cranes, see Vitruvius (*On Architecture*) X, 2.10, in Casson (1995), p. 370, n. 41: *ad onerandas et exonerandas naves sunt paratae, aliae erectae, aliae planae in carchesiis versatilibus conlocatae*, 'for loading and unloading ships there are derricks, some fixed vertically, others horizontally on revolving platforms'.
7. Marsden, p. 22.

8. Peacock (1978) p. 49ff. Dressel 30 is the second-most common type found in London.

9. Rodriguez, quoted in Opper (2008), p. 40.

10. The instructions are given by Pliny the Elder (*Natural History*) XXXII, 21; see Milne (1985), p. 95.

11. Pliny the Elder (*Natural History*) XXXI, 93.

12. RIB 2492.11 *Cod(ae) ting(tae) ve(tus) penuar(ium)*, though there are other possible readings, see RIB II, Fascicle 6 (1994), p. 5.

13. Such a boat was found in Thames mud in 1962 at Blackfriars. Its trees were felled between AD 130 and AD 175. It plied the waters of the Thames Estuary for perhaps another couple of decades, before being wrecked in the middle of the century near the mouth of the River Fleet. Merrifield (1983), p. 50, and Milne (1985), p. 38.

14. On the north side of the basilica are offices with shops adjoining them, separated by partition walls and accessible only from the street.

15. It is possible—as suggested in Brigham with Crowley (1992), pp. 96–113.

16. Tacitus (*Annals*) XIV, 33: *copia negotiatorum et commeatuum maxime celebre.*

17. For statues in fora and decoration with garlands, see, for example, the vivid depictions of the forum from wall-paintings found in the House of Julia Felix at Pompeii. The originals are badly faded, but there is a fine set of eighteenth-century engravings in *Le antichità di Erocolano*, Vol. III (1762).

18. Millar (1992), pp. 348–9. See Pliny the Younger (*Letters*) II, 11.2, for an example.

19. Millar (1992), pp. 348 and 389.

20. Tacitus (*Annals*) XIV, 32, for an account of Boudicca's destruction of Colchester.

21. Cowan *et al.* (2009), pp. 100–1.

22. RIB 2491.147, *Austalis dibus xiii vagatur sib[i]cotidim*, found in Warwick Lane and now in the Museum of London.

23. Tacitus (*Annals*) XIV, 33.

24. (*Digest*) 1.15.3, quoting Paulus (*On the Duty of the Prefect of the Guard*), in Croom (2011), p. 83.

25. (*Digest*) 33.7.12, 18, quoting Ulpian (*On Sabinus*) XX.

26. Pliny the Younger (*Letters*) X, 33.2.

27. This is at what became Pudding Lane, Perring (1991), pp. 73–4 and Milne

(1985), p. 140. It was in Pudding Lane that the 'Great Fire of London' broke out in 1666.

28. As shown in the correspondence of Pliny the Younger (*Letters*) X, with the Emperor Trajan.

29. (*Digest*) 1.16.8, quoting Ulpian (*On the Edict*) 39: *Et ideo maius imperium in ea provincia habet omnibus post principem*, 'Therefore the proconsul in his own province has greater authority than anyone else except the emperor.'

30. Birley (1981).

31. A third-century inscription from a villa at Combe Down in Somerset names Naevius 'freedman and assistant of the procurators' who restored a 'headquarters' (RIB 179). The reference to procurators in the plural indicates that this inscription dates from after the division of Britannia into two provinces.

32. One of the clearest examples of a rift between governor and procurator in Britannia occurred during the reign of Nero, in the aftermath of Boudicca's revolt. The newly arrived procurator Gaius Julius Alpinus Classicianus, who came from northern Gaul, objected to the 'scorched earth' policy being pursued by Governor Suetonius Paullinus, even in areas that had remained loyal, a situation that not only created economic hardship (and hence the risk of a fall in future revenues) but also caused considerable suffering and was thereby exacerbating hostility to the Roman presence in Britannia. Classicianus complained to Nero, and the situation was investigated, with Paullinus being replaced early with a more placatory governor, Publius Petronius Turpilianus. Classicianus died in post in the mid-60s, and his wife erected a handsome memorial to him in London (RIB 12). Relationships between procurator and governor met their nadir in AD 69, when one procurator put a governor to death, albeit under the orders of the sleazy Emperor Galba. See Tacitus (*Histories*) I, 7, for the Galba episode. An example of a more cordial relationship is given in Tacitus (*Agricola*) IX, where Tacitus commends Agricola for getting on so well with his procurator when he was governor of Aquitania; Pflaum (1950), pp. 157–160.

33. Pflaum (1950), but for scepticism about the extent of the Hadrianic reorganization, see Brunt (1983), pp. 42–75.

34. Tacitus (*Agricola*) XV, albeit describing an earlier period, tells how the procurator of Britannia used freedmen to exercise power.

35. The legal document written on a wooden tablet recording the sale of Fortunata was found in London and has been dated to *c.* AD 7–125. Incidentally, when the tablet states that the slave is called 'Fortunata or whatever she was known by', this does not in itself reflect a casual disregard for her name but was a legal phrase to cover the eventuality that she might have been known by other names. This concern with nomenclature is also expressed in prayers to deities and the belief that no deity who was wrongly addressed would respond to a prayer. In a world of multiple gods and goddesses with their multiplicity of names, qualifications are found such as 'to the nymphs or whatever name you wish to be called'. See Tomlin (2003). For a whole entourage of slaves owned by slaves see ILS 1514, a funerary monument dedicated to Musicus Scurranus—a slave accountant (*dispensator*) of the Emperor Tiberius, who worked at the Treasury for the province of Gallia Lugdunensis—by the sixteen sub-slaves of his own, including secretaries, cooks, footmen, a valet, a doctor and others, who were all with him when he died on a visit to Rome.

36. A man called Rufus, instructing his Celtic correspondent Epillicus in London; *diligenter cura(m) agas ut illam puellam ad nummum redigas*; RIB II, 4,2443.7.

37. There is a record of a case presided over by a certain *iuridicus* Lucius Javolenus Priscus in the AD 70s or 80s, regarding the estate of a helmsman in the *classis Britannica* whose son had predeceased him. It is quoted in (*Digest*) 36.1.48. An important document (RIB 2504.29) found in London, dated 14 March 118, refers to a dispute over the tenure of a wood in Kent called Verlucionum. It is the type of case that a judicial legate might have heard, and it demonstrates that land and property in Britannia was now firmly under Roman law.

38. CIL XI 384; Birley (2005), pp. 272–3.

39. Hassall (2012), pp. 158–63.

40. The wood might have been recycled from barrels containing imported goods from other northern provinces. Cowan *et al.* (2009), p. 98.

41. In one letter found at Vindolanda just south of the northern frontier, for example, a secretary presumes that his boss has said '*et hiem*', 'and winter' (the 'h' being pronounced silently), following something about *tempestates* (storms). But he has to cross out '*et hiem*' when he realizes that *etiam si*, 'even if', was meant. Vindolanda Tablet 234; see Bowman

and Thomas's commentary on the text for the suggestion that this was a phonetic dictation error.

42. At the time, he was looking for an applicable legal ruling, implying that he was drawing on an extensive archive or library, although it is not clear whether this was his personal library or one at his disposal in the province. Pliny the Younger (*Letters*) X, 65.

43. Tomlin (2003), p. 41; Suetonius (*Nero*) 17.

44. Jones (1949), pp. 38–55.

45. See the late-first-century figure of an officer from a funerary monument found in Camomile Street, London, which depicts him in military dress but carrying a scroll and writing tablets. See Bishop (1983), pp. 31–48.

46. Hassall (1996), p. 20.

47. Hassall (1996), p. 21.

48. RIB 235, from Dorchester: M. Varius Severus, *beneficiarius consularis*; and RIB 88 from Winchester, a shrine to the Matres dedicated by Antonius Lucretianus, *beneficiarius consularis*; and also at many other places, especially on the northern frontier.

49. Such as Veldedeius, the recipient in Londinium of a letter sent from his old mess-mate Chauttius from Vindolanda, who was seconded from the north to serve the governor in Londinium for a while. Vindolanda Tablet 310.

50. SHA (*Hadrian*) XIV, for gladiatorial weapons; SHA (*Hadrian*) XIX, on building and games in every city.

51. This took place in either AD 125–6 or 128–9.

52. Dio (*Epitome*) LXIX, 10.2; SHA (*Hadrian*) XIX, 2–4. Jennison (1937), p. 84.

53. This is speculative. The south gate of the London amphitheatre is more elaborate than the other entrances and its twin passage walls could well have supported a box for the governor. For a discussion about the entrances and *tribunalia*, see Bateman (2011), pp. 98, 105 and 125.

54. Suetonius (*Claudius*) 25.

55. Dio Cassius (*Epitome*) LXIX, 8.2; see also SHA (*Hadrian*) XVIII.

56. Suetonius (*Augustus*) 44.3.

57. Fifty-three items of personal adornment have been found, such as brooches, rings, bracelets, hairpins and shoes, including a fine gold and pearl necklace clasp and bone hairpins with the head of Minerva. See Bateman, Cowan and Wroe-Brown (2008), pp. 132–3.

58. Fragments of these *clibani* or portable ovens, together with a miniature Samian-ware bowl depicting a gladiatorial scene, were found outside the Chester amphitheatre, together with specially brought-in yellow sand containing a human tooth; see Wilmott (2008), p. 178 and fig. 27.

59. A fragment of first-century South Gaulish Samian ware was found in the arena depicting this scene, RP 172. See Bird in Bateman, Cowan and Wroe-Brown (2008), pp. 135–40 and fig. 129. For human bone in the arena, see ibid., pp. 128–9.

60. Bateman, Cowan and Wroe-Brown (2008), p. 128.

61. Scobie (1988). The ivory inlaid rollers are hinted at in a poem from Nero's time regarding the pre-Colosseum amphitheatre at Rome.

62. Such an iron ring has been found in the legionary amphitheatre at Chester, and a wooden stake that could have served the same purpose (as well as for tethering people) has been found at St Albans. A near complete bull's skull was found in a drain at the London amphitheatre, as has part of a red deer skull and a fragment of bear bone. See Bateman, Cowan and Wroe-Brown (2008), pp. 128–9.

63. Martial (*de Spectaculis*) IX, 3–5, 'On Shows': *nuda Caledonio sic viscera praebuit urso/ non falsa pendens in cruce Laureolus*, 'Laureolus hanging on a real-life cross offers his naked flesh to a Caledonian bear'.

64. Martial (*de Spectaculis*) VI, 5: *Iunctam Pasiphaen Dictaeo credite tauro./ vidimus, accepti fabula prisca fidem./ nec se miretur, Caesar, longaeva vetustas:/ quidquid Fama canit, praestat harena tibi*, 'Believe that Pasiphae had union with a Cretan bull/ we have seen it and accept that the old myth is true; long ago antiquity shouldn't rest on its laurels, Caesar,/ whatever fame boasts about is presented to you in the arena.'

65. RIB 9. Alfidus Olussa died in London, at the age of seventy; his tombstone was erected near Tower Hill.

66. RIB 3014 was found in 2002 in Tabard Street, Southwark, buried in a pit between two Romano-Celtic temples: *num(inibus) Aug(ustorum) deo Marti Ca/mulo Tiberini/us Cerlerianus c(ivis) Bell(ovaus) moritix Londiniensi/um primus...*, 'To the divinities of the emperors and to the god Mars Camulus. Tiberinius Celerianus, a citizen of the Bellovaci, *moritix*, of Londoners the first...' For a commentary, see Roger Tomlin in *Britannia* (2002), p. 364. The inscription dates from the 160s.

VI. WESTWARDS TO CALLEVA ATREBATUM

1. RIB 725 from Catterick, AD 191. Roman inscriptions used abbreviations in a similar way to those found in text messages. 'SC' probably stands for *summus curator*, meaning chief supply officer or accounts manager, a man whose job depended on good roads to ensure supplies reached the auxiliary fort at Catterick, which was an important supply centre. The 'SC' in this inscription has also been translated as *singularis consularis*, meaning the governor's bodyguard, but the former definition is more likely in the context—although a governor's bodyguard might also be grateful to the gods for good roads. 'FVLLM' is a standard abbreviation for *votum, laetus, libens merito*, 'joyfully, willingly, deservedly fulfilled his vow'. 'BF COS' stands for *beneficiarius consularis*, a soldier seconded to the governor's staff on 'special duty'. 'COS' stands for *consulares*, 'consuls'.

2. Pitt (2006), pp. 50–3.

3. The line of Watling Street from Kent to Verulamium in fact points towards Westminster and suggests a crossing further west rather than directly into the City: see Margary (1973), p.54; but no traces of such a road have been found and this theory is questioned. See Perring (1991), p. 5, for a brief summary of conflicting views.

4. Margary (1973), p. 47.

5. For the use of ablative-locatives in British place names, see Rivet and Smith (1979), pp. 34 and 441.

6. It is mentioned in the Antonine Itinerary. There was possibly a *mansio* here, although no evidence has yet been found for one.

7. P. Jones (2010).

8. Margary (1973), p. 82: the fact that there are no known branches along the road's length indicate that it might have been forested.

9. Few milestones survive, here or anywhere else in Britain. Two miles east of Silchester is a possible milestone known locally as the Imp Stone, being inscribed 'IMP'. Local tradition says it was 'thrown by a giant from Silchester'. *Victoria County History of Hampshire and the Isle of Wight*, Vol. IV (1912), p. 433.

10. Hyland (1990), p. 259. Traction animals seem occasionally to have been provided with a form of temporary 'hook on' iron shoes, known as hipposandals, to prevent them slipping in particularly muddy or wet

conditions. The remains of several have been found at Ware, for example, where Ermine Street crossed the River Lea, suggesting animals needed extra help descending slippery slopes down to the river during a late period when roads were less well maintained. Allason-Jones (2011), p. 61, referencing Crummy in O'Brien and Roberts (2006), p. 24.

11. Davies (1998), p. 71.
12. (*Digest*) 19.2.13.1, quoting Ulpian (*On the Edict*) 32: ... *si cisiarius, id est carucharius, dum ceteros transire contendit, cisium evertit et servum quassavit vel occidit.*
13. Cunliffe (1973), p. 16.
14. Noviomagus was perhaps his base. There is a much disputed reading of very hard-to-read letters from the only surviving inscription referring to him which may describe him as 'a great king of Britain'; see Bogaers (1979), pp. 243–54.
15. For a summary of Cogidubnus's life, see Malcom Todd's entry 'Cogidubnus (*fl. c.* AD 47–70)' in the *Oxford Dictionary of National Biography* (2004).
16. Dating evidence is poor. This first-phase timber amphitheatre is thought to date from *c.* AD 55–75. It is possible that the amphitheatre had, by AD 130, already been replaced, or was in the process of being replaced, by one more elliptical in shape. In the third century, the amphitheatre was rebuilt in stone in conventional form. There is no evidence for seating arrangements. See Fulford (1989).
17. Nigel Sunter in Fulford (1989), pp. 161–76.
18. The largest of them contains a *cella* 3.9 metres (42 feet) square with a 4.11-metre (13 foot 6 inch) wide portico running around it. Fulford (1989). See also Boon (1990), pp. 397–400, suggesting a possible connection between the amphitheatre and temples. The larger northern temple had a concrete floor, while the smaller floors were of plain red tesserae. Bath stone and fragments of Purbeck marble are associated with the site. There is evidence to suggest at least one other temple in the precinct, possibly a fourth. The date the precinct was established is unknown. Wacher (1995), p. 281.
19. A small figure of Harpocrates, the god of secrecy and silence, who had once been attached to a charcoal-burning brazier, of a type and quality seen in prosperous homes in Italy was found in a first-century rubbish heap in Calleva. See Crummy (2011), pp. 157–65.

20. RIB 69–71. See Frere and Fulford (2002), pp. 167–75.

21. Ravens are also significant in the cult of Mithras. Also buried beneath the foundations of the new forum was a small bronze figure of an eagle, once part of a larger statue, perhaps that of an early-first-century Jupiter or the emperor in the persona of Jupiter. This find, now in Reading Museum, inspired Rosemary Sutcliff's children's novel *The Eagle of the Ninth*. See Boon (1974), pp. 119ff., and Durham (2013), pp. 78–105, for a reappraisal.

22. Ritual deposits are found from the late first century BC right through to the fifth century AD, throughout Britain. They occur in major towns and cities, such as London and St Albans, through to small towns, rural sites and military camps. Some of the deposits seem to have been the result of private or familial acts of devotion, but others, involving metal or large numbers of animals, suggest communal activity. The deposits seem to have fulfilled a variety of needs, although what these were is rarely clear. It is often hard to distinguish between what was deposited as a deliberate act of ritual, and what was simply thrown into a random pit. What is to say that the glasses discarded at Calleva did not form part of a Roman bottle bank? Even if items were arranged carefully and seem to be deposited deliberately, that still leaves the questions of what motives lay behind the depositions and under what circumstances they were carried out. Some were apparently foundation deposits, made when new buildings were erected, and some were associated with marking boundaries, while others may have been part of funerary rituals, or practices associated with the changing seasons, or linked to people's work or sporting activities. In London a carefully articulated skeleton of an adult horse, a dog and a juvenile red deer—all arranged nose to tail— were found in a pit. It must signify the hunt in some way, but whether its purpose was to secure good hunting, or to commemorate the life of someone who loved hunting and ensure he would have good hunting in the afterlife (with his horse and his favourite hound beside him), is not known. For a discussion, see Fulford (2001).

23. In Silchester, there is evidence perhaps of a vet at work in late Roman times, in the form of a lame dog that has had its paw cleaned and immobilized to prevent infection. Clarke (2006), p. 195.

24. Columella (*De Res Rustica*) X, 342–4. Ovid tells us that dogs' or sheep's entrails could also be used: Ovid (*Fasti*) IV, 901–10. Inscription about

healing dogs from Epidaurus IG IV, 952, 1.36–8, cited in Jenkins (1957), pp. 60–76. See also Green (1992). At the fourth-century shrine at Lydney, Gloucestershire, dedicated to the Celtic god Nodens, pilgrims offered votive objects including cockerels and many images of dogs. The objects included a breathtaking copper-alloy figure of a deerhound, now in the collection of Bristol City Museum. It is not known whether real dogs played a part in either the proceedings at Lydney or at Sequanna's shrine in France.

25. Clark (2011).
26. Diodoros Siculus V, 28.
27. Timby (2011).
28. Robinson (2011).
29. Whether or not they scooped out their ears in public is not known. For nail cleaners, see Crummy and Eckhardt (2003).
30. N. Crummy (2012), pp. 105–25.
31. Perring (2002), pp. 49–50.
32. Gaius Caligula is said to have been so incensed by (the future emperor) Vespasian's failure to keep the streets clean when he was an *aedile* and charged with that duty that he ordered Vespasian's senatorial toga to be heaped with mud. Suetonius (*Vespasian*) 5.3.
33. Croom (2011), p. 116.
34. P. Dark (2011), pp. 294–300.
35. Galen (*De Compositione Medicamentorum Secundum Locos*) XII, 786. See Boon (1983). And note also the strength report of the first cohort of Tungrians based at Vindolanda at the end of the first century listing fifteen men as sick and ten as having inflammations of the eye. Vindolanda Tablet 154.

VII. AQUAE SULIS

1. Margary (1973), p. 135.
2. Corney (2001), pp. 15–16.
3. Draper (2006), p. 20, and Hostetter and Noble Howe (1997), p. 41. At this period Littlecote Park was still nothing more than a wooden house and barn. It was rebuilt in stone with a brick and flint barn in the 170s. At least thirty-five villas or possible villas have been identified in the area.

4. Draper (2006), p. 12.
5. Dark and Dark (1997), p. 95.
6. Margary (1973), p. 136 and footnote 4, p. 137.
7. There may have been a Roman shrine or temple south of the hill, adjacent to the road west. For a discussion of the shafts, and of Roman activity on the hill, see Leary, Field and Campbell (2013), pp. 274–84.
8. Leary and Field (2010), p. 159. There was an inn there by the third or fourth century. It has been suggested that the buildings to the north of the road may have been temple precincts around Silbury Hill.
9. Pliny the Elder (*Natural History*) XXXVI, 16–20, for marvellous monuments in Egypt.
10. Plutarch (*Moralia*) 976C: 'they open their mouths to let their teeth be cleaned by hand and wiped with towels. Recently our excellent Philinus came back from a trip to Egypt and told us that he had seen in Antaeopolis an old woman sleeping on a low bed beside a crocodile which was stretched out beside her in a perfectly decorous way' (Loeb translation, VII, 1957); and Strabo (*Geography*) XVII, 812, for his charming account of feeding the sacred crocodile at Arsinoe.
11. In fact, this was a memorial to Pharoah Amenhotep III (1400 BC), which had split in an earthquake and thereafter could 'speak' at dawn. See Casson (1994) for bibliography on this subject and for sacred crocodiles (above).
12. Pliny the Younger describes the resort in detail in (*Letters*) VIII, 8.6. A site that vividly evokes this account in the twenty-first century and where thermal waters still run into the ruins of the Roman baths, situated by the river, is Fordioganus (Forum Traianii) in Sardinia.
13. Tacitus (*Agricola*) 16.
14. Tacitus (*Agricola*) 21: *inde etiam habitus nostri honor et frequens toga; paulatimque discessum ad delenimenta vitiorum, porticus et balinea et conviviorum elegantiam. Idque apud imperitos humanitas vocabatur, cum pars servitutis esset.*
15. See Pliny the Younger (*Letters*) X, 32, concerning condemned criminals cleaning baths.
16. Pseudo Lucian (*Erotes*) 8 describes avoiding the guides on Rhodes who do just this: 'two or three fellows rushed up to me offering....'
17. See Casson (1994), Chapter 16, for numerous references to dodgy tourist guides.

18. For example, Demetrius the silversmith at Ephesus, mentioned in the Acts of the Apostles, made copies of the temple of Diana for tourists. He provoked a riot in the city among other craftsmen, who feared that Christianity, with its abhorrence of idolatry, would destroy their business. Acts of the Apostles 19.22.

19. For illustrations of the silver pan, of a second-century date, and other offerings thrown into the sacred spring, see Cunliffe (1988); for souvenirs from Hadrian's Wall and other enamelled objects, see Breeze (2012).

20. It was a viewpoint apparently much favoured by gay men, who could fantasise that they were seeing the handsome young Ganymede. See Pseudo Lucian (*Erotes*) 8–18 for the entertaining account of a visit there.

21. Cunliffe and Davenport (1985), p. 24; the courtyard measures 52 metres (170 feet) by 72 metres (236 feet).

22. Pliny the Elder (*Natural History*) XVI, 251.

23. Caesar (*Gallic War*) VI, 13–14.

24. Lucan (*The Civil War*) III, 453ff.

25. Suetonius (*Claudius*) 25.5.

26. Caesar (*Gallic War*) VI, 14.

27. Tacitus (*Annals*) XIV, 30. The Latin is particularly enjoyable: *Stabat pro litore diversa acies, densa armis virisque, intercursantibus feminis; in modum Furiarum veste ferali, crinibus deiectis faces praeferebant; Druidaeque circum, preces, diras sublatis ad caelum manibus fundentes, novitate aspectus perculere militem ut quasi haerentibus membris immobile corpus vulneribus praeberent.*

28. Lucan (*The Civil War*) III, 453–57.

29. Statius (*Silvae*) V, 2.147–9. (The shield may possibly be that of Venutius, ex-husband of pro-Roman Queen Cartimandua of the Brigantes.)

30. Solinus (*Collection of Curiosities*) XXII, 10.

31. RIB 155: *sacerdos deae Sulis*.

32. Such as the votive bronze axe found near Canterbury in the form of a bull. See Henig (1995), p. 118.

33. The inscription that accompanies the statue's dedication shows that his job title was originally abbreviated to 'HAR', in nicely spaced regular letters, but had 'USP' crammed in at the end at a later date. Perhaps the temple authorities felt its meaning was being lost and needed to be spelled out more explicitly, see Cunliffe (2000), p. 49. Confraternities of *haruspices* are attested in the Rhineland CIL XIII 6765 (Mainz); see

Cunliffe (1969), p. 189, no. 1.60.

34. RIB 143; RIB 144.

35. RIB 149.

36. RIB 151.

37. RIB 105, possibly the same person. It was discovered in what might have been his mason's yard, together with several pieces cut from Bath stone, and is now in Corinium Museum, Cirencester.

38. During the late second or early third century, the baths were extended and entirely re-roofed with an enormous barrel vault.

39. SHA (*Hadrian*) XVIII: *lavacra pro sexibus separavit*; also mentioned in Dio (*Epitome*) LXIX, 8.2. For a Hadrianic inscription stating separate bathing hours for men and women, see Lex Metalli Vipascensis (no. 282) and Fagan (1999), p. 184.

40. Plutarch (*Life of Cato the Elder*) XX, 5–6, who tells us in the same passage that at the time fathers avoided bathing with their sons-in-law because they were ashamed about being naked. Later, however, having caught the Greek habit, they even taught the Greeks to bathe when women were present.

41. Martial (*Epigrams*) III, 68.3–4: *Gymnasium, thermae, stadium est hac parte: recede! Exuimur, nudos parce videre viros!*

42. As depicted on the fourth-century mosaics at Piazza Armerina in Sicily. It is often said that the women in bikinis in these pictures are professional acrobats or dancers, but the context is the baths.

43. A leather bikini was found in a well in Queen Street in London and is now in the Museum of London.

44. For the reference to *paxsa(m) ba(ln)earum et [pal]leum* from Bath, see Tab. Sulis 32 in Fagan (1999), p. 37, footnote 65. As it might have been stolen in the baths, it may point to being used as a bathrobe rather than a swimming costume. See also SHA (*Alexander Severus*) XLI, 1, for reference to sets of bathing clothes.

45. Juvenal (*Satires*) VI, 419ff.

46. (*Digest*) 3.2.4.2–3, quoting Ulpian (*On the Edict*) 6.

47. (*Digest*) 48.17.0. A short chapter is devoted to bath thieves, *de furibus balneariis*, recommending different types of punishment according to the severity of the crime and the rank of the thieves. If thieves defended themselves or hit anyone, they could be condemned to the mines; people of higher rank could be sent into exile; a soldier caught stealing from the

baths would be dishonourably discharged.

48. More than half of the 500 or so Latin curse tablets discovered throughout the empire come from Britain, and most of these are from Bath and the surrounding area (the other thousand are written in Greek). Tomlin, in Cunliffe (1988), p. 60.

49. Greek Magical Papyri vii, 398–9, cited by Tomlin in Cunliffe (1988), p. 60.

50. At Bowness-on-Solway, a merchant called Antonianus dedicated a shrine to the Matres—the Mother Goddesses—and promised them in verse that if they helped his venture he would gild the letters of his poem in return. RIB 2059.

51. Late second century, cited by Tomlin in Cunliffe (1988), p. 169.

52. No two are written by the same hand, with the exception of one where the writer ran out of room and had to continue on a fresh sheet. Tab. Sulis 95 and 96.

53. Tab. Sulis 16.

54. One tablet, citing eight Celtic names, is written in a stylish hand: Tab. Sulis 30. See Tomlin in Cunliffe (1988). For the Latin text in Greek letters, see Uley 52.

55. The spelling of *Patarnianus filius* and *Matarnus ussor*, for example, instead of *Paternianus* and *Maternus*, indicates that the writer spoke Latin with a heavy accent, pronouncing their 'e' as an open 'a' when followed by 'r'. Bath curse tablets 30.2–3. See Tomlin in Cunliffe (1988), pp. 146–7. This is something that occurs too in Latin loan-words in Welsh, e.g. *taberna* becomes *tafarn*; *serpens*, *sarff*; see Adams (1992) and Smith, in *Aufstieg und Niedergang der Römischen Welt* (*ANRW*) (1983), p. 900.

56. The only possible votive offerings found in the spring representing body parts are one amulet of breasts made of elephant ivory and another small copper-alloy breast. Cunliffe (1988), pp. 7, 8 and 36.

57. The elaborately carved blocks associated with the *tholos* are comparable in workmanship to the baths at Sens in northern France. Cunliffe (2000), p. 110.

VIII. INTO WALES:
TO THE LEGIONARY FORTRESS
OF ISCA AUGUSTA

1. Text from Lanna (2013), p. 231. This poem written by Hadrian's court musician Mesomodes captures the hypnotic and inescapable beauty and attraction of Nemesis. Mesomodes of Crete, a freedman of Hadrian, worked at the Museion in Alexandria and is said to have been the composer of the panegyric written to celebrate the life of Hadrian's beloved Antinous. His hymn to Nemesis is one of four that preserve the ancient musical notation written over the text. According to the SHA (*Antoninus Pius*) VII, 8, his state salary was reduced after Hadrian's death, but he was honoured by a cenotaph erected by Caracalla 100 years after his death.

2. Abonae may possibly have been a base for a squadron of the fleet. See Burnham and Davies (2010), p. 38.

3. Margary (1973), p. 138.

4. Bennett (1985), pp. 3–4.

5. For the etymology of the name, see Rivet and Smith (1979), pp. 450–1.

6. It has been conjectured that there might also have been a ferry crossing running from Aust to Sudbrook, on the Welsh side of the Severn, with other ferry terminals at Black Rock and Magor on the Welsh coast. See Burnham and Davies (2010), p. 99.

7. Tacitus (*Agricola*) 11: *Silurem colorati vultus, torti plerumque crines et posita contra Hispania Hiberos veteres traiecisse easque sedes occupasse fidem faciunt.* While the geography may be a little dodgy, the people of northern Spain and Brittany and the Celtic people of Cornwall, Wales, Ireland and western Scotland are now considered to be of common descent: see Cunliffe (2001).

8. Tacitus (*Annals*) XII, 32: *atrocitate non clementia.*

9. Tacitus (*Annals*) XII, 38.

10. Tacitus (*Annals*) XII, 39.

11. Tacitus (*Annals*) XII, 39.

12. Tacitus (*Agricola*) 17: *validamque et pugnacem Silurum.*

13. It is most exposed from the north-west, where the land rises steeply to the site of an imposing former hillfort at Lodge Wood, which overlooks the mouth of the Usk and parts of the Severn Estuary.

14. From where the River Usk ultimately derives its name. (Welsh *Wysg* is connected but the etymology is complicated; see Rivet and Smith (1979) pp. 376–8.) The modern name 'Caerleon' is derived from the Welsh for 'fortress of the legion', first referred to around AD 800 as *Cair Legeion guar Uisc*.

15. There are parallels for large courtyard buildings situated outside legionary forts at Nijmegen (in the Netherlands) and Carnuntum (in Austria), and also at Mirebeau (in France) and Vindonissa (in Switzerland), where they are similarly close to the amphitheatre as is the case at Caerleon. It is not clear what they were used for. See Guest, Luke and Pudney (2012), p. 8 and *passim*, for a description of excavations of the courtyard building and associated structures in the southern *canabae*.

16. RIB 369. The tombstone also remembers their mother, Tadia Vallaunius, who died at the age of sixty-five.

17. A fragment of a wooden tablet found at Caerleon provides such a list and is on display at the National Roman Army Museum.

18. As cited on a papyrus from Dura Europos, early third century: P. Dura 82.

19. The devastating effects of Roman gold-mining techniques and their vast scale are still vividly apparent at Las Médulas in north-western Spain.

20. Pliny the Elder (*Natural History*) XXXIII, 21.

21. Pliny the Elder (*Natural History*) XXXIV, 49.

22. The exact location of the mines is unknown; they were possibly near Wirksworth. See Rivet and Smith (1979), pp. 403–4.

23. Tylecote (1964), p. 34.

24. As on a lead pig from Lutudarum (Wirksworth?, Derbyshire) RIB 2404.39: *IMP CAES HADRIANI AUG MET LUT*.

25. Pliny the Elder (*Natural History*) XXXIV, 50.18: 'the orator Calvus is said to have cured himself by these plates and so preserved his bodily energies for labour and study'; see Boulakia (1972), pp. 139–44.

26. Suetonius (*Vespasian*) 4.1.

27. For the porticoed courtyard building at Caerleon, see Guest, Luke and Pudney (2012), pp. 91–2. Gardens and fountains were common features of such buildings elsewhere.

28. Zienkiewicz (1986), Vol. I, pp. 115ff.

29. Zankiewicz (1986), Vol. II, pp. 226ff.

30. They are comparable in scale with the surviving Roman baths at Cluny in Paris.

31. A fragment of a round basin (*labrum*) found at 'Castle' baths outside the fortress walls in 1849 was carved from Purbeck marble and decorated with a Gorgon's head.

32. Zankiewicz (1986), Vol II, p. 223.

33. The strigil is thought to date from *c.* AD 150–200 and was possibly made in Syria or Egypt. See Zankiewicz (1986), Vol. II, p. 166.

34. Two dates in May are given for the *rosaliae signorum*—the 10th and 31st of the month. All military units celebrated a calendar of festivals: the *Feriale Duranum*, a papyrus believed to date from the AD 220s and found at Dura Europos, Syria, where the Cohort XX Palmyrenorum was stationed, is the only surviving example. For a reference in the *Feriale Duranum* to the *rosaliae feriale*, see col. II.II. 8, 14. For an interesting discussion about evidence for the celebration of military festivals on other inscriptions, see Fishwick (1988), pp. 349–61.

35. Valerius Maximus (*Factorum et Dictorum Memorabilium,* 'Memorable Deeds and Sayings') II, 4.7, on the date on which gladiatorial spectacles were first celebrated at Rome in the Forum Boiarum. Gladiatorial games seem to have had their origins in Campania in funeral games, which included forced combat and which are commemorated on wall-paintings found at Paestum and elsewhere, dating from 370–340 BC.

36. SHA (*Hadrian*) XVIII: *lenoni et lanistae servum vel ancillam vendi vetuit causa non praestita.*

37. See Petronius (*Satyricon*) XIV, 117: *tanquam legitimi gladiatores domino corpora animasque religiosissime addicimus,* 'and like real gladiators we bound ourselves religiously to our master, body and soul'.

38. Galen (*De Compositione Medicamentorum per Genera*) III, 2; see also Celsus (*De Medicina*) Prooemium, 43, on doctors learning about internal organs from examining injured gladiators, soldiers wounded in battle and travellers set upon by robbers.

39. CIL IV 4397; see Varone (2002), p. 69.

40. CIL X 6012 in Hopkins and Beard (2005), p. 89.

41. See, for example, Dio (*Epitome*) LXVIII, 15.1, and Wiedemann (1992), Chapter 1.

42. CIL XIII 12048 for Bonn; Martial (*de Spectaculis*) VII, 3, for Caledonian bears. See Epplett (2001), pp. 210–22 *passim,* for descriptions of soldiers

in all parts of the empire engaged in capturing animals for shows; and pp. 213–14 for possible British examples. Two hundred British stags were provided for a *venatio* given by the Emperor Gordian in the third century AD: SHA (*The Three Gordians*) III, 6 and 7. Gordian held the show as *aedile* under Septimius Severus.

43. Symmachus writing in the fourth century is the magistrate who suffers such problems: (*Letters*) II, 46 (for the deaths of the twenty-nine Saxons); II, 76, for the pitiful bears; IX, 141, for similar trouble with crocodiles. See Jennison (1937), pp. 96–7.

44. The only places where there is the slightest evidence for gladiatorial combat in Britain are the legionary amphitheatres of Caerleon, Chester and London.

45. *Per Galliam Bretanniam Hispanias Germaniam* (CIL III 249, Dessau, 1396) in Sordi (1953), pp. 104ff.

46. At Bignor Roman Villa, Sussex, the fourth-century mosaics depict twelve Cupids—three dressed as trainers; nine as gladiators. See Neal and Cosh (2009), Vol. III.

47. Green glass cups of the mid-first century made in Gaul, depicting eight named gladiators, one of whom holds a victory palm, have been found at Colchester; a less complete one has been found in Leicester. See Allason-Jones (2011), p. 221, for a round-up of gladiatorial scenes in Britain and bibliographical references.

48. Hull (1963), pp. 47–74.

49. Known as Nene Valley Ware. Examples of both hunt scenes and a 'Gladiator Cup' are to be found at Peterborough Museum. Whether many Britons were ever entertained by the sight of a female acrobat vaulting from a horse to a panther in real life, as depicted on a pottery beaker from Durobrivae, is a moot point. Toynbee (1962), p. 190.

50. A rare ivory knife showing two gladiators fighting, possibly third century, was found in *insula* XIV of Venta Silurum (Caerwent). Bartus and Grimm (2010), pp. 321–4.

51. Another piece of surviving graffito from Caerleon depicts a central rosette flanked by a shoulder guard and what may represent the arm-guard of a *retiarius*. See Brewer (1986), Vol. 1, Fascicle 5, nos 37 and 38.

52. Marcus Aurelius (*Meditations*) I, 5: 'My tutor taught me not to side with the Greens or the Blues at the races, nor the *palmularius* (Thracian's shield) or *scutarii* (rectangular shields of the *secutor*)'.

53. A relief found at Chester in 1738 made from local north Welsh slate depicts a *retiarius* holding his trident and net. He wears a belted loincloth (*subligaculum*), his right arm is protected by a padded sleeve (*manica*) secured by leather straps, and on the right shoulder he carries a metal shoulder guard (*galerus*) protecting neck and face. His opponent is a *secutor* with a sword (*gladius*) and curved rectangular shield. The scene may have been part of a frieze, perhaps even adorning the amphitheatre. The Chester *retiarius* uniquely holds his trident in his right hand and his net in his left, with his *manica* and *galerus* worn on his right arm rather than on his left: it has been suggested that this depicts a known gladiator. The relief is in the Saffron Walden Museum. See Jackson (1983), pp. 87–95.

54. The sherd was found in 1851 when a drain was being dug. See Wilmott (2008), p. 162, for an overview and illustration Pl.21. RIB 2501.586 in S. Frere and R.S.O. Tomlin, *The Roman Inscriptions of Britain*, Vol. II, Fascicle 7, *Graffiti on Samian Ware* (Oxford, 1995). Had Lucius been killed and Verecunda kept the little fragment of pot as a memento, or were these names scratched by a fan who had seen them both perform? Verecunda means 'shy' or 'coy' and could perhaps be a stage name. There is so little to go on that the romantic possibilities are endless. The only other names of gladiators to survive from Britain are those commemorated on the spectacular 'Colchester Vase' (AD 170s) on display in Colchester Museum. It depicts scenes from the arena, and bears an inscription cut onto the vessel after firing, which reads: *MEMNON SAC VIIII VALENTINU LEGIONIS XXX.* This could mean that Memnon, the *secutor*, who had nine victories, defeated Valentinus 'of the legion', who had thirty victories. Surviving thirty fights would be a record achievement, and so Memnon's victory would be all the more worthy of note. See Wilmott (2008), pp. 168–70. Another suggestion is that it refers to the 30th Legion stationed in Xanten, in Lower Germany, and perhaps these gladiators were part of a troupe managed by the 30th Legion and on tour in Britain. 'Of the legion' may mean that Valentinus was a gladiator owned by a legion or the favourite of the legion.

55. Juvenal (*Satires*) VI, 103: *quid vidit propter quod ludia dici sustinuit?*

56. Juvenal (*Satires*) VI, 82–109.

57. CIL V 3466.

58. On Nemesis and games, see Hornum (1993).

59. A building just outside the amphitheatre has been proposed as a shrine to Nemesis by analogy with one in the same position at Carnuntum, in Austria. See Boon (1972), p. 100. One of the chambers of the amphitheatre was possibly used as a shrine to Nemesis in a later phase of its development. At Chester, a small stone altar found in a chamber near the entrance to the arena at the main north entrance was converted into a Nemeseum: *Deae Nemesi Sext Marcianus ex visu*, 'To the Goddess Nemesis Sextius Marcianus, the centurion set this up after a vision.'

60. RIB 316. An inscription records that a temple of Diana was restored by Titus Flavius Postumius Varus, legionary legate. Nothing is known about the temple itself.

61. RIB 323. The lead tablet was found in the arena of Caerleon's amphitheatre. In contrast to Mesmodes' courtly poem, the humble curse from Caerleon reduces Nemesis to some sort of provincial vigilante: *Dom(i)na Nemesis do tibi palleum et galliculas qui tulit non redimat ni[si] vita sanguine suo*, 'Lady Nemesis, I give thee a cloak and a pair of Gallic sandals; let him who took them not redeem them (unless) with his own blood'.

62. For the curse tablet found in London's amphitheatre, see Hassall and Tomlin (2003), pp. 362–3.

63. Tertullian (*To the Nations*) I, 10, and also mentioned in Tertullian (*Apology*) XV. Tertullian, an early Christian writer *c.* AD 160–*c.*225, from Carthage, was himself said to be the son of a centurion.

64. Tacitus (*Annals*) XI, 19, describes how, following the defeat of the rebellious Frisii at the hands of the Roman general Corbulo in AD 47, hostages were handed over, after which Corbulo demarcated land and allocated a senate, magistrates and laws. Tacitus adds: *ac ne iussa exuerent praesidium immunivit*, 'should they forget these orders, Corbulo also constructed a fort'.

65. It is not entirely clear how far the Silures' territory extended outside the town—possibly to the east as far as the River Wye, which probably marked the boundary with the neighbouring Dobunni.

66. An open yard to the east probably forms part of a large timber workshop premises of a late-first- or early second-century date. It has comfortable living quarters to its north end and a workshop with several hearths to the south, and was the site of a Romano-Celtic temple in the fourth century.

67. It measured about 38 metres (126 feet) long and 19 metres (62 feet) wide.

68. Black (1995), pp. 26–7.
69. Black (1995), p. 27.
70. Vegetius (*Epitome of Military Science*) III, 6.
71. It is possible that leagues were also used as a unit of measurement in Britain. A medieval copy of a late Roman itinerary, known as the Peutinger map (now held in the Austrian National Library, Vienna), shows the main roads throughout the empire and beyond, from Britain to China, in twelve sheets, of which the twelfth, representing most of Britain and Spain, is—frustratingly—lost. The only surviving fragment of Britain depicts its south and eastern corner, which happened to extend beyond the lost first sheet of parchment and onto the second. The Peutinger map is a parchment roll, 6.4 metres (21 feet) long and 30 centimetres (1 foot) wide, and seems to be a conflation of earlier maps from different periods. Presumably a traveller could have used just one or two sheets as necessary, depending on the length of his journey.
72. Margary (1973), pp. 318–19.

IX. VIROCONIUM CORNOVIORUM: CAPITAL OF CATTLE COUNTRY

1. Rivet and Smith (1979), pp. 505–6.
2. As mentioned in 'Speech of Thanks to Constantine Panegyric V by a native of Autun': on receiving the emperor in Autun, 'we decorated the streets which lead to the palace, with mean enough ornament no doubt but we brought out the banners of all the colleges and the images of all our gods and produced our paltry number of musical instruments, which by means of shortcuts were to greet you several times over'. Translation from Nixon and Rodgers (1994).
3. For a discussion about the lettering being provincial rather than imperial quality, see White and Barker (1998), pp. 78–9.
4. (*Digest*) 1.16.7, quoting Ulpian (*Duties of a Proconsul*) II.
5. When the basilica was excavated, inkwells and part of an auxiliary soldier's discharge certificate (that of Mansuetus) were found among the ashes, dating to the occasion on which the forum burnt down in about AD 165–175, and thus suggesting that the city record office was here. White and Barker (1998), p. 86.

6. For Hadrian pronouncing judgement in public from a tribunal in the forum, see Dio Cassius (*Epitome*) LXIX, 7.1, on Trajan, and Millar (1992), p. 229.

7. (*Digest*) 1.16.9.4, quoting Ulpian (*On the Duties of a Proconsul*) I.

8. Martial (*Epigrams*) VI, 82, for the Batavian ear. Marcus Aurelius was chided by his tutor Fronto for writing sloppy Latin. Fronto (*To Marcus Aurelius*) III, 13. See Woolf (2002), pp. 181–8.

9. SHA (*Hadrian*) III.

10. From a speech of thanks to Constantine (*Panegyric* V) by a native of Autun, delivered at Trier on behalf of his city in thanks for tax relief before the emperor, his retinue of friends and imperial officials in AD 311. For a critical edition and translation, see Nixon and Saylor Rodgers (1994).

11. Although gaining audience sympathy (*captatio benevolentiae*) is part and parcel of such a speech, the sentiments are true enough. Speech made *c.* AD 313 (XII Panegyric of Constantine Augustus). Translations from Nixon and Saylor Rodgers (1994).

12. Tacitus (*Agricola*) 21.

13. Jackson (1953), pp. 76–121.

14. As seems to have happened to one of the commanding officer's boys at Vindolanda, near Hadrian's Wall. See Vindolanda Tablet 118, which has a line from Virgil's *Aeneid* IX (473) written on the back of a letter, partly in clumsy capital letters. The line should read *interea pavidam volitans pinnata per urbem*, 'meanwhile winged [rumour] flying through the fearful city', but the 'r' is missing from *urbem*, as is the 'er' from *per*. Another hand has written '*seg*' after it, which Bowman and Thomas suggest might read *segniter*—'lazy': see www.vindolanda.casad.ox.ac.uk/TVII-118.

15. See Goetz (1892), a textbook with Greek and Latin parallel text from the fifth century.

16. Vindolanda Tablet 343. See Bowman and Thomas at www.vindolanda.csad.ox.ac.uk/TVII-343.

17. (*Digest*) 47.14.1, quoting Ulpian (*On the Duties of a Proconsul*) VIII (citing a rescript sent by Hadrian to the provincial council of Baetica about appropriate punishments for cattle rustlers).

18. Doloney (2001), pp. 36–45.

19. Martial (*Epigrams*) VI, 93; XII, 48.8, and see Bradley (2002) and Wild (1970), pp. 82–6, on fulling in the northern provinces.

20. Tacitus (*Agricola*) 21.
21. See Bradley (2002), p. 22.
22. No fullers are securely attested in Britain. Fullers' guilds are known to have existed in the Rhineland, and given that British wool products were so highly rated it is more than likely that they operated in Britain too. See Wild (1970), p. 82.
23. Vedica the Cornovian died aged thirty at Ilkley. Her tombstone (RIB 639) depicts her sitting sturdily, her hair in two thick plaits. It does not record her marriage to a soldier, but it is a possibility given that there was an auxiliary fort there.
24. Martial (*Epigrams*) XI, 21.9: *quam veteres bracae Brittonis pauperis.*
25. A poor man's Tyrian purple, the whelks are related to the *Murex brandaris* of the eastern Mediterranean, from which true purple derived. See Wild (1970), p. 81.
26. Wild (1970).
27. A *tossiam Brit(annicam)*, or British rug or bedspread, was among the presents listed in a copy of a letter, from a certain Tiberius Claudius Paulinus, sent from Britain in AD 238 to a Gallo-Roman aristocrat called Titus Sennius Sollemnis and proudly published on the Thorigny inscription found at Vieux in Gaul: CIL XIII, 3162. In Diocletian's *Edict of Prices* listing prices for goods and services across the empire in AD 301, the only British products to be mentioned are the *birrus*, or hooded woollen cape, which is ranked—in terms of price and quality—equal sixth out of fourteen types, while British rugs (*tapetia*) of both first-class and second-class grades are second to none. A British coverlet, 1st form, is worth 5,000 *denarii*; British coverlet, 2nd form is 4,000 *denarii*; a British hooded cloak is valued at 6,000 *denarii*.
28. RIB 2491.79 (a possible 'Attius, you bugger'). See RIB (Collingwood and Wright), Fascicle 4, p. 117.
29. RIB 2491.157 (Colchester); RIB 2491.215 (Silchester).
30. RIB 2447.1 (a); see RIB II, Fascicle 4 (1992), p. 63.
31. RIB 2447.28(a); RIB 2447.28(d); see RIB II, ibid., pp. 74–6.
32. RIB 2450.3; RIB II, ibid., p. 102.

X. TO THE WALL

1. Latin text from Speidel (2007), p. 10.
2. Mason (1988).
3. The bridge lay on or near the site of the present one – Margary (1973), p. 297.
4. Towards the end of the second century, a new and extremely elaborate amphitheatre was built at Chester on the site of its predecessor. Building work also began on the fortress at the start of the third century, indicating that the Legion XX Valeria Victrix had returned there. They remained there into the fourth century.
5. For a useful summary and bibliography, see *Cheshire Historic Towns Survey: Middlewich—Revised Archaeological Assessment*, revised and updated by Malcolm Reid (2013), available online.
6. The River Mersey is crossed close to Warrington Parish Church: Margary (1973), p. 367.
7. Rogers and Garner (2007), pp. 45–6.
8. For a discussion of the *ala* Asturum and the Sarmatians garrisoned here from *c.* AD 175, see Edwards (2000), pp. 49–50.
9. See Edwards (2000), pp. 4–5, and Margary (1973), p. 377. Between Ribchester and Low Borrow Bridge there was a fort at Burrow-in-Lonsdale on the Lune about which little is known.
10. *praefectus arcend(is) latroc[in(is)]* CIL XIII 5010 = ILS 7007; CIL XIII 6211. Such men are recorded in Noviodunum (Nyon, Switzerland), Bingium (Bingen, on the Rhine) and also in Normandy. See Grünewald (2004), p. 22.
11. Just as Fronto did, on being elected governor of Asia Minor in the mid-150s. He appointed to his staff his friend Julius Senex of Mauretania, who had an excellent track record of hunting down bandits, though in the end he did not take up his post. Fronto (*To Antoninus Pius*) 8.
12. CIL III 2399.
13. CIL VIII 2728 and 18122 = ILS 5795 (Lambaesis): *profectus sum et inter vias latrones sum passus. Nudus saucius evasi cum meis*, 'I set out and on the highways I was attacked by bandits. Naked and injured I escaped from them with my retinue.' See Grünewald (2004), p. 21.
14. Pliny the Younger (*Letters*) VI, 25.
15. The Gospel According to St Luke 10.25–37.

16. Celsus (*de Medicina—On Medicine*) Introduction, 43 (first century).

17. Travellers coming from Condate could also have chosen the road via Wilderspool, which continued north through undulating farmland to Coccium (Wigan), cutting through great stretches of moss to east and west. From there it was about 16 miles to Preston, where the route entered the Ribble Valley, crossing the river a little to the north of Walton-le-Dale (west of Ribchester).

18. For the *mansio*, see Black (1995), pp. 37–8. The fort was built on Castle Hill, where Lancaster Castle and the Priory Church of St Mary now stand.

19. RIB 3185 *Dis Manibus Insus Vodulli [...] Cive Trevereques Alae Aug [.] Victoris Curator Domitia [...]*, see Bull (2007) and Iles and Shotter (2010).

20. As their name 'Aelia' suggests, they seem to have been raised during the time of Hadrian.

21. The Roman name for Ambleside may have been Clanovanta, 'the market beside the shore', rather than Galava: see Shotter (2004), p. 63. Hardknott's Roman name is not certain—it has been suggested that Mediobogdum would be better ascribed to the fort at Watercrook, near Kendal: see, e.g., Shotter (2004), p. 68. For the date of the fort and the inscription recording the presence of the cohort of Dalmatians, see Wright (1965), pp. 169–75.

22. For a table of altars and a discussion of Maenius Agrippa's career and uncertainties over dates in light of recent excavation at Maryport, see Breeze, Dobson and Maxfield (2012), pp. 17–30.

23. Emperors received frequent requests for military posts to further equestrian careers, although Pliny's correspondence shows that imperial legates might also have had the power to grant them. For Pliny attempting to secure a job for the young Suetonius, see Pliny the Younger (*Letters*) IV, 4. The letter mentioned above (Chapter IX, Note 27) from the *legatus* serving in Britannia Inferior to his friend and client in Gaul promises him a letter of appointment as a tribune with a salary of 25,000 *sestertii* as soon as there is a vacancy. See also Millar (1992), pp. 284–5.

24. He was at Maryport in about AD 132, and was promoted as a centurion in the Legion X Fretensis, serving in Judaea (under Severus's son or nephew, Gnaeus Julius Verus). In AD 133 Julius Severus was sent to Judaea: see Postscript. See Piso (1993), p. 46, citing Petersen, in E. Groag

et al. (eds), *Prosopographia Imperii Romani* (*PIR*), 2nd edition (Bonn, 1933–), I, 618.

25. Birley (1981), pp. 151–5. The Fourth Cohort of Lingones is attested at Wallsend in the third century but its whereabouts in Britannia in the early AD 130s is not known. M. Statius Priscus was decorated with a military flag by Hadrian for his part in the Judaean war and later admitted to the Senate. He returned to Britain as its governor in AD 161.

26. Suetonius (*Vespasian*) 8.3.

27. Named after the River Derwent, which was also called Derventio: Rivet and Smith, p. 334.

28. SHA (*Hadrian*) XI, 2.

29. SHA (*Hadrian*) V, 2. And for trouble in the reign of Antoninus Pius, see also SHA (*Antoninus Pius*) V, 4, and Pausanias (*Description of Greece*) VIII, 43.4: 'He also took away from the Brigantes in Britain the greater part of their territory because they too had begun an unprovoked war...'

30. There is much debate as to the date of the *expeditio Britannica*. Because the word *expeditio* seems to be used only of a military campaign at which the emperor himself is present, this may indicate that the war was fought around AD 122. Whatever its date, the sources surrounding Britannia's troublesome reputation are consistent. As Fronto later wrote in a letter to Emperor Marcus Aurelius, 'under the rule of your grandfather, Hadrian, what numbers of soldiers were killed by the Jews, what numbers by the Britons!': Fronto (*On the Parthian War*) 2, *Avo vestro Hadriano imperium obtinente quantum militum a Judaeis, quantum ab Britannis caesum?* See Breeze, Dobson and Maxfield (2012), pp. 17–30.

31. RIB 3364. His tombstone records his death in war. The Tungrians were at Vindolanda in the AD 90s, and from *c*.105 until possibly as late as 146, so it is unclear to which war it refers—although a date between AD 100 and AD 125 has been suggested, based on the style of the inscription.

32. In Egypt, Karus served as military tribune of the III Cyrenaica Legion, AE 1951.88.

33. SHA (*Hadrian*) XII, 6.

34. Breeze (2011), pp. 56–8, for the character and extent of the Upper German-Raetian limes.

35. Zant (2009), Vol. I, Chapter 6 ('The Second Fort') and Vol. II, pp. 763ff.

36. Birley (1979), p. 63. RIB 812. The altar is second- or third-century and is in the British Museum.

37. The turf wall was thus similar in height to the stone wall, which was an estimated 15 Roman feet high (4.4 metres). The walls of the forts may have been a little higher, at 15 feet (4.5 metres). See Breeze and Dobson (2000).

38. Caesar (*Gallic War*) VII, 73.

39. Breeze and Dobson (2000), p. 41.

40. The *falx* is shown on Trajan's Column, which commemorates the conquest of Dacia. It is depicted on two building inscriptions from Birdoswald Fort, where the Dacians were stationed from the early third century for the next 200 years. Intriguingly, the *falx* inscriptions and the tombstone recording the name 'Decebal' date from a hundred years or more after the unit was raised, where all the original recruits from Dacia would have been long dead. This raises the possibility that fresh recruits from Dacia continued to be brought over to join the cohort into the third century, a phenomenon for which there is otherwise no evidence. For a discussion, see Wilmott (2001).

41. As a result of unrest in Dacia at the start of his reign, Hadrian had reorganised the area, hiving off territories north of the Danube, which had formerly belonged to the neighbouring province of Moesia Inferior, to create a new province, Dacia Inferior, with Trajan's original province of Dacia renamed 'Dacia Superior'. It was to the newly named Dacia Superior that Julius Severus was appointed governor by June 120. He oversaw a further change in AD 123, splitting Dacia Superior by creating *Dacia Porolissensis*, which roughly corresponds to north-western Transylvania. Julius Severus might well have had similar plans for reorganizing Britannia, had he not been required to leave the province prematurely. See Piso (2013), pp. 27–8, for the reorganization of Dacia.

42. Vindolanda Tablet 164.

43. It has been suggested that this, the most lavish building found at Vindolanda, was to accommodate Hadrian on his visit in AD 122. See, for example, Birley (2002), pp. 75–6.

44. Fragmentary Inv. 1503B lists these items 'ordered through an *Adiutor* from London'.

45. Bowman and Thomas (*Tabulae Vindolandenses III*, 2003), 581, for example, implies that the governor was entertained to a lunch of chicken: lines 95–7.

46. Vindolanda Tablet 208: www.vindolanda.csad.ox.ac.uk/TVII-208

47. Aelius Aristides (*Orations*) XXVI, 83; Behr (1981), pp. 90–1.

48. Tacitus (*Histories*) IV, 64: *quod contumeliosius est viris ad arma natis, inermes ac prope nudi sub custode et pretio coiremus.*

49. It is unclear whether the no-man's-land north of the Wall was imposed as a deliberate policy or whether the presence of such a formidable barrier, with its consequent confiscation of land, made it impossible for communities to sustain a living there. What happened to these people is unknown. For a summary of recent research on the impact of the Wall on the native population, see Hodgson (2013).

50. Northern Britain continued to be troubled. Two soldiers serving at the fort at Galava (Ambleside) in Cumbria in the fourth century were killed in the camp 'by enemies', *in cas(tris) inte(rfectus ab hosti(bus).* See *Journal of Roman Studies*, Vol. 53, No. 4 (1963), and Breeze (1993).

51. Vindolanda Tablet 164: *equites gladis non utuntur equites nec resident Brittunculi ut iaculos mittant,* 'the cavalry do not use swords nor do the Britlings stay in their saddles to throw javelins'.

52. Arrian (*Periplus Ponti Euxini*) 11.

53. For hides from the Frisii for military use, see Tacitus (*Annals*) IV, 72. The virtual absence of any coins found at native sites on the northern frontier indicates that this was not a cash economy.

54. Tax-gatherers are equated with prostitutes and other sinners in the New Testament, their reputation for extortion and enriching themselves at the expense of others made plain in the story of the conversion of Zacchaeus, a chief tax collector in Jericho, who declares, following Jesus's visit to his house, that 'Here and now I give half of my possessions to the poor and if I have cheated anybody out of anything, I will pay back four times the amount.' (The Gospel according to St Luke) 19, 1–10.

55. CIL 5213. The inscription from Haterius Nepos's home town describes him as *censitor Brittones Anavionesium,* 'census officer of the Britons in Annandale'.

56. Tacitus (*Annals*) IV, 72.

57. *Codex Theodosianus* 10.2 and 7.8.5.1.

58. Vindolanda Tablet 344: *virgis cruentatum* (line 17), 'bloodied by the birch', and *innocentem virgis castigatum* (line 6), 'an innocent man chastised by the birch'. Apuleius (*Metamorphoses*) IX, 39: *Latini sermonis ignarus tacitus praeteribat,* 'ignorant of the Latin language he kept quiet and rode on'. For the soldier's hobnail boot, see Juvenal

(*Satires*) III, 247–8, and for brutal military life in general, see Juvenal (*Satires*) XVI.

59. In a *pridianum*, an annual inventory of personnel recorded by the Cohort I Hispanorum Veterana serving in Moesia. BM Papyrus 2851, dating from *c*. AD 99.

60. (*Digest*) 49.16.14.

61. Dated 18 May, the year is uncertain, though it dates no later than AD 97. Bowman and Thomas (*Tabulae Vindolandenses III*, 2003), 154.

62. Livy (*History of Rome*) XLIII, 3.

63. RIB 1065.

64. Pliny the Younger (*Letters*) X, 65–66, on the problem of foundlings in Bithynia.

65. P.*Oxy*.IV.744, 'Letter of Hilarion', dated 17 June 1 BC; and see Apuleius (*Metamporphoses*) 10.23 for a story about a man who similarly goes abroad, instructing his pregnant wife that if she has a girl she should have it killed.

66. A letter from Vindolanda refers to being prevented from travelling to Catterick for fear of injuring the animals because the roads are bad. Bowman and Thomas (*Tabulae Vindolandenses III*, 2003), 343. (This is the same letter quoted earlier concerning the delivery of hides and sinew: Chapter IX, Note 16. Brocchus, however, managed to visit his friend Cerialis in December and January.)

67. RIB 725. He might alternatively have been a *singularis consularis*, or bodyguard of the governor.

68. RIB 1550 restored: [...Se]verus, [Pro-P]raetorian Legate [of Augustus], the 1st Cohort of Aquit-[anians] built this [under...] Nepos the [Pr]efect.

69. This is based on Speidel's translation.

70. Austen and Breeze (1979); the *Discipulina* altar at Chesters is the earliest known in Britain.

71. SHA (*Hadrian*) X, 4: *triclinia de castris et porticus et cryptas et topia dirueret.*

72. As seen adapted for an urban context at Calleva.

73. Blagdon Park 1 and 2, see Hodgson (2013).

74. Glass bangles of a type known as Kilbride Jones Type 2.

75. Active Iron Age construction plots have been found and excavated at numerous points beneath the construction levels of the Wall and its forts. See Hodgson (2013).

76. The parties were destined not to last, and towards the end of the century the site was abandoned. See Proctor (2012).

77. Vindolanda Tablet 233. When Brocchus was later transferred to Pannonia he took his passion for the chase with him, dedicating an altar there to Diana, goddess of the hunt. CIL III 4360, and see notes to Vindolanda Tablet 233 at: www.vindolanda.csad.ox.ac.uk/TVII-233.

78. Bowman and Thomas (*Tabulae Vindolandenses III*, 2003), 594.

79. Arrian (*Cynegetica*) 3–4.

80. Arrian (*Cynegetica*) IX, based on Sestili's Italian translation and commentary (2011).

81. Dio (*Epitome*) LXIX, 10. For the inscription in Gaul: CIL XII 1122.

82. Aymard (1951).

83. SHA (*Hadrian*) XX, 12–13.

84. RIB 1041: *silvano invicto… formae captum quem multi antecessores eius praedari non potuerunt.*

85. See Hetherington, Lord and Jacobi (2006) for recent carbon-dating evidence that shows lynx to have been present in Yorkshire into the early medieval period.

86. Pliny the Younger (*Letters*) III, 5.15 which describes admiringly how even in winter the workaholic elder Pliny kept a secretary constantly at his side, whose hands 'were well protected by sleeves so that the bitterness of the weather could not snatch any time away from study', and so Pliny could continue to dictate notes to him.

87. Croom (2011), pp. 78–82.

88. Bowman and Thomas (*Tabulae Vindolandenses III*, 2003), 660. A fragment of a character reference found at Vindolanda recommends: *viri boni accedit etiam liberalium studiorum amor e[iu]s profectus morum denique te[m]peramentum et cu-.*

89. RIB 1319: *Neptuno le(gio) VI Vi(ctrix) P(ia) F(idelis)*; and RIB 1320 *Ociano leg(io) VI Vi(ctrix) P(ia) F(idelis)*. See Bidwell and Holbrook (1989) for a discussion.

90. Bidwell and Holbrook (1989), pp. 99–103.

91. Fronto (*Principia Historiae*) 11: *Eius itinerum monumenta videas per plurimas Asiae atque Europae urbes sita, cum alia multa tum sepulcra ex saxo formata*, 'And so you may see monuments of his journeys through many cities of Asia and Europe with many other types of buildings as well as tombs made out of stone.'

92. RIB 1051a and 1051b for the very, very heavily restored text from two fragments of a second-century inscription from St Paul's Church, Jarrow, which has been interpreted as a possible speech by Hadrian.

POSTSCRIPT: BEYOND AD 130

1. Julius Severus is attested in Britain on a diploma dated 9 December AD 132 ('*et sunt in Britannia sub Iulio Severo*'). See Piso (2013), pp. 25 and 28, which means that he probably did not set off to Judaea until spring AD 133.

2. Dio Cassius (*Epitome*) LXIX, 13.3–14.1. Julius Severus had a statue erected in his honour at Burnum in his native Dalmatia, ILS 1056 (= CIL III 2830 = 9891), which records that he was awarded the *ornamenta triumphalia*. This description gives the fullest account of his career. Monuments were also erected in his home town of Aequum. AE 1904, 9, states that he was governor of Syria Palaestina—the province of Judaea having been extinguished as punishment.

3. See Piso (1993), p. 45 and footnote 19, for Syme on Syrian inscriptions attesting Severus's presence in the province, and footnote 20 for Eck expressing doubts.

4. Claudian (*On the Consulship of Stilicho*) II, 247ff.: *Inde Caledonio velata Britannia monstro, ferro picta genas, cuius vestigia verrit/ caerulus Oceanique aestum mentitur amictus…*

Acknowledgements

———

Dᴜʀɪɴɢ the course of my work as series editor of English Heritage Red Guides, I have had the pleasure of commissioning new guidebooks to many of the Roman sites in the care of English Heritage and have had the good fortune to learn much from both the authors of these guides on site visits and during the whole stimulating exercise of creating a guidebook: David Breeze (Hadrian's Wall); Jim Crow (Housesteads); Nick Hodgson (Corbridge); Tony Wilmott (Birdoswald and Richborough and Reculver); Roger White (Wroxeter); Pete Wilson (Lullingstone), and from the editors of these guides past and present for their searching questions, diligent picture research and brilliant editing: Katy Carter, Jennifer Cryer, Katherine Davey, Catriona Howatson, Susannah Lawson and Sarah Yates.

Essential ingredients of these guidebooks are the reconstruction drawings which illustrate how a building or settlement may have looked during a particular phase of its existence. Although we know that they will never capture exactly how something looked at a particular moment in time, these drawings add walls, roofs, interiors, landscape and people to ruins which are sometimes little more than wall-footings in a much changed environment. They help to breathe life over archaeological sites which are often presented in such a way that many different phases of building over several centuries are laid bare, making it difficult to unravel them in the mind's eye and picture them at one or other points in their existence. It was in thinking about these drawings (and I am grateful to John Goodall, Richard Lea, and David Robinson from whom I learned so much in this respect) and gazing at Mark Fenton's brilliant phased plans that I began to think about how it might be possible to evoke one particular period of Roman Britain and this book is the result of these thoughts. I am indebted to English Heritage for allowing me research leave and to my colleagues there for their patience and understanding, particularly Anna Eavis, Jeremy Ashbee, Rob Campbell, Katy Carter, Jennifer Cryer, Katherine

Davey, Poppy David, Susannah Lawson, Clare Loughlin, Sam Kinchin-Smith, Richard Lea and Mark Fenton.

I am deeply grateful to Nick Hodgson and Pete Wilson who read an early draft and offered invaluable comments and corrections and drew my attention to articles and debates, and also to Mike Fulford who read the chapter on Silchester and to Peter Guest who read the chapter on Caerleon and to David Breeze who early supplied me with invaluable references. Both my father and sister Meg also read early chapters and made comments and suggestions for which I thank them. All errors and infelicities remain my own.

Particular thanks must go to Kwasi Kwarteng, who has been an ever motivating presence, and to Gerard Wales and Simon Lawrance for providing at various times sanctuary, diversions and delicious treats. I wrote the first words of this book seeking solace in the Howgills near Ravenstonedale while staying with Tom and Annie Reeves and I would like to thank my friends in the North for being so kind and so hospitable throughout, particularly my cousin Victoria Brown, Sarah Dunning, Charlotte Fairbairn, Stephen Gorton and Tatiana Harrison. My agent, Georgina Capel, merits a special mention for being ever uplifting in Wardour Street, while my commissioning editor, Richard Milbank has shown me the utmost patience, over many cups of tea and macaroons, in Smithfield.

* * *

THIS BOOK is dedicated to my parents. To my father who first showed me the remains of the Romans in Britain and to my mother who made it all possible. I thank them for this, and for all the love, support and encouragement they have always given me. I would also like to thank especially my brother Rupert for his most steadfast support while I wrote this book, and my daughter Connie, who has had to share me with the Romans for rather a long time now. Although early driven to parody, she patiently accompanied me round many sites and museums and has even come round to admitting a mild interest in the subject.

Index

A

Abonae (Sea Mills) *129, 149, 150, 232*

Achilles *130*

Achilles Tatius (Greek novelist) *62, 66*

acta (governor's records of official decisions and directives) *104*

actors *159*

administration *see also* record-keeping
of Britannia *16, 102*
collapse of *223*
of imperial property *103*
of military affairs *153*
census of occupied Britannia *37*
civil administration in Rome *35*
local administration *see* individual towns
high-salaried positions *103*
reforms under Diocletian (AD 284) *218*
reforms under Tetrarchy (AD 312–314) *219*

administrators *see* financial accountants, secretaries, procurators, tax collectors

Aegean Sea *64*

Aelius Aristides (orator) *21, 42, 196*

Aelii *see also* Hadrian *29*

Aequum (Dalmatia) *35, 65*

Aethelred *223*

Afon Lwyd (River) *152*

Africa *21, 23, 27, 64*
fossatum Africae (defensive ditch, North Africa) *190*
products *48*

Agricola (Roman general)
born at Forum Julii *65*
raised at Massilia *65*
governor of Britannia (AD 77–83) *18*

agriculture *128*
arable farming *88, 113, 115, 169, 182*
Celtic field systems *128*
cereals *182*
cereals in lieu of taxes *200*
crops *182, 200*
fields with lynchets *128*
livestock *see* cattle, sheep
Robigo (goddess of crops) *122*

Alauna (Maryport) *14–15, 18, 36, 187, 192, 219*

Aldborough *see* Isurium Brigantum

Alemanni (Germanic tribe) *218*

Alesia, siege of (Gaul, 52 BC) *193*

Alexander Severus (emperor, r. AD 222–235) *228*

Alexandria *50, 64*

Allectus (emperor) *218*

Alresford, graffiti *180*

altars *133, 138, 140, 145, 187, 219, 220*

Ambleside *see* Galava

Amiens *see* Samarobriva

amphitheatres *see also* games
arenas *106–107*
carceres (beast pens)
female spectators *107*
protection for spectators *108*
seating *107*
stalls for snacks and souvenirs *108*
tribunal (box for sponsor of games) *107*

amphorae *67*

E